An Introduction to Koranic and Classical Arabic

An Introduction to Koranic and Classical Arabic

Wheeler M. Thackston

Ibex Publishers,
Bethesda, Maryland

An Introduction to Koranic and Classical Arabic:
An Elementary Grammar of the Lanuage
by Wheeler M. Thackston

ISBN: 978-0-936347-40-0

A Key to Exercises is available for this book (978-0-936347-51-6)

Manufactured in the United States of America

The paper used in this book meets the minimum requirements of the American National Standard for Information Services—Permanence of Paper for Printed Library Materials, ANSI Z39.48–1984

Ibex Publishers strives to create books which are complete and free of error. Please help us with future editions by reporting any errors or suggestions for improvement to the address below or: corrections@ibexpub.com

Ibex Publishers, Inc.
Post Office Box 30087
Bethesda, Maryland 20824
Telephone: 301–718–8188
www.ibexpublishers.com

Library of Congress Cataloging-in-Publication Data

Thackston, W.M. (Wheeler McIntosh), 1944-
An introduction to Koranic and Classical Arabic : an elementary grammar of the lanuage / Wheeler M. Thackston.
p. cm.
Includes bibliographical references and index.
ISBN 0-936347-40-6 (alk.)
1. Arabic language—Grammar. 2. Koran—Language, style.
I. Title.
PJ6307 1994
492 .782421—dc20 94-1289

Contents

Preface

ARABIC, A MEMBER of the large and widespread Semitic language family, is one of the latest of these languages to be literarily attested. Although this obviously does not mean that Arabic is not at least as ancient as Babylonian or Ugaritic—indeed it is the closest of all its akin languages to reconstructed proto-Semitic and has presumably been spoken in the heartland of the Arabian peninsula from time immemorial—there is no literary evidence of Arabic until well into the Christian era.

The languages to which Arabic is related are (1) Northeast Semitic: Babylonian and Assyrian (Akkadian), (2) Southeast Semitic: Ancient South Arabian (Sabaean, Minaean, Qatabanian, Hadramitic) and Ethiopic (Geʻez), (3) Northwest Semitic: Canaanite (Ugaritic, Phoenician, Hebrew) and Aramaean (Babylonian Aramaic, Palestinian Aramaic, Syriac, Samaritan), and (4) Southwest Semitic: Arabic (old Arabian dialects, classical Arabic, medieval and modern Arabic dialects).

Scattered fragments and lapidary inscriptions have been found in Arabic from around the fourth century A.D., but Arabic gained universal prominence as the language par excellence of Islam, which was born in the Hejaz in Arabia in the seventh century. Wherever Islam afterwards spread, Arabic was taken; and although it never displaced a language to which it was not related, it became for centuries the medium of education and culture for all Muslims and was one of the most important unifying factors in Islamic civilization. In the non-Arab parts of the Muslim world Arabic gradually gave way after around the year 1000 to Persian as the language of high culture, but it remains to this day the ecumenical language of religion and is cultivated to some extent by all Muslims.

In the Semitic-speaking regions Arabic rapidly became the dominant tongue, gradually displacing all other Semitic languages with which it came in contact, and gave rise to the regional dialects as we know them today. Although there has naturally been great change in the various spoken idioms over the centuries, written Arabic has changed all but imperceptibly from the seventh century.

The first book written down in Arabic, and the one that has been responsible not only for establishing Arabic as an important written language but also for maintaining the language and isolating it from external impetus to change, was the Koran, which Muslims hold to be the Word of God revealed to the Prophet Muhammad. Islamic tradition holds that the Koran was written fragmentarily during the Prophet's lifetime (d. 632) and that the recension that exists today was compiled and standardized during the caliphate of 'Uthmān ibn 'Affān (644–56). More than any other source, the Koran formed the basis of life, law and language for the Muslim community; and a knowledge of it is indispensible for anyone who pretends to familiarity with the Islamic world—past or present.

More importantly for our purposes, the Koran established an unchanging norm for the Arabic language. There are, of course, certain lexical and syntactic features of Koranic Arabic that became obsolete in time, and the standardization of the language at the hands of the philologians of the eighth and ninth centuries emphasized certain extra-Koranic features of the old Arabian poetic *κοινη* while downplaying other, Koranic usages; yet by and large not only the grammar but even the vocabulary of a modern newspaper article display only slight variation from the established norm of classicized Koranic Arabic.

It is the grammar of that classicized Koranic Arabic that is presented to the student in this book. With very few exceptions (and those in the initial lessons only), all examples and readings have been taken directly from the text of the Koran and the body of *hadith,* the reports of Muhammad's sayings, and supplemented with extracts from other classical sources. Every effort has been made to limit the vocabulary to which the student is exposed to common lexical items: obscure and highly idiosyncratic words have been avoided as unsuitable for an elementary grammar. By the end of the forty lessons, which are designed to cover a normal academic year, the student will have an active basic vocabulary of over 450 words and/or productive roots (from which many times that number of individual lexical items can be regularly and predictably formed); and in the course of readings, passive exposure is given to more than 400 additional items of vocabulary. Items intended for active acquisition are intentionally repeated as often as possible in the exercises for reinforcement.

From the very beginning of this book Arabic is presented in its normal state, i.e., unvocalized. Most grammars of Arabic accustom the student to reading Arabic fully vocalized and then gradually eliminate the vowels in an effort to wean the learner from them. However, no matter how gradual the withdrawal process may be, when the final inflectional vowels are removed, most students panic at the sight of a "naked" Arabic word. It is felt to be preferable to train the learner from the beginning to recognize words as they will be seen ever afterwards. It is true, of course, that the Koran is always fully vocalized; but a student who can read Koranic text unvocalized as an exercise can cope with any other text he is likely to encounter later.

Preliminary Matters

1 The Sounds of Arabic. A discussion of the sounds not found in English is given below, but the student should imitate the instructor or a native speaker of Arabic to acquire correct pronunciation.

1.1 CONSONANTS. The following sounds are quite similar to their English counterparts and hence need no special explanation:

b as in "bit"	*s* as in "sun"	*n* as in "noon"
t as in "ten"	*z* as in "zoo"	*w* as in "wet"
d as in "den"	*j* as in "judge"	*y* as in "yet"
k as in "kit"	*h* as in "hat"	
f as in "fan"	*m* as in "moon"	

The following special symbols also have exact English counterparts:

'	the glottal stop: this sound occurs in English dialect pronunciations of "li'l" (for "little") and "bo'l" (for "bottle"); it also occurs in words such as "uh-oh."
θ	the *th* in "thin"
ð	the *th* in "then." Although these two sounds are spelled alike in English, they are quite distinct.
š	the *sh* in "ship"

The following sounds require explanation, as they have no counterparts in English:

ṭ a velarized *t*, pronounced like *t*, but the tongue is raised high against the velar ridge. Pronunciation of all the velarized consonants is accompanied by pharyngealization, or constriction in the back of the throat, which produces a *t*-like sound with a heavy, thudding overcast, the effect of which is most clearly heard in the following vowel.

ḍ the voiced counterpart to *ṭ*. This is the *d*-sound produced in the same manner as *ṭ*.

ṣ a velarized *s*, similar to *s* but produced by elevating the tongue toward the velar ridge. This sound, like all the velarized consonants, imparts a "cloudy" quality to surrounding vowels as a secondary articulation.

ẓ this is pronounced either (1) as the voiced counterpart to *ṣ* or (2) as the velarized counterpart to *ð*. Most modern pronunciations favor the former, although the choice among speakers of modern Arabic is conditioned largely by dialectal considerations.

q a uvular plosive stop, pronounced like *k* but further back in the throat. The correct point of articulation is against the soft palate.

x the voiceless velar fricative, a scrape in the back of the throat as in the German *Bach* and Scottish *loch*.

ğ the voiced velar fricative, the "gargling" sound similar to but stronger than the Parisian French and German *r*. It is the voiced counterpart to *x* and is produced in exactly the same manner but with the addition of voice.

ḥ the voiceless pharyngeal fricative, produced like an *h* but further forward in the throat. A constriction in the pharynx produces a low, hissing sound with no trace of scraping. In learning this sound care must be taken to distinguish it properly from *x* on the one hand and from *h* on the other.

ʿ the voiced pharyngeal fricative, the most characteristic sound of Arabic, but by far the most difficult for learners to produce. As with *ḥ*, the throat muscles are highly constricted with the vocal cords vibrating to produce a sound close to a gag.

l the clear *l* of French and Italian, not the "dull" *l* of English, except in the word *allāh-* ('God') when it is preceded by the vowel *a* or *u*.

r an alveolar flap as in Italian or Spanish—never the constriction of American English. Doubled *rr* is a roll like the *rr* of Spanish.

1.2 VOWELS. Arabic has only three vowels, *a*, *i* and *u*. They occur, however, as long and short and contrast vividly with each other. The consonantal environment also has an effect on the quality of each of the vowels.

a (short *a*) in an ordinary (front) environment pronounced similarly to the *a* in "cat"; in a velar or back environment, i.e., when in the same syllable as any of the velarized consonants (*ḍ*, *ṭ*, *ṣ*, *ẓ*), *r* or any of the guttural consonants (*ḥ*, *x*, *q*, *ğ*, ʿ), short *a* is more like the *o* in "cop."

ā (long *a*) in ordinary environments pronounced like short *a* but held for a much longer duration, something like the *a* in "cab" but even longer; in velar and back environments it is like the *a* in "calm" but longer.

i (short *i*) pronounced like the *i* in "bit" in nonvelarized environments; in the vicinity of a velarized consonant it is closer to the *i* of "bill."

ī (long *i*) similar to the *ea* of "bead"; in velarized environments the quality is significantly "clouded"—rather like the *ea* of "peal."

u	(short *u*) between the *oo* of "boot" and the *u* of "put"; being a back vowel, it is only marginally affected by velarization but is slightly fronted.
ū	(long *u*) like the *oo* of "moon"; in velar and back environments it is slightly fronted.
ay	is pronounced like the *i* in "bite"
aw	is pronounced like the *ow* in "cow"

2 Syllabification. Every syllable in Arabic begins with a single consonant and is followed by a vowel (short or long). Thus, wherever two consonants occur together, including doubled consonants, the syllabic division falls between them. Examples:

ja'altu > *ja-'al-tu* I made/put
ba'aθanī > *ba-'a-θa-nī* he sent me
nabīyunā > *na-bī-yu-nā* our prophet
yaktubūnahā > *yak-tu-bū-na-hā* they write it
walākinnahunna > *wa-lā-kin-na-hun-na* but they (fem.)

When initial vowels are dropped, resulting phrases should be divided syllabically as isolated words are:

bismi llāhi > *bis-mil-lā-hi* in the name of God
li-mra'atin > *lim-ra-'a-tin* for a woman
mina l-'arḍi > *mi-nal-'ar-ḍi* from the earth
fi l-'arḍi > *fil-'ar-ḍi* on the earth

Clusters of more than two consonants do not occur in classical Arabic.

A syllable that ends in a short vowel is a **short syllable**; a syllable that ends in a long vowel is a **long syllable**. Syllables that end in a consonants are also long but are said to be **closed**. Closed syllables with long vowels are rare in Arabic.

3 Stress. There are two simple rules for determining the placement of stress (accent) in Arabic:

(1) The final syllable (ultima) *never* receives stress.

(2) Not counting the final syllable, the first syllable from the end of the word that is long or closed receives stress.

ḍarabatnā	>	*ḍa-ra-'bat-nā* (*-bat-* is closed)
yaqtulannaka	>	*yaq-tu-'lan-na-ka* (*-lan-* is closed)
yaqtulūnī	>	*yaq-tu-'lū-nī* (*-lū-* is long)
madīnatī	>	*ma-'dī-na-tī* (*-dī-* is long)

As to how far back stress may recede, there are two schools of practice.

(a) One school allows stress to recede indefinitely until a stressable syllable is found, or to the first syllable of the word.

ḍarabahum	>	*'ḍa-ra-ba-hum*
yaqtulunī	>	*'yaq-tu-lu-nī*
madīnatuhum	>	*ma-'dī-na-tu-hum*

(b) The other school does not allow stress to recede farther back than the third syllable from the end (the antepenult).

ḍarabahum	>	*ḍa-'ra-ba-hum*
yaqtulunī	>	*yaq-'tu-lu-nī*
madīnatuhum	>	*ma-dī-'na-tu-hum*

Native speakers of Arabic normally impose the stress patterns of their own dialects upon Classical Arabic. This will acount for the wide variety the student may encounter from native speakers.

4 The Arabic Script. Arabic is written in letters related to the Aramaic and Syriac and known as the Arabic alphabet. This alphabet, which is written from right to left, has a total of twenty-eight characters, all but one of which represent consonants. The Arabic script does not normally represent the short vowels; only the long vowels and diphthongs have graphic representations as the script is usually employed.

This alphabet is a "script" in that most letters must be connected one to another. There are no separate letter forms corresponding to the "printing" of the Latin alphabet. Because the letter shapes vary slightly depending upon their position in a word, all letters have at least two forms and at most four.

Most letters connect on both sides (i.e., from the right and to the left) and have four forms: (1) the "initial" form, used as the first letter in a word or when following a nonconnecting letter and followed by any other letter; (2) the "medial" form, used when the letter is both preceded and followed by other connecting letters; (3) the "final" form, used when the letter is preceded by a connecting letter and is also the last letter in the word; and (4) the "alone" form, used only when the letter is the last letter in a word and is preceded by a nonconnecting letter.

Those letters that do not connect forward (i.e., to the left) have only two forms: (1) the "initial-alone" form, used (a) when the letter is the first letter in a word and (b) when it is preceded by a nonconnecting letter; (2) the "medial-final" form, used when preceded by a connecting letter. The six nonconnecting letters are marked by asterisks in the chart below.

5 The Alphabet.

NAME OF LETTER	ALONE FORM	FINAL FORM	MEDIAL FORM	INITIAL FORM	TRANS-SCRIPTION
**'alif*	ا	ـا	ـا	ا	–
bā'	ب	ـب	ـبـ	بـ	*b*
tā'	ت	ـت	ـتـ	تـ	*t*
θā'	ث	ـث	ـثـ	ثـ	*θ*
jīm	ج	ـج	ـجـ	جـ	*j*
ḥā'	ح	ـح	ـحـ	حـ	*ḥ*
xā'	خ	ـخ	ـخـ	خـ	*x*
**dāl*	د	ـد	ـد	د	*d*
**ðāl*	ذ	ـذ	ـذ	ذ	*ð*
**rā'*	ر	ـر	ـر	ر	*r*
**zāy*	ز	ـز	ـز	ز	*z*

sīn	س	ـس	ـسـ	سـ	*s*
šīn	ش	ـش	ـشـ	شـ	*š*
ṣād	ص	ـص	ـصـ	صـ	*ṣ*
ḍād	ض	ـض	ـضـ	ضـ	*ḍ*
ṭā'	ط	ـط	ـطـ	طـ	*ṭ*
ẓā'	ظ	ـظ	ـظـ	ظـ	*ẓ*
'ayn	ع	ـع	ـعـ	عـ	'
ğayn	غ	ـغ	ـغـ	غـ	*ğ*
fā'	ف	ـف	ـفـ	فـ	*f*
qāf	ق	ـق	ـقـ	قـ	*q*
kāf	ك	ـك	ـكـ	كـ	*k*
lām	ل	ـل	ـلـ	لـ	*l*
mīm	م	ـم	ـمـ	مـ	*m*
nūn	ن	ـن	ـنـ	نـ	*n*
hā'	ه	ـه	ـهـ	هـ	*h*
**wāw*	و	ـو	ـو	و	*w*
yā'	ى	ـى	ـيـ	يـ	*y*

Additional Combinations and Signs

**lām-'alif*	لا	ـلا	ـلا	لا	*lā*
tā' marbūṭa	ة	ـة			*-at-*
hamza	ء				'
šadda	ّ				(doubling)
'alif-madda	آ	ـآ	ـآ	آ	*'ā*

The only two-letter combination to have a separate form in the alphabet is the combination *lām* + *'alif*. The initial *lām*+*mīm* combination is conventionally written لمـ and should not be confused with *mīm* + *lām* (ـملـ).

Numerals. Compound numerals are written, like English, from left to right (365 = ٣٦٥).

١ 1	٣ 3	٥ 5	٧ 7	٩ 9
٢ 2	٤ 4	٦ 6	٨ 8	١٠ 10

6 The Vowel Signs.

6.1 The short vowels and the sign of quiescence:

(1) *fatḥa,* the sign for *a,* is a short diagonal stroke placed over the consonant it follows in pronunciation, as in كَتَبَ *kataba* and خَرَجَ *xaraja.*

(2) *kasra,* the sign for *i,* is the same diagonal stroke placed under the consonant it follows in pronunciation, as in مِنَ *mina* and بِهِ *bihi.*

(3) *ḍamma,* the sign for *u,* is a small *wāw* placed over the consonant it follows in pronunciation, as in كُتُبُ *kutubu* and رَجُلُ *rajulu.*

(4) In fully vocalized texts such as the Koran, every consonant must be marked, hence the existence of *sukūn,* the sign for no vowel at all (quiescence), usually written as a small circle above the consonant, as in كَتَبْتُ *katabtu* and مِنْ *min.*

6.2 The long vowel signs are as follows:

(1) *ā* is indicated by *fatḥa* plus *alif,* as in كَاتَبَا *kātabā* and قَامَ *qāma.* Note that *ā* is often, especially in the Koran, written defectively as "dagger *alif*" above the consonant, as in الله *allāhu* and إِبْرٰهِيمُ *'ibrāhīmu*

(2) *ī* is indicated by *kasra* plus *yā'*, as in كَبِير *kabīr-* and دِين *dīn-.*

(3) *ū* is indicated by *ḍamma* plus *wāw,* as in رَسُول *rasūl-* and ثُوم *θūm-*

6.3 The diphthong signs are a combination of the short vowel *a* and consonant:

(1) *ay* is indicated by *fatḥa* plus *yā'*, as in أَيْنَ *'ayna*

(2) *aw* is indicated by *fatḥa* plus *wāw*, as in دَوْر *dawr-*

6.4 Otiose *alif*. In certain conjugational forms an *alif* is appended to a lengthening *wāw*, as in كَتَبُوا *katabū*. This *alif* is not pronounced and serves merely to indicate the verbal form. It owes its existence to early orthographic conventions.

6.5 *Alif maqṣūra*. The *alif maqṣūra*, also called *alif bi-ṣūrati l-yā'* (*alif* masquerading as *yā'*), occurs word-finally only. Written like a *yā'*, it is pronounced exactly like a lengthening *alif*, as in المعنى *al-ma'nā* and رمى *ramā*. When any enclitic suffix is added to *alif bi-ṣūrati l-yā'* it becomes "tall" *alif*, as in معناه *ma'nā-hu* and رماه *ramā-hu*.

7 Additional Orthographic Signs.

7.1 *Hamza*, the sign of the glottal stop ('). Word-initially it is invariably written on *alif*. When the vowel of the *hamza* is *a* or *u*, the *hamza* is commonly written above the *alif*, as in أرض *'arḍ-* and أن *'an*.

But when the vowel is *i*, the *hamza* is commonly written beneath the *alif*, as in إنسان *'insān-* and إن *'in*.

Non-initially the "bearer" of the *hamza* may be:

(1) *alif*, as in سأل *sa'ala*
(2) *wāw*, as in سؤال *su'āl-*
(3) *yā'* without dots, as in رئيس *ra'īs-*
(4) nothing, as in نساء *nisā'-*

For a full treatment of the orthography of the *hamza*, see Appendix G.

7.2 *Waṣla*, a small initial *ṣād*, is the sign of elision. Many initial vowels, notably the vowel of the definite article, are elided when not in sentence-initial position. When such elision occurs, the *waṣla* sign is placed over the *alif*. E.g., when sentence initial, الأرض *'al-'arḍu,* but فى آلأرض *fi l-'arḍi.*

In the vocabularies, words that begin with *hamza* non-elidible will be indicated by the apostrophe (glottal stop), as *'arḍ-* and *'insān-*. Words beginning with elidible vowels will be indicated by the absence of the apostrophe, as *imra'at-* and *ibn-,* the initial vowel of which is elided, as in *mini mra'at-* and *li-bn-*.

7.3 *Šadda,* the sign of gemination. Doubled consonants are never written twice in Arabic but are indicated by placing the sign *šadda* over the doubled consonant. In unvocalized texts the *šadda* may be indicated sporadically, but it is not normally given.

جنّة	*jannat-*	مكّة	*makkat-*
سيّد	*sayyid-*	نبيّ	*nabīy- (nabiyy-)*
ردّ	*radda*	نبوّة	*nubūwat- (nubuwwat)*

7.4 *Alif-madda,* the sign of glottal stop *(')* followed by *ā*. Word-initially *'ā* is written with *alif-madda* in order to avoid the conjunction of two *alif*s, a situation that is not ordinarily permitted orthographically.

آمن	*'āmana*	الآية	*al-'āyat-*

7.5 *Tā' marbūṭa* occurs word-finally only. It is written like a *ha'* with two dots above. Invariably preceded by the vowel *a* (long or short), it is pronounced exactly like a *t* except in pausal form (for which see Appendix F). The *tā' marbūṭa* is generally a sign of feminization, although not all words that end in it are feminine by any means. Since *tā' marbūṭa* occurs word-finally only, when any suffix is added to it the *tā' marbūṭa* is written as an ordinary *tā'*. Thus:

	مدينة	*madīnatu*	حياة	*ḥayāti*
but	مدينتنا	*madīnatunā*	حياتهم	*ḥayātihim*

7.6 Omission of Orthographic Signs. The following orthographic signs are omitted from Arabic texts as they are normally printed (other than the Koran, which is always fully vocalized, and poetry, which is generally heavily vocalized);

(1) all vowels and *sukūn*. An occasional vowel may be supplied to avoid ambiguity;

(2) initial *hamza*. Internal and final *hamzas* are fairly consistently given;

(3) *waṣla.* This sign almost never appears in ordinary texts;

(4) *madda,* seldom omitted from careful texts;

(5) the dagger *alif,* normally omitted from the few words in which it occurs. It is seldom omitted from the word *allāh-* ('God'), for which a special symbol exists in most type fonts;

(6) *šadda,* occasionally given where ambiguity might otherwise arise.

8 Orthography of the Indefinite Inflectional Endings (nunation). The grammar involved in these endings will be taken up in Lesson One. For now, simply learn the orthography.

8.1 The indefinite nominative ending *-un* is written by doubling the *ḍamma* of the definite ending, conventionally written ـٌ:

رجلٌ	*rajulun*	مدينةٌ	*madīnatun*
بيتٌ	*baytun*	امراةٌ	*imra'atun*

8.2 The indefinite genitive ending *-in* is written by doubling the *kasra* of the definite:

رجلٍ	*rajulin*	مدينةٍ	*madīnatin*
بيتٍ	*baytin*	امراةٍ	*imra'atin*

8.3 The indefinite accusative ending *-an* is written by doubling the *fatḥa* of the definite ending **and** adding *alif* to all words except those that end in *tā' marbūṭa, alif maqṣūra* and *alif-hamza (-ā'-).* The double *fatḥa* is conventionally placed on top of the *alif.*

رجلاً	*rajulan*	مدينةً	*madīnatan*
بيتاً	*baytan*	معنًى	*ma'năn*

اسماءً *'asmā'an*

8.4 Nouns that end in *alif maqṣūra* are indeclinable, but many of them show state by suffixing the *-n* termination of the indefinite, which has the secondary effect of shortening the long *ā*.

المعنى *al-ma'nā* (definite) معنًى *ma'năn* (indefinite)

8.5 Most nouns that end in "tall" *alif* are invariable: they show neither case nor state.

دنيا *dunyā* (all cases, all states) عليا *'ulyā* (all cases, all states)

A few of these show state like the previous class:

العصا *al-'aṣā* (definite) عصًا *'aṣăn* (indefinite)

The Grammar of Koranic and Classical Arabic

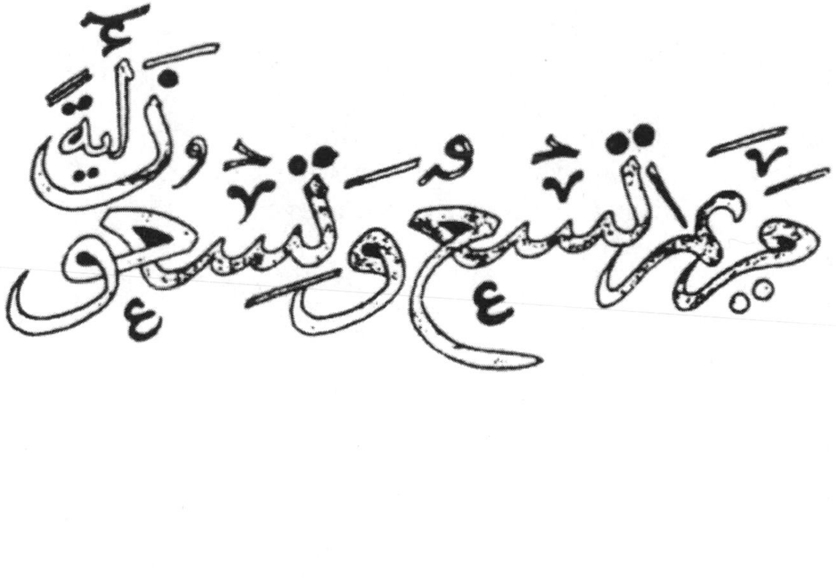

Ic...wolde þas lytlan boc awendan to Engliscum gereorde of þæm stæftcræfte þe is gehatten *grammatica*...for þæm þe stæftcræfte is seo cæg þe þara boca andgiet unlycþ.

(I wanted to translate this little book on the art of letters called *grammatica* into the language of the English, for that art is the key that unlocks the sense of books.)

—Aelfric's preface to his Latin grammar

Lesson One

1 The Definite Article. The Arabic definite article, which corresponds roughly to the English article 'the,' is invariably written as *alif-lām* attached to the noun. When the article is the initial element in a sentence or phrase, which does not occur frequently, it is pronounced *al-;* in any other position the article is necessarily preceded by a vowel, in which case the *a* vowel of the article is elided. The *-l-* of the article is pronounced as *-l-* when followed by any of the consonants in the left-hand column below; when followed by any of the consonants in the right-hand column, the *-l-* assimilates to the consonant, which is then doubled in pronunciation. This assimilation is indicated in vocalized texts by leaving the *lām* with no marking at all and by placing a *šadda* over the initial consonant of the word, as shown by the first two examples.

NON-ASSIMILATING CONSONANTS			ASSIMILATING CONSONANTS[1]		
'	اَلأَرْضُ	*al-'arḍu*	*t*	اَلتَّابُوتُ	*at-tābūtu*
b	اَلْبَيْتُ	*al-baytu*	*θ*	اَلثَّمَنُ	*aθ-θamanu*
j	الجنة	*al-jannatu*	*d*	الدّنيا	*ad-dunyā*
ḥ	الحليم	*al-ḥalīmu*	*ð*	الذكر	*að-ðikru*
x	الخبر	*al-xabaru*	*r*	الرجل	*ar-rajulu*

---

[1]It may be helpful when learning the assimilating consonants to note that they consist of all the "dentals" (all *t*'s, *d*'s and *th*), all the sibilants (all *s*'s and *z*'s) and the "liquids" (*r, l, n*).

ʻ	العرب	*al-ʻarabu*	z	الزمن	*az-zamanu*
ğ	الغنى	*al-ğanīyu*	s	الستر	*as-sitru*
f	الفاكهة	*al-fākihatu*	š	الشمس	*aš-šamsu*
q	القرآن	*al-qur'ānu*	ṣ	الصبر	*aṣ-ṣabru*
k	الكتاب	*al-kitābu*	ḍ	الضال	*aḍ-ḍāllu*
m	المدينة	*al-madīnatu*	ṭ	الطويل	*aṭ-ṭawīlu*
h	الهدى	*al-hudā*	ẓ	الظلم	*aẓ-ẓulmu*
w	الولد	*al-waladu*	l	الليل	*al-laylu*
y	اليوم	*al-yawmu*	n	النبى	*an-nabīyu*

2 Case and State of the Noun. Arabic nouns are subject to desinential inflection, that is, endings are added to the base of the noun to indicate what grammatical function the noun serves in the phrase in which it occurs.

2.1 The states are two, **definite** and **indefinite**. The definite corresponds generally to the English noun with the definite article "the" and also to generic uses. The indefinite corresponds generally to the English noun with the indefinite article "a" (plural "some"). Nouns are grammatically definite if they are (1) preceded by the definite article, or (2) the first member of a construct state (this will be introduced in §7). A noun that does not meet one of these two criteria is grammatically indefinite.

2.2 The cases are three, **nominative, genitive** and **accusative.** Fully inflected nouns, or noun that have different endings for each of the three cases in both states, are called **triptotes**. The triptote endings are:

	INDEFINITE			DEFINITE		
CASE	ENDING	EXAMPLE		ENDING	EXAMPLE	
nom.	*-un*	رجلٌ	*rajulun*	*-u*	الرجلُ	*ar-rajulu*
gen.	*-in*	رجلٍ	*rajulin*	*-i*	الرجلِ	*ar-rajuli*
acc.	*-an*	رجلاً	*rajulan*[1]	*-a*	الرجلَ	*ar-rajula*

2.3 A second class of inflected nouns is called **diptote.** Diptotes never have the *-n* termination of the indefinite state, and the genitive and

[1]For the *alif* termination, see Preliminary Matters §8.3.

accusative cases are identical. Where the genitive and accusative cases share the same inflectional ending, it will be referred to as the **oblique** case. Nouns classed as diptotes are diptote in the indefinite state only; **ALL NOUNS ARE INFLECTED AS TRIPTOTES WHEN DEFINITE.** The diptote endings are:

CASE	INDEFINITE ENDING	INDEFINITE EXAMPLE		DEFINITE ENDING	DEFINITE EXAMPLE	
nom.	*-u*	انبياء	*'anbiyā'u*	*-u*	الانبياء	*al-'anbiyā'u*
gen.	*-a*	انبياء	*'anbiyā'a*	*-i*	الانبياء	*al-'anbiyā'i*
acc.	*-a*	انبياء	*'anbiyā'a*	*-a*	الانبياء	*al-'anbiyā'a*

2.4 The nominative case is used (1) for the subject of a verb, which normally follows the verb directly.

خلق الله	*xalaqa llāhu*	God created.
دخل رجل	*daxala rajulun*	A man entered.

(2) for both subject and predicate of nonverbal, equational sentences (Arabic has no verb 'to be' in the present tense).

محمد رسول	*muḥammadun rasūlun*	Muhammad is an apostle.
الرجل مؤمن	*ar-rajulu mu'minun*	The man is a believer.

2.5 The genitive case is used (1) for complements of all prepositions.

فى مدينة	*fī madīnatin*	in a city
فى المدينة	*fi l-madīnati*	in the city
من مؤمن	*min mu'minin*	from a believer
من المؤمن	*mina l-mu'mini*	from the believer

(2) for the second member of a construct state (see §7).

2.6 The accusative case is used (1) for all verbal complements and direct objects.

خلق الارض	*xalaqa l-'arḍa*	He created the earth.
دخل الجنة	*daxala l-jannata*	He entered the garden.

دخل مدينة	*daxala madīnatan*	He entered a city.
كان رسولاً	*kāna rasūlan*	He was an apostle.

(2) following the sentence-head particle *'inna*.

ان محمداً رسول	*'inna muḥammadan rasūlun*	Muhammad is an apostle.
ان الرجل مؤمن	*'inna r-rajula mu'minun*	The man is a believer.

(3) for adverbial expressions of time.

اليوم	*al-yawma*	today
الليلة	*al-laylata*	tonight
ليلاً	*laylan*	at night, by night

Vocabulary

Note: All triptote nouns will be indicated in the vocabularies by a hyphen; diptote nouns will be given in full with the *-u* ending. Prepositions that belong idiomatically with verbs will be indicated in the vocabularies, and they should be learned along with the verb.

VERBS

خرج *xaraja* he went out (*min* of), he left (*min* someplace)

خلق *xalaqa* he created

دخل *daxala* he entered

كان *kāna* he was (takes complement in the accusative)

NOUNS

الله *allāhu* God (declined with definite case endings)

ارض *'arḍ-* (fem.) earth

جنة *jannat-* garden; paradise

رجل *rajul-* man, male human being

رسول *rasūl-* messenger, apostle

مدينة *madīnat-* city, town

مؤمن *mu'min-* believer (in the religious sense)

نبى *nabīy-* prophet

OTHERS

ان *'inna* (+ acc.) this word, a sentence-head particle, must be followed by a noun or enclitic pronoun (see §15), introduces a nominal clause; it is usually best left untranslated

اين *'ayna* where?

من *min(a)*[1] (+ gen.) from, among, of (in a partitive sense)

فى *fī* (+ gen.) in[2]

و *wa-* (proclitic) and

PROPER NAMES[3]

احمد *'aḥmadu* Ahmad

محمد *muḥammad-* Muhammad

موسى *mūsā* (invariable) Moses

Exercises

(a) Vocalize, then read and translate:

١ دخل الرجل المدينة

٢ خرج النبى من المدينة

٣ الرجل نبى

٤ كان الرجل نبياً

٥ اين محمد وموسى

٦ ان الرجل فى المدينة

٧ اين كان احمد

٨ الرسول فى الجنة

٩ ان محمداً فى المدينة

(b) Give the Arabic for the following:

---

[1]The prosthetic vowel that consonant-final words acquire when followed by an elidible *alif* will be so indicated in the vocabularies.

[2]When *fī* is followed by an elidible *alif*, it is pronounced with a short vowel, *fi*.

[3]Note that proper names may be diptote (*'aḥmadu*), triptote (*muḥammadun*) or invariable (*mūsā*). Triptote proper names, like *muḥammadun*, behave grammatically like indefinite nouns; semantically, however, they are definite.

1. a city, the city, in the city, from the city
2. a man, the man, from a man, from the man
3. a garden, the garden, in the garden, from a garden
4. a man entered, the man entered, the believer entered
5. a messenger left, the messenger left, Ahmad left, Moses left

(c) Translate into Arabic:

1. God created the earth.
2. The prophet entered the city.
3. Where are the apostle and the prophet?
4. Ahmad was in the garden.
5. The believer went out of the city.
6. Muhammad is in the city.

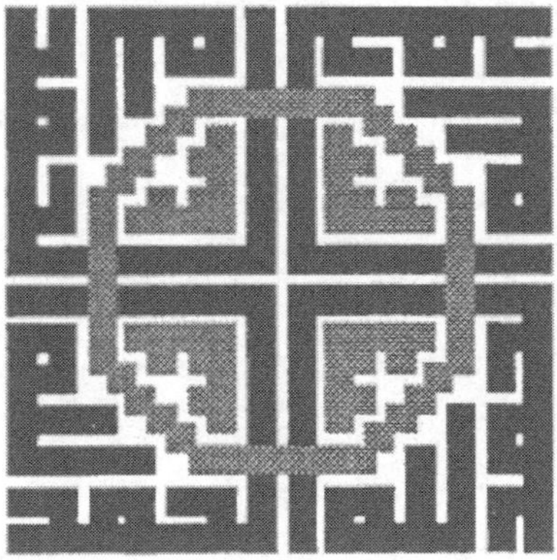

Lesson Two

3 Gender of the Noun. Arabic has two grammatical genders, masculine and feminine. These tend to follow natural gender, as naturally male persons and things are usually masculine, and naturally feminine persons and things are usually feminine; but it does not necessarily follow that all grammatically feminine nouns refer exclusively to females, as there are many examples to the contrary. The following types of nouns may be classed as feminine:

(1) nouns referring to intrinsically female beings, like *'umm-* 'mother,' *'uxt-* 'sister,' and *bint-* 'daughter.'
(2) names of towns and cities (*Baǧdādu* 'Baghdad'), countries (*Miṣru* 'Egypt'), tribes, etc.
(3) parts of the body that occur in pairs, like *'ayn-* 'eye,' *'uðn-* 'ear,' *yad-* 'hand,' etc.
(4) most, but not all, singular nouns ending in ة, like *madīnat-* 'city,' *laylat-* 'night,' etc.
(5) collective nouns, like *'arab-* 'Arabs,' as well as many plurals when treated as collective.

In general, nouns that do not fall into one of these categories are masculine—with the exception of a very few nouns with no external indication of grammatical femininity that are feminine by convention, such as *'arḍ-* 'earth' and *šams-* 'sun.' Such words will be marked in the vocabularies.

4 Adjectives and Adjectival Agreement. The distinction between noun and adjective in Arabic is basically one of usage, that is, the function of a given word in a sentence determines whether it is a noun or adjective. All adjectives may be used as nouns (but not necessarily vice versa).

4.1 Attributive adjectives invariably follow the nouns they modify and **agree completely in (1) case, (2) number, (3) gender, and (4) determination (state).** Thus, an indefinite masculine singular noun in the nominative case must be modified by a similar adjective.

ملك كبير	*malikun kabīrun*	a great king

If the noun is definite, the adjective must also be definite:

الملك الكبير	*al-maliku l-kabīru*	the great king
من الملك الكبير	*mina l-maliki l-kabīri*	from the great king

4.2 Feminine singular adjectives are formed by adding *tā' marbūṭa (-at-)* to the masculine base (the word without its inflectional endings).

مدينة كبيرة	*madīnatun kabīratun*	a great city
المدينة الكبيرة	*al-madīnatu l-kabīratu*	the great city
فى مدينة صغيرة	*fī madīnatin ṣağīratin*	in a small city
فى المدينة الصغيرة	*fi l-madīnati ṣ-ṣağīrati*	in the small city

4.3 Predicate adjectives and verbal complements agree with their subjects in gender and number. They occur in the **indefinite state** and hence do not agree in determination (state). The case of the predicate adjective is determined by the syntax of the sentence.

الملك كبير	*al-maliku / kabīrun*	The king is great.
ان المدينة كبيرة	*'inna l-madīnata / kabīratun*	The city is large.
كان الملك كبيرا	*kāna l-maliku kabīran*	The king was great.

5 Predication of Existence. Existential predication (English "there is, there are") is accomplished by reversing the normal order of a sentence, that is, by placing the subject (necessarily indefinite) after the predicate.

في المدينة رجل	*fī l-madīnati rajulun*	There is a man in the city.

Such sentences are almost always introduced by the sentence-head particle *'inna,* which will put the subject into the accusative case.

ان في المدينة نبيا كبيرا	*'inna fī l-madīnati nabīyan kabīran*	There is a great prophet in the city.
ان في البيت امرأة كبيرة	*'inna fī l-bayti mra'atan kabīratan*	There is an old woman in the house.

6 The Preposition *li-*. The preposition *li-* ('to, for') is proclitic, i.e., it is attached directly to the following word. Like all prepositions it takes the genitive case.

لرجل	*li-rajulin*	to/for a man

Words that begin with elidible *alif* lose their initial vowels in favor of the vowel of *li-*. The *alif* is retained orthographically.

لامرأة	*li-mra'atin*	to/for a woman

When *li-* is followed by the definite article, however, the *alif* of the article is dropped and the *l-* of the preposition is added to the remaining *-l-* of the article.

للبنت	*lil-binti*	to/for the girl

When *li-* is added to words that begin with *l* and that already have the definite article, such as *al-laylat-,* giving *lil-laylati,* only two *lāms* are written, the second and third coalescing with *šadda.* In an unvocalized text the definite and indefinite of *li-* + *l*-initial words are written the same (i.e., *li-l-* and *lil-l-* are written identically with two *lāms*).

لليلة (لِلَيْلَةٍ)	*li-laylatin*	for a night
لليلة (لِلَّيْلَةِ)	*lil-laylati*	for the night

When the word *allāhu* is preceded by *li-*, it is treated similarly.

لله	*li-llāhi*	to/for God

6.1 As Arabic has no verb 'to have,' *li-* is commonly used to express possession in the following manner:

ان الارض لله	*'inna l-'arḍa li-llāhi*	The earth is God's.
ان الحديقة للمرأة	*'inna l-ḥadīqata lil-mar'ati*	The garden belongs to the woman.

In such constructions the *li-* phrase precedes an indefinite noun (see §5).

للرجل بنت	*lir-rajuli bintun*	The man has a daughter.
ان للمرأة ولدأ	*'inna lil-mar'ati waladan*	The woman has a child.

Vocabulary

NOUNS

امرأة (المرأة) *imra'at-* woman; wife (with the definite article this word becomes المرأة *al-mar'at-*)[1]

بنت *bint-* (f.) girl; daughter

حديقة *ḥadīqat-* garden

عين *'ayn-* (f.) eye; spring

ليل/ليلة *layl-* night(time); *laylat-* night (one night); الليلة *al-laylata* tonight

ولد *walad-* boy, child

يد *yad-* (f.) hand, arm

ADJECTIVES

صغير *ṣaġīr-* small, little; young

قريب (من) *qarīb-* close, near, nearby *(+ min* to)

كبير *kabīr-* big, large; old; great

---

[1]Note that the change in the word occurs only when the definite article is attached to the word.

OTHERS

هنا *hunā* (invariable) here

ل *li-* (proclitic + genitive) to, for

Exercises

(a) Give the Arabic for the following:

1. a small boy, the small boy, from the small boy, for a small boy
2. an old woman, the old woman, from an old woman, to an old woman
3. a small hand, the small hand, in the small hand
4. a large garden, the large garden, in the large garden, in a large garden
5. a great prophet, the great prophet, for a great prophet, for the great prophet
6. a nearby city, the nearby city, from the nearby city, for the nearby city

(b) Vocalize, then read and translate:

١ العين الكبيرة قريبة من المدينة.
٢ البنت الصغيرة قريبة من المرأة.
٣ خرج الولد الصغير من المدينة اليوم.
٤ ان الحديقة الصغيرة قريبة من هنا.
٥ ان فى الحديقة الكبيرة عيناً صغيرة.
٦ البنت الكبيرة فى المدينة.
٧ ان الارض كبيرة.
٨ المرأة فى المدينة الليلة.
٩ الجنة للمؤمن.
١٠ للرجل الكبير بنت صغيرة.

(c) Translate into Arabic:

1. The small boy was here
2. The large city is close to a spring.
3. The old man was a believer.
4. Ahmad went out from the garden near the city.
5. The city has a great prophet.
6. The small girl is a believer
7. There is a spring in the city.
8. The woman has a small garden.

Lesson Three

7 The Construct State. This characteristic feature of Semitic languages has no true parallel in Indo-European tongues. Stated simply, the construct state, or "chain," consists of two nouns and indicates a possessive or limiting relationship between the two.

7.1 The first member of the construct, the thing possessed or limited, may **never** have the definite article; it is, however, **grammatically definite by definition** in a formal sense by virtue of its position in the construct: it is ordinarily declined with the definite case endings. The second member of the construct, the possessor or limiter, is in the genitive case and may be definite or indefinite. With the sole exception of the demonstrative adjective (to be introduced in §17), **NOTHING MAY INTERVENE BETWEEN TWO MEMBERS OF A CONSTRUCT.**

When the second member of the construct is indefinite, the entire construct has an indefinite sense.[1]

كتاب رسول	*kitābu rasūlin*	an apostle's book
بيت امرأة	*baytu mra'atin*	a woman's house

When the second member of the construct is definite, the entire construct has a definite sense.

[1] An indefinite first member of the construct is not possible. For phrases such as "a book of the apostle," a periphrastic construction such as *kitābun lir-rasūli* ('a book belonging to the apostle') or *kitābun min kutubi r-rasūli* ('a book from among the apostle's books') is used.

| كتاب الرسول | *kitābu r-rasūli* | the book of the apostle / the apostle's book |
| بيت المرأة | *baytu l-mar'ati* | the house of the woman / the woman's house |

The case of the first member is in no way affected by the construct state. The first member takes normal definite case endings according to the syntax of the sentence.

بيت الرجل صغير	*baytu̱ r-rajuli ṣaḡīrun*	The man's house is small.
دخل بيت الرجل	*daxala bayta̱ r-rajuli*	He entered the man's house.
خرج من بيت الرجل	*xaraja min bayti̱ r-rajuli*	He went out from the man's house

The construct chain may be extended indefinitely by making the second member of one construct the first member of a second, etc.

| بيت امرأة شيخ المدينة | *baytu mra'ati šayxi l-madīnati* | the city elder's wife's house |

7.2 Adjectives with the construct. Since nothing can intervene between the members of a construct, all attributive adjectives describing either member must follow the construct. Case and/or gender agreement usually makes it clear which of the two members a given adjective is modifying.

بيت الملك الكبير	*baytu̱ l-maliki l-kabīru̱*	the king's great house
بيت الملك الكبير	*baytu l-maliki̱ l-kabīri̱*	the great king's house
بيت ملك كبير	*baytu malikin kabīrin*	a great king's house[1]
مدينة الرسول الكبيرة	*madīnatu̱ r-rasūli l-kabīratu̱*	the apostle's great city

---

[1]Another, but rare, possibility for reading this string is *baytu malikin kabīrun*, where *baytu malikin* is taken as an indefinite construct forming a "compound noun" meaning 'king-house, royal residence' and modified by the indefinite adjective *kabīrun*. Such "compound nouns" are exceedingly rare in Arabic.

If the first member is in the genitive case and both members are of the same gender, ambiguity can arise. Context and/or sense, however, should indicate which noun the adjective is modifying.

فى بيت الملك الكبير	*fī bayti l-maliki l-kabīri*	in the king's great house *or* in the great king's house

Vocabulary

VERBS

ذهب *ðahaba* he went

وجد *wajada* he found

NOUNS

ابن *ibn-* son

اسم *ism-* name (the *alif* of *ism-* is dropped in the phrase بسم الله *bi-smi llāhi* 'in the name of God'; elsewhere the *alif* is retained)

بيت *bayt-* house, dwelling

رب *rabb-* lord, master

شيخ *šayx-* old man, elder, chief

كتاب *kitāb-* book

ملك *malik-* king

مكة *makkatu* Mecca

يوم *yawm-* day; *al-yawma* today

ADJECTIVES

جميل *jamīl-* handsome, beautiful

عظيم *'aẓīm-* great, huge, magnificent

OTHERS

الى *'ilā* (+ genitive) to (generally implies motion or direction toward)

بـ *bi-* (proclitic + genitive) in, by (instrumental), with, for (this preposition is highly idiomatic; usages will be indicated in the vocabularies)

Exercises

(a) Read and translate:

٧ شيخ المدينة	٤ بيت ملك	١ اسم البنت
٨ كتاب بنت	٥ رب البيت	٢ ملك الارض
٩ فى جنة الله	٦ لابن الرجل	٣ ولد امرأة

(b) Give the Arabic:

1. God's earth
2. a prophet's city
3. the apostle's book
4. Muhammad's child
5. for the king's wife
6. from the man's garden
7. the woman's daughter
8. the old man's master
9. Ahmad's son
10. the lord's house

(c) Translate into English:

١ خرج شيخ المدينة الكبيرة من بيت المرأة الجميلة.
٢ ذهب ابن الرجل الى حديقة الملك العظيمة اليوم.
٣ كان كتاب الرسول فى بيت الملك.
٤ وجد الشيخ الكبير كتاب الولد الصغير فى البيت.
٥ كان اسم ابن الرجل المؤمن محمداً.
٦ دخل الرجل بيت ابن الملك.
٧ ذهب الى بيت المرأة المؤمنة الليلة.
٨ ان كتاب الرسول للمؤمن.
٩ وجد النبى امرأة جميلة قريبة من العين.

(d) Translate into Arabic:

1. The child's lord's house is near here.
2. The apostle of God went to the city of the great king.
3. The man's son found a big book in the house.
4. The beautiful garden is for the king's wife.

5. The prophet's city is near Mecca.
6. The woman's child is a believer in *(bi-)* the Apostle of God.

Lesson Four

8 The Dual Number. For two of anything Arabic employs the dual number, which is completely regular in its formation.

NOMINATIVE	*-āni*
OBLIQUE	*-ayni*

8.1 The dual nominative suffix, which is added to the base of the noun (i.e., the noun without its inflectional endings), is *-āni*.

رجل > رجلان	*rajul- > rajulāni*	two men (nom.)
المرأة > المرأتان	*al-mar'at- > al-mar'atāni*	the two women (nom.)

The dual oblique (genitive and accusative) suffix is *-ayni*.

من رجلين	*min rajulayni*	from two men
وجد امرأتين	*wajada mra'atayni*	He found two women.

8.2 When a dual noun is first member of a construct, the *-ni* ending is dropped from all cases. The resulting *-ā* of the nominative is pronounced short before an elidible *alif.* A prosthetic *-i* usually occurs with the oblique before an elidible *alif.*

امرأتا الملك	*imra'atā̆ l-maliki*	the king's two wives (nom.)
لامرأتي احمد	*li-mra'atay 'aḥmada*	for Ahmad's two wives
لامرأتي الملك	*li-mra'atayi l-maliki*	for the king's two wives

8.3 Adjectival agreement with the dual is formed completely according to the rule for adjectives.

رجلان كبيران	*rajulāni kabīrāni*	two great men (nom.)
من رجلين كبيرين	*min rajulayni kabīrayni*	from two great men
وجد امرأتين جميلتين	*wajada mra'atayni jamīlatayni*	He found two beautiful women.

9 The Plural Number: Sound Plurals. The "sound," or regular, plural is formed by adding a suffix to the base of the noun.

9.1 The base of the masculine noun is formed, as was the dual, by dropping the inflectional endings. The **sound masculine plural** suffix that is then added serves both the indefinite and definite states. Like the dual suffix, it has only nominative and oblique forms.

CASE	SUFFIX	INDEFINITE	DEFINITE
nom.	*-ūna*	مؤمنون *mu'minūna*	المؤمنون *al-mu'minūna*
obl.	*-īna*	مؤمنين *mu'minīna*	المؤمنين *al-mu'minīna*

9.2 When the first member of a construct, the masculine plural ending drops the *-na* termination of both *-ūna* and *-īna*. The resulting final vowels, though written long, are shortened in pronunciation when followed by elidible *alif.*

مؤمنو مكة	*mu'minū makkata*	the believers of Mecca
مؤمنو المدينة	*mu'minu l-madīnati*	the believers of the city
لمؤمني مكة	*li-mu'minī makkata*	for the believers of Mecca
لمؤمني المدينة	*li-mu'mini l-madīnati*	for the believers of the city

9.3 The **sound feminine plural** is formed by dropping the *-at-* ending of words that end in *tā' marbūṭa* and adding the plural suffix. For nouns that do not end in *-at-*, the plural suffix is added to the base. Like the masculine plural, the feminine plural has only nominative and oblique forms. Unlike the masculine plural, it shows definite and indefinite states.

STATE	CASE	SUFFIX	EXAMPLE
indefinite	nominative	*-ātun*	جنات *jann<u>ātun</u>*
	oblique	*-ātin*	جنات *jann<u>ātin</u>*
definite	nominative	*-ātu*	الجنات *al-jann<u>ātu</u>*
	oblique	*-āti*	الجنات *al-jann<u>āti</u>*

Note that the sound feminine plural suffix **never takes *-a* as an inflectional vowel.** As expected, feminine plurals as first member of the construct use the definite plural forms.

مؤمنات المدينة	*mu'minātu l-madīnati*	the faithful women of the city
فى جنات الارض	*fī jannāti l-'arḍi*	in the gardens of the earth

10 Broken Plurals; Triliteral Roots. In addition to the sound plurals formed by suffixing regular endings onto the singular base, Arabic has the so-called "broken," or internal, plural, formed by a rearrangement of the vowel pattern around the triliteral root of the singular base. Study the plurals of the following nouns:

SINGULAR	PLURAL
رجل *rajul-*	رجال *rijāl-*
رسول *rasūl-*	رسل *rusul-*
مدينة *madīnat-*	مدن *mudun-*
كتاب *kitāb-*	كتب *kutub-*
عين *'ayn-*	عيون *'uyūn-*
رب *rabb-*	ارباب *'arbāb-*
ملك *malik-*	ملوك *mulūk-*
شيخ *šayx-*	شيوخ *šuyūx-*
كبير *kabīr-*	كبار *kibār-*
ولد *walad-*	اولاد *'awlād-*

If we group these plurals according to vocalic pattern, we can easily distinguish several categories:

XiXāX	XuXuX	XuXūX	'aXXāX
rijāl-	*mudun-*	*šuyūx-*	*'arbāb-*
kibār-	*kutub-*	*'uyūn-*	*'awlād-*
	rusul-	*mulūk-*	

Notice that there is no predictable correspondance between the vocalic pattern of the singular and that of the plural. What remains stable in each word is the succession of three consonants. The tri-consonantal, or triliteral, root system is the distinguishing characteristic of Semitic languages in general and of Arabic in particular. Nouns and verbs in Arabic behave in predictable fashions according to set patterns of vowels superimposed onto the triliteral roots. Thus, extracting the consonants from *malik-* as *m-l-k,* one can say that the word belongs to the triliteral radical √*MLK*, all of the derivatives of which share in some sense the basic meaning of the radical, which in the case of √*MLK* has to do with rule and possession. Other words produced from this root are *mulk-* 'kingship,' *milk-* 'property,' *mamlakat-* 'kingdom,' *malaka* 'to rule,' and a host of other predictable derived forms.

The vocalic pattern of *malikun* can then be said to be a short *a* after the first radical consonant and a short *i* after the second radical consonant, with the case ending (triptote) following the third radical consonant. A shorthand way of expressing the same thing would be to give the vocalic pattern as $\mathbf{C_1aC_2iC_3un}$, where C_1 stands for any first radical, C_2 for the second, and C_3 for the third. This device is convenient and will be used occasionally in this book; unfortunately it cannot be pronounced. In order to have a "dummy" root to stand for any series of three consonants, the Arabic grammarians settled upon the root *F'L*, meaning 'to do'; thus, *malikun* is said to be on the pattern FA'ILUN, and its plural *mulūkun* on the pattern FU'ŪLUN.

The four plural patterns introduced in this lesson are (1) FI'ĀLUN, (2) FU'ULUN, (3) FU'ŪLUN, and (4) 'AF'ĀLUN. The triptote ending of these four tells us that any and all plurals on these patterns are triptote. The plural of *nabīyun, 'anbiyā'u*, is on the pattern 'AF'ILĀ'U, a diptote pattern; this means that all plurals on this pattern are diptote, as *walīyun* 'friend' with its plural *'awliyā'u*.

Learn the plurals of these nouns, which have already been introduced in the singular. Note that some nouns have more than one plural.[1]

SINGULAR	PLURAL		SINGULAR	PLURAL	
ابن	بنون	*banūna*	عظيم	عظام	*'iẓām-*
	ابناء	*'abnā'-*		عظماء	*'uẓamā'u*
ارض	اراضٍ	*'arāḍin*[2]	عين	عيون	*'uyūn-*
اسم	اسماء	*'asmā'-*	كبير	كبار	*kibār-*
	اسامٍ	*'asāmin*	كتاب	كتب	*kutub-*
امراة	نساء	*nisā'-*	ليل	ليالٍ	*layālin*
بنت	بنات	*banāt-*	مدينة	مدن	*mudun-*
بيت	بيوت	*buyūt-*	ملك	ملوك	*mulūk-*
جنة	جنات	*jannāt-*	مؤمن	مؤمنون	*mu'minūna*
حديقة	حدائق	*ḥadā'iqu*	نبي	انبياء	*'ambiyā'u*[3]
رب	ارباب	*'arbāb-*	ولد	اولاد	*'awlād-*
رجل	رجال	*rijāl-*	يد	ايدٍ	*'aydin*
رسول	رسل	*rusul-*		اياد	*'ayādin*
شيخ	شيوخ	*šuyūx-*	يوم	ايام	*'ayyām*
صغير	صغار	*ṣiğār-*			

Vocabulary

آية/آيات *'āyat-* pl *'āyāt-* sign, token; verse of the Koran

ذلك *ðālika* (invariable) that (masc. sing. demonstrative)

خير *xayr-* good, a good thing

---

[1]Nouns with more than one connotation usually have different plurals for the different meanings, as is the case with the plurals of *ibn-*: *banūna* is used almost exclusively for the names of tribes and clans, and *'abnā'-* serves all other uses of 'sons.'

[2]This form falls into a pattern not yet introduced, as do the plurals of *ism-*, *laylat-* and *yad-* that end in *-in*.

[3]Note that the combination *-nb-* is pronounced "*-mb-*" wherever it occurs; *nabīy-* also forms a sound masculine plural, *nabīyūna*.

سماء/سموات *samā'*- (masc. and fem.) pl *samāwāt*- sky, heaven (usually occurs in the def. pl.)

عبد/عباد *'abd*- pl *'ibād*- slave, servant (of God)

مخلص *muxliṣ*- pl *-ūna* sincere, devoted (*li*- to)

Exercises

(a) Give the Arabic:

1. the names of the prophets
2. the small (ones) of the city
3. the kings of the earth
4. the adults (big ones) of the house
5. the sincere believers of Mecca
6. the sons of elders
7. a man's two children
8. the men of the two cities
9. the masters of books
10. the woman's two small daughters

(b) Vocalize, then read and translate:

١ ملوك المدينة الكبار
٢ مدينة الانبياء العظام
٣ ارباب المدينة الكبيرة
٤ ابنا الملك الصغيران
٥ نساء رجال مؤمنين
٦ بيوت رجال المدينة
٧ لمؤمنى الارض
٨ لشيخى مكة الكبيرين
٩ نساء الانبياء المؤمنات
١٠ لرسل الله العظام
١١ عباد الله المخلصون
١٢ شيوخ المدينة الكبار
١٣ شيوخ المدينة الكبيرة
١٤ فى حدائق بيوت الرجال
١٥ فى حديقة بيت المراة
١٦ فى حديقتى بيتى المراتين
١٧ ولدا المراة
١٨ اولاد المراة الصغار

(c) Vocalize, read and translate:

١ ان الله رب السموات والارض.
٢ وجد موسى عبداً من عباد الله المخلصين.
٣ ان للعبد المؤمن خيراً.
٤ خلق الله السموات والارض، وفى ذلك آية للمؤمنين.

٥ ان المؤمنين عباد الله.
٦ ذلك كتاب كبير لعبدين من عباد الله.
٧ للمرأة بنتان كبيرتان وابن صغير.
٨ موسى ومحمد اسما نبيين مخلصين لله.
٩ كان العبد مخلصاً لرب البيت.
١٠ للانبياء نساء مؤمنات واولاد مؤمنون.

(d) Translate into Arabic:

1. The man is devoted to God, the Lord of heaven and earth.
2. That was in the books of the apostles.
3. The man's two children were (*kāna*) in the king's garden.
4. The large spring is near the city gardens.
5. A prophet's book is a good thing for the believers.
6. The cities of kings (use def. art.) are here on earth, and God's paradise is in heaven.

Lesson Five

11 Adjectives and Adjectival Agreement (Strict and Deflected Agreement). As has been seen, attributive adjectives agree with the nouns they modify in determination, case, gender, and number. Of gender/number agreement there are two types, (1) strict and (2) deflected.

11.1 Strict Agreement. (1) Strict agreement applies to all singular nouns, i.e., a masculine singular noun is modified by a masculine singular adjective, and a feminine singular noun is modified by a feminine singular adjective.

رجل مخلص	*rajulun muxliṣun*	a sincere man
امرأة مخلصة	*imra'atun muxliṣatun*	a sincere woman

(2) Strict agreement also applies to all duals without exception.

رجلان مخلصان	*rajulāni muxliṣāni*	two sincere men
امرأتان مخلصتان	*imra'atāni muxliṣatāni*	two sincere women

(3) Strict agreement also applies to the plurals of words referring to people, but not to things.

رجال مخلصون	*rijālun muxliṣūna*	sincere men
نساء مخلصات	*nisā'un muxliṣātun*	sincere women

A broken plural referring to people takes a broken plural adjective if one exists; otherwise, the adjective is sound plural.

شيوخ كبار	*šuyūxun kibārun*	great elders
شيوخ مخلصون	*šuyūxun muxliṣūna*	sincere elders

Plurals referring to female persons take sound feminine plurals.

بنات كبيرات	*banātun kabīrātun*	big girls
نساء مخلصات	*nisā'un muxliṣātun*	sincere women

(4) In Koranic Arabic all sound feminine plurals, even of inanimate objects, tend to take strict adjectival agreement.

آيات بينات	*'āyātun bayyinātun*	evident signs
جنات معروشات	*jannātun ma'rūšātun*	trellised gardens

In post-Koranic classical Arabic, however, feminine plurals referring to things (not people) tend to take deflected agreement (see below).

11.2 Broken plurals of nouns referring to other than people take **deflected agreement**, that is, the adjective is feminine singular.[1]

مدن كبيرة	*mudunun kabīratun*	large cities
بيوت صغيرة	*buyūtun ṣaǧīratun*	small houses

11.3 The chart below describes the range of gender/number agreement of adjectives.

NOUN	ADJECTIVE	AGREEMENT	EXAMPLE	
FOR PERSONS				
masc. sing.	masc. sing.	strict	رجل كبير	*rajulun kabīrun*
dual	masc. dual	strict	رجلان كبيران	*rajulāni kabīrāni*
sound masc. pl.	sound masc. pl.	strict[2]	مؤمنون مخلصون	*mu'minūna muxliṣūna*
"	broken pl.	by sense	مؤمنون كبار	*mu'minūna kibārun*[3]
broken pl.	broken pl.	strict	رجال كبار	*rijālun kibārun*
"	sound masc. pl.[4]	by sense	رجال مخلصون	*rijālun muxliṣūna*

[1]A broken plural adjective or a feminine plural adjective may also be found with a broken plural noun, i.e., *mudunun kibārun* and *mudunun kabīrātun* are both possible, though uncommon, constructions.

[2]When neither noun nor adjective has a broken plural.

[3]Such a combination is exceedingly rare. Stylistically the construct phrase *kibāru l-mu'minīna* would be preferred.

[4]Only where a broken plural of the adjective does not exist.

fem. sing.	fem. sing.	strict	امراة كبيرة	*imra'atun kabīratun*
dual	fem. dual	strict	امراتان كبيرتان	*imra'atāni kabīratāni*
sound fem. pl.	fem. pl.	strict	بنات كبيرات	*banātun kabīrātun*
FOR THINGS				
masc. sing.	masc. sing.	strict	بيت كبير	*baytun kabīrun*
masc. dual	masc. dual	strict	بيتان كبيران	*baytāni kabīrāni*
fem. sing.	fem. sing.	strict	مدينة كبيرة	*madīnatun kabīratun*
fem. dual	fem. dual	strict	مدينتان كبيرتان	*madīnatāni kabīratāni*
broken pl.[1]	fem. sing.	deflected	بيوت كبيرة	*buyūtun kabīratun*
broken pl.	fem. pl. (rare)	deflected	بيوت كبيرات	*buyūtun kabīrātun*
broken pl.	broken pl. (rare)	strict	بيوت كبار	*buyūtun kibārun*
sound fem. pl.[2]	fem. sing.	deflected	جنات كبيرة	*jannātun kabīratun*
sound fem. pl.	fem. pl.	strict[3]	جنات كبيرات	*jannātun kabīrātun*

12 Pronouns. There are two sets of pronouns in Arabic, independent and attached.

12.1 The independent pronouns are:[4]

	SINGULAR		DUAL		PLURAL	
3 m	هو	*huwa*	هما	*humā*	هم	*hum(u)*
f	هى	*hiya*	هما	*humā*	هن	*hunna*
2 m	انت	*'anta*	انتما	*'antumā*	انتم	*'antum(u)*
f	انت	*'anti*	انتما	*'antumā*	انتن	*'antunna*
1 c[5]	انا	*'ana*[6]	—	(lacking)	نحن	*naḥnu*

[1]Note that for things the gender of the singular has no relevance to how the plural is construed.

[2]There are many nouns that are masculine in the singular but take the sound feminine plural.

[3]Rare outside of Koranic Arabic.

[4]For those who have studied Indo-European languages, this paradigm will appear upside-down. In Semitic languages, however, it is convenient to begin paradigms with the 3rd masc. sing. form, the reason for which will become apparent when the verbal structure is presented.

[5]The first person is of common gender.

[6]The final *alif* of *'ana* is otiose, i.e., it is merely a spelling device and does not indicate a long vowel.

The vowels given in parentheses for the 3rd masc. pl. and the 2nd masc. pl. are for use when the pronoun is followed by an elidible *alif.*

12.2 These pronouns are used (1) as independent subjects of non-verbal sentences.

انا شيخ المدينة	*'ana šayxu l-madīnati*	I am the city elder.
هو ولد صغير	*huwa waladun ṣağīrun*	He is a small boy.
هم من المدينة	*hum mina l-madīnati*	They are from the city.
هم الشيوخ	*humu š-šuyūxu*	They are the elders.

(2) to divide subject from predicate in non-verbal sentences when the predicate has the definite article.

ان عبد الله هو المخلص	*'inna 'abda llāhi <u>huwa</u> l-muxliṣu*	The servant of God is the sincere one.

Such a construction, literally "the servant of God, he is the sincere one," avoids the ambiguity of *'inna 'abda llāhi l-muxliṣa* ('the devoted servant of God'), where *l-muxliṣa* would be an attributive adjective agreeing with *'abda llāhi.*

Vocabulary

VERBS

سجد *sajada* he prostrated himself, fell/bowed down (*li-* before)

نزل *nazala* he came/went down, descended, stopped; he brought (*bi-* something)

NOUNS

اصبع/اصابع *'iṣba'-* (masc. and fem., usually fem.) pl. *'aṣābi'u* finger

امر/اوامر *'amr-* pl *'awāmiru* order, command; *bi-'amri* (+ construct) at the order of

انسان *'insān-* (no plural) human being, person, man

الرحمن *ar-raḥmān-* The Merciful (attribute of God)

طين *ṭīn-* mud, clay

عدو/اعداء *'adūw-* pl *'a'dā'-* enemy

قلب/قلوب *qalb-* pl *qulūb-* heart
ملك/ملائكة (ملائك) *malak-* pl *malā'ikat-/malā'iku* angel

PREPOSITIONS

بين *bayna* (+ gen.) between, among (note the construction *bayna X wa-bayna Y* 'between X and Y')
على *'alā* (+ gen.) on, onto; against; over

OTHERS

أ *'a-* (proclitic) an interrogative particle, not generally used before the definite article
الا *'illā* (+ acc.) except for

PROPER NAMES

آدم *'ādamu* Adam
ابليس *'iblīsu* Iblis, the Islamic proper name for Satan

Exercises

(a) Give the Arabic for the following noun-adjective combinations in the singular, dual and plural (nominative):

1. beautiful name
2. beautiful finger
3. huge house
4. small girl
5. large spring
6. nearby city
7. imminent (near) sign
8. small boy
9. devoted servant
10. large hand (sing. & dual only)

(b) Vocalize, read and translate:

١ خلق الله آدم من طين الارض
٢ سجد الملائكة[1] لآدم الا ابليس وهو للانسان عدو
٣ ان قلب المؤمن بين اصبعين من اصابع الرحمن
٤ أهو من المؤمنين برسول الله

---

[1]Here and in sentence 6 of this exercise, a singular verb is followed by a plural subject. This construction will be taken up in the next lesson.

٥ قلب المؤمن بيت الله
٦ نزل الملائكة من السموات بامر الرب على قلب النبى
٧ سجد العبد المخلص لله
٨ سجد لله العبد المخلص
٩ أانتم اولاد شيخ المدينة
١٠ ذلك من امر الله وهو خير للمؤمنين

(c) Translate into Arabic:

1. Iblis was an enemy to Adam and Adam's wife.
2. The king's son went to the small cities.
3. That was at the order of the king of the city.
4. The men's young wives have little children.
5. The girl's (two) hands are small.
6. The angel brought down the book from heaven.
7. They are old men, and we are young.
8. She is the king's daughter, and I am an enemy to the king.
9. Are you from among (use the partitive *min*) the men of the cities near here?
10. The elder of the city has two beautiful, large gardens.[1]

[1] Adjectival order in Arabic is of little importance. As a rule of thumb, the adjectives closer to the noun in English should be retained as the closer to the noun in Arabic.

Lesson Six

13 Verbal Inflection: The Perfect Active. The Arabic perfect generally translates into an English simple past or present perfect tense.

دخل البيت	*daxala l-bayta*	He entered (has entered) the house.

The perfect has other translational values that are contextually conditioned. These will be noted as encountered.

The perfect, or suffix, inflection is formed by adding personal endings to the stem of the verb. Since there is no infinitive in Arabic, verbs are quoted by convention in their simplest form, the third-person masculine singular perfect, which is one of the following patterns: FA'ALA, FA'ILA, or FA'ULA.

13.1 To form the perfect inflectional stem, the final *-a* is removed from the 3rd masc. sing. form to give a stem of *fa'al-/fa'il-/fa'ul-*. To this stem are added the personal endings. It will be convenient when dealing later with several classes of verbs to distinguish personal endings that begin with vowels ("V-endings") from personal endings that begin with consonants ("C-endings"). Note in the list of endings below that all 3rd-person endings except the 3rd fem. pl. begin with vowels; all the endings of the other persons begin with consonants.

	SINGULAR	DUAL	PLURAL
3 m	*-a*	*-ā*	*-ū*
f	*-at*	*-atā*	*-na*
2 m	*-ta*	*-tumā*	*-tum(u)*
f	*-ti*	*-tumā*	*-tunna*

1 c	*-tu*	—	*-nā*

There are several types of verbs in Arabic and, although the personal endings of the inflection remain unchanged, the base-forms of the several types undergo predictable changes. The various types are:

(1) "sound," verbs that consist of three radical consonants, none of which is *w* or *y*. This inflection will be introduced immediately below.

(2) "hollow" (C_2*w/y*, §18), verbs whose second radical consonant is *w* or *y*.

(3) "weak-lām" (C_3*w/y*, §20), verbs whose third radical consonant is *w* or *y*.

(4) "geminate" or "doubled" (§22), those verbs whose second and third radical consonants are identical.

A typical inflection of a "sound" verb is given as paradigm—of the verb *nazala:*

	SINGULAR		DUAL		PLURAL	
3 m	نزل	*nazala*	نزلا	*nazalā*	نزلوا	*nazalū*
f	نزلت	*nazalat(i)*	نزلتا	*nazalatā*	نزلن	*nazalna*
2 m	نزلت	*nazalta*	نزلتما	*nazaltumā*	نزلتم	*nazaltum(u)*
f	نزلت	*nazalti*	نزلتما	*nazaltumā*	نزلتن	*nazaltunna*
1 c	نزلت	*nazaltu*	—	—	نزلنا	*nazalnā*

REMARKS:

(1) The 3rd masc. pl. ending *-ū* is spelled with otiose *alif*, which is purely an orthographic device and is dropped when any enclitic ending is added.

(2) The only endings that are consonant-final and thus require prosthetic vowels before elidible *alif* are the 3rd fem. sing. and 2nd masc. pl., as in *daxal<u>ati</u> l-bayta* "she entered the house" and *daxal<u>tumu</u> l-bayta* "you (pl) entered the house."

(3) When followed by an enclitic pronoun, the 2nd masc. pl. ending *-tum* becomes *-tumū-*, as in *daxal<u>tumū</u>hu* "you entered it" (see §15).

(4) The 2nd dual is of common gender; there is no 1st dual—the plural is used instead.

13.2 The negative perfect is made by prefacing the negative particle *mā*. Although translational values are conditioned to a large extent by context, it is helpful to think of the Arabic negative perfect as equivalent to the English negative present perfect.[1]

ما سمع	*mā sami'a*	He has not heard.
ما دخلنا	*mā daxalnā*	We have not entered.

13.3 For added emphasis on the completeness or finality of an affirmative perfect verb, the particle *qad* may precede. *Qad* may be further strengthened by the addition of the emphatic particle *la-*. The Arabic perfect has several different uses, but the affirmative perfect preceded by *qad* is exclusively past perfective (past definite) in meaning.

قد دخل البيت	*qad daxala l-bayta*	He did enter / has entered / has already entered the house.
لقد ذهب	*la-qad ðahaba*	He did go / has really gone / has already gone.

14 Verb-Subject Agreement. All verbs agree with their subjects in gender, either strictly or by deflection. Number agreement depends upon the position of the subject in relation to the verb.

14.1 When the subject of a verb follows the verb—the normal order for rhetorically unmarked sentences—the verb agrees with its subject in *gender* but remains *singular* regardless of the number of the subject.

ذهب الرجل	*ðahaba r-rajulu*	The man went.
ذهب الرجال	*ðahaba r-rijālu*	The men went.
خرجت المرأة	*xarajati l-mar'atu*	The woman went out.
خرجت النساء	*xarajati n-nisā'u*	The women went out.

If the subject is grammatically but not intrinsically feminine, the placement of any word other than an enclitic object between the verb and subject is liable to nullify verb-subject gender agreement, and the verb remains masculine singular.

[1] The negative past definite is expressed differently, to be introduced in §46.

قد كان لكم آية	*qad kāna* <u>*lakum*</u> *'āyatun*	There was a sign for you.

As previously stated (§3(5)), tribes, classes, peoples and broken plurals that can be construed as collective tend to be considered feminine.

قالت الاعراب	*qālati l-'a'rābu*	The bedouins said.
آمنت به بنو اسرئيل	*'āmanat bihi banū 'isrā'īla*	The Children of Israel believed in him.
كذبت رسل من قبلك	*kuððibat rusulun min qablika*	Apostles before you have been called liars.

Sentences or clauses of the above type, where the verb is the first element, are called **verbal sentences** or clauses.

14.2 When the subject precedes the verb, the verb agrees with its subject in *both gender and number*.

ان الرجل ذهب	*'inna r-rajula ðahaba*	The man went.
ان الرجلين ذهبا	*'inna r-rajulayni ðahabā*	The two men went.
ان الرجال ذهبوا	*'inna r-rijāla ðahabū*	The men went.
ان المرأة ذهبت	*'inna l-mar'ata ðahabat*	The woman went.
ان المرأتين ذهبتا	*'inna l-mar'atayni ðahabatā*	The two women went.
ان النساء ذهبن	*'inna n-nisā'a ðahabna*	The women went.

As in adjectival agreement, plural things are usually construed as feminine singular for purposes of verbal agreement. The chart given on p. 20f. shows the gender/number agreement applicable between verbs and preceding subjects.

ان الحدائق كانت قريبة من هنا	*'inna l-ḥadā'iqa kānat qarībatan min hunā*	The gardens were near here.

Vocabulary

VERBS

خرج على *xaraja ʻalā* go out against, appear to

دخل على *daxala ʻalā* go into (the presence of)

سمع *samiʻa* hear

قال *qāla* say (followed by *'inna* "that...")

منع *manaʻa* hinder access (*min* to); prevent (acc., someone) (*min* from); forbid

NOUNS AND ADJECTIVES

آخر *'āxir-* last, final; end

خير *xayr-* better (*min* than), occurs in this meaning almost exclusively as a predicate, never as an attributive adjective; *xayr-* is a noun and does not agree in gender and number as an adjective would

دين/اديان *dīn-* pl *'adyān-* religion; *yawmu d-dīni* day of judgment, doomsday

صالح *ṣāliḥ-* pl *-ūna* pious

غنى/اغنياء *ğanīy-* pl *'ağniyā'u* rich

فقير/فقراء *faqīr-* pl *fuqarā'u* poor

قول/اقوال *qawl-* pl *'aqwāl-* voice, words, speech

كافر *kāfir-* pl *-ūna/kuffār-* unbeliever, infidel

كفر *kufr-* infidelity, unbelief

OTHERS

اذ *'ið* when (conjunction + perfect verb)

ف *fa-* (proclitic) and then, and so (sequential conjunction)

قد *qad(i)* a particle that emphasizes the perfective aspect of a perfect verb (not usually translated)

PROPER NAMES

جبريل *jibrīlu* Gabriel

لوط *lūṭ-* Lot

نوح *nūḥ-* Noah

Exercises

(a) Give the Arabic orally, then give the negative:

1. we heard
2. they (2 f) were
3. you (f pl) went down
4. you (m pl) created
5. they (f) found
6. they bowed down
7. they (2 m) heard
8. you (m s) left
9. she said
10. I went
11. you (2 m) entered
12. you (f s) left

(b) Read aloud and translate; then reverse the order to make nominal sentences with *'inna,* making necessary changes in the verb:

١ خرج الاولاد
٢ ذهب الرجلان
٣ نزل الصالحون
٤ سمعت البنتان
٥ دخل الفقراء
٦ كانت المراتان
٧ قال الشيوخ
٨ سجدت الصالحات
٩ وجد الانبياء
١٠ ما سمع الرجال
١١ كان المؤمنون
١٢ ذهب الملوك

(c) Vocalize, read and translate:

١ منعتم العباد الصالحين من بيت الله
٢ خرجت المراة على رجال المدينة فقالوا قد خرجت من دين الله
٣ قد سمع الله قول الكفار وهم قالوا ان الله فقير ونحن اغنياء
٤ انتم اين سمعتم آيات الله
٥ هم مؤمنون بالله والملائكة واليوم الآخر وكتب الرسل
٦ كان ابليس عدوا لله وللملائكة وللرسل ولجبريل فان الله عدو للكافرين
٧ نزل امر الله على قلوب بنى آدم
٨ ان امراة نوح وامراة لوط كانتا لعبدين من عباد الله صالحين[1]
٩ دخل النبى على الفقراء المؤمنين

(d) Translate into Arabic:

1. We have not bowed down before a human being.
2. The women heard the prophet's words and then left the city.
3. The pious poor (men) went to the king's house.
4. Is the rich (man)'s house better than the poor (man)'s house?

---

[1] A rhetorical order often found in Koranic Arabic with the partitive *min;* normal order would be لعبدين صالحين من عباد الله.

5. Gabriel came down to (on) the earth at God's command for (some) clay.
6. When they heard the signs of God, they went out and fell down before the apostle.
7. God said, "I created Adam from clay."
8. The pious woman prevented the children from disbelieving [use the def. art.].

Lesson Seven

15 The Attached (Enclitic) Pronouns.

	SINGULAR		DUAL		PLURAL	
3 m.	ـه	*-hu/-hi*	ـهما	*-humā/-himā*	ـهم	*-hum(u)/-him(u)*
f.	ـها	*-hā*	ـهما	*-humā/-himā*	ـهن	*-hunna/-hinna*
2 m.	ـك	*-ka*	ـكما	*-kumā*	ـكم	*-kum(u)*
f.	ـك	*-ki*	ـكما	*-kumā*	ـكن	*-kunna*
1 c.	ى	*-ī/-iya/-ya*	—	—	ـنا	*-nā*

Uses of the enclitic pronouns:

(1) as possessive pronouns, which form a construct with the noun modified.

كتابه	*kitābu-hu*	his book
كتابها	*kitābu-hā*	her book
كتابك	*kitābu-ka*	your (m s) book
كتابك	*kitābu-ki*	your (f s) book
كتابى	*kitāb-ī*	my book
كتابهما	*kitābu-humā*	their (dual) book
كتابكما	*kitābu-kumā*	your (dual) book
كتابهم	*kitābu-hum*	their (m pl) book
كتابهن	*kitābu-hunna*	their (f pl) book
كتابكم	*kitābu-kum*	your (m pl) book

كتابكن	*kitābu-kunna*	your (f pl) book
كتابنا	*kitābu-nā*	our book

REMARKS:

(1) The 3rd-person enclitics, with the exception of the 3rd fem. sing. *-hā*, harmonize with the vowel that precedes immediately. When the immediately preceding vowel is *u* or *a*, the vowel of the enclitic is *u;* when immediately preceded by *i* or *ay*, the vowel of the enclitic is *i*.

كتابُهُ	***kitābuhu***	his book (nom.)
كتابَهُ	***kitābahu***	his book (acc.)
كتابه	***kitābihi***	his book (gen.)
كتاباهُ	***kitābāhu***	his two books (nom.)
كتابيه	***kitābayhi***	his two books (obl.)

(2) The 2nd and 3rd masc. forms *-kum* and *-hum* add a prosthetic *-u* when followed by elidible *alif.*

بيتهم الكبير	*baytuhum**u** l-kabīru*	their big house
بيتكم الكبير	*baytukum**u** l-kabīru*	your big house

(3) The 1st-person sing. enclitic *-ī* supersedes all short inflectional vowels. *Kitābī* ('my book') thus serves all cases. When the 1st sing. enclitic is preceded by a long vowel or diphthong, it is *-ya.*

كتاباى	*kitābā-ya*	my two books (nom.)
كتابىّ	*kitābay-ya*	my two books (obl.)

When preceded by a consonant, the enclitic ending is *-ī;* when followed by an elidible *alif*, the enclitic may become *-iya.*

بيتى كبير	*baytī kabīrun*	My house is large.
بيتى الكبير	*baytiya* (or *baytī*) *l-kabīru*	my large house

(2) as sentence subjects after the head-particle *'inna.* When *'inna* is followed by the 1st-person enclitic *-ī*, it produces alternative forms, انى

'innī and انني *'innanī*. Similarly, when the 1st-person plural enclitic *-nā* follows *'inna,* it gives انا *'innā* and اننا *'innanā*. All others are predictably formed.

(3) as direct objects of verbs. In this case the 1st-person singular enclitic is not *-ī* but *-nī*. All others remain the same.

امرني	*'amara-nī*	he ordered me
امروك	*'amarū-ka*	they ordered you
امرتك	*'amartu-ki*	I ordered you (f)
امرناه	*'amarnā-hu*	we ordered him

Pronominal objects are added directly to the verbs as they appear in the paradigm—with the exception of the 2nd masc. pl., which becomes *-tumū-* before any pronominal enclitic, as

امرتموني	*'amartumūnī*	you (pl) ordered me

Remember that the otiose *alif* of the 3rd masc. pl. verb is dropped before the addition of any enclitic (امروا *'amarū* > امروني *'amarūnī).*

(4) as complements of prepositions. Two prepositions, *min* and *'an,* double the *n* before the 1st sing. enclitic (see below). The prepositions *fī* and *bi-* predictably take the *i*-forms of the 3rd-person enclitics.

مني	*minnī*	عني	*'annī*	فيّ	*fīya*	بي	*bī*
منك	*minka*	عنك	*'anka*	فيك	*fīka*	بك	*bika*
منه	*minhu*	عنه	*'anhu*	فيه	*fīhi*	به	*bihi*
منها	*minhā*	عنها	*'anhā*	فيها	*fīhā*	بها	*bihā*

Prepositions ending in *alif maqṣūra*, like *'alā* and *'ilā,* recover the *y* inherent in the base before adding the enclitics. The preposition *li-* changes to *la-* when followed by any enclitic other than the 1st sing., which is regularly formed.

عليّ	*'alayya*	لي	*lī, liya*
عليك	*'alayka*	لك	*laka*
عليه	*'alayhi*	له	*lahu*
عليها	*'alayhā*	لها	*lahā*

16 *Kull-*. The noun *kull-* ('totality, whole') functions as "every" and "all." When followed by an indefinite singular noun in construct, it means "every."

كل نفس	*kullu nafsin*	every soul
من كل مدينة	*min kulli madīnatin*	from every city

When followed by a definite noun in construct, it means "all."

كل المدينة	*kullu l-madīnati*	all (of) the city
لكل الاولاد	*li-kulli l-'awlādi*	for all (of) the children

Kull- is often set in apposition to the noun it modifies, in which case it takes a resumptive pronoun and means "all."

سجد كل الملائكة	*sajada kullu l-malā'ikati* or	All the angels fell prostrate.
سجد الملائكة كلهم	*sajada l-malā'ikatu kulluhum*	
وجد كل الفقراء	*wajada kulla l-fuqarā'i* or	He found all the poor people.
وجد الفقراء كلهم	*wajada l-fuqarā'a kullahum*	

Vocabulary

VERBS

امر *'amara* order, command (acc., someone; *bi-* to do something)

جعل *ja'ala* make, put

كتب *kataba* write; prescribe (acc. something; *'alā* for someone)

كفر *kafara* be ungrateful; disbelieve (*bi-* in), perform an act of infidelity

لعن *la'ana* curse (acc., someone; *bi-/li-* for something)

NOUNS

اذن/آذان *'uð(u)n-* (f) pl *'āðān-* ear

انف/آناف ، انوف *'anf-* pl *'ānāf-/'unūf-* nose

روح/ارواح *rūḥ*- (m & f) pl *'arwāḥ*- spirit

زوج/ازواج *zawj*- pl *'azwāj*- mate, spouse

سن/اسنان *sinn*- pl *'asnān*- tooth; age

شيء/اشياء *šay'*- pl *'ašyā'u* (diptote!) thing

كل *kull*- all, every, whole

لعنة/لعنات *la'nat*- pl *la'anāt*- curse

نار/نيران *nār*- (f) pl *nīrān*- fire

نفس/انفس *nafs*- (f) pl *'anfus*- -self (reflexive pronoun);[1] pl *nufūs*- soul

واحد *wāḥid*- one (adj.)

OTHERS

لما *lammā* when (+ perf.)

مع *ma'a* (prep.) with

عن *'an* (prep.) away from, out of (the various meanings of this highly idiomatic preposition are best learned along with the nouns and verbs with which it occurs)

Exercises

(a) Read and translate:

١ في ناره	٤ عدوك	٧ ازواجكن	١٠ صالحوكم
٢ اغنياؤها	٥ بانفسهم	٨ بيتاهما	١١ من مخلصينا
٣ من امرى	٦ لفقرائنا	٩ لنسائكم كلهن	١٢ وجد ابرهيم ربه

(b) Give the Arabic:

[1]The enclitics are not used as reflexive direct objects ("he saw himself"). For such constructions *nafs-/'anfus-* is generally used as the reflexive direct object along with the appropriate enclitic, e.g., *sami'a nafsahu* "he heard himself," *sami'ū 'anfusahum* "they heard themselves" (cf. *sami'ahu* "he heard him," i.e., someone else). The enclitics do sometimes occur as reflexives as prepositional complements.

1. my two hands
2. their (m) prophets
3. in your (m s) garden
4. your (f pl) daughters
5. their (2) eyes
6. your (f s) child
7. our messengers
8. in their (f) city
9. your (m pl) houses
10. her slave
11. his wife
12. for his wife

(c) Read and translate the following verb + object forms:

١ لعنّاهم
٢ امروكم
٣ كتبتماه
٤ ما سمعتِهن
٥ لعناك
٦ لعنّنا
٧ جعلتُها
٨ دخلتموه
٩ منعتْنى منه
١٠ وجدتاهم
١١ امرتنهما
١٢ امرتِه به
١٣ ما كتب لكما
١٤ منعكن
١٥ وجدوهم
١٦ امرتَنى

(d) Vocalize, read and translate:

١ ان ربكم خلقكم من نفس واحدة وجعل منها زوجها
٢ كتبنا عليهم ان النفس بالنفس والعين بالعين والانف بالانف والاذن بالاذن والسن بالسن
٢ جعل الكفار اصابعهم فى آذانهم
٤ قال انى عبد الله وانه جعلنى نبيا
٥ انى كتبت عليهم ذلك فدخلوا النار الى آخر ايامهم
٦ ان الله جعل لكم من انفسكم ازواجا
٧ ولقد امركم بذلك الله ربى وربكم

(e) Translate into Arabic:

1. The poor (man) cursed all the rich (men) until the end of their days.

2. When God created everything on the earth, he said, "The earth is for humankind, and the heavens are for the angels."

3. They cursed Lot and his wife, and so they left the city with their children.

4. The two women barred the men from their spring and said, "We are two poor (women), and the spring is ours."

5. I put my hands over my ears and so did not hear his words.

6. The angels brought down the spirit at God's command.

7. The last day will be [use perfect] a great thing.

Lesson Eight

17 Demonstratives. There are two sets of demonstratives in Arabic, near ("this, these") and far ("that, those"). The same words serve as both adjectives and pronouns.

17.1 The near demonstratives are:

	SING	DUAL	PLURAL
masc. nom.	هذا *hāðā*	هذان *hāðāni*	
obl.		هذين *hāðayni*	
			هؤلاء *hā'ulā'i*
fem. nom.	هذه *hāðihi*	هتان *hātāni*	
obl.		هتين *hātayni*	

The far demonstratives are:

	SING	DUAL	PLURAL
masc. nom.	ذلك *ðālika*	ذانك *ðānika*	
obl.		ذينك *ðaynika*	
			اولئك *'ulā'ika*
fem. nom.	تلك *tilka*	تانك *tānika*	
obl.		تينك *taynika*	

REMARKS:

(1) Only the dual forms are subject to inflection; all others are indeclinable.

(2) The *wāw* in *'ulā'ika* is otiose and does not indicate a long *ū*.

17.2 As pronouns, the demonstratives agree in gender and number **by deflected agreement** with the words to which they refer.

هذا هو النبى	*hāδā huwa n-nabīyu*	This is the prophet.
تلك آيات الله	*tilka 'āyātu llāhi*	Those are God's signs.
اولئك هم المؤمنون	*'ulā'ika humu l-mu'minūna*	Those are the believers.

17.3 When the demonstratives are used as adjectives, they usually precede the nouns they modify. The noun, however, **must have the definite article** for the demonstrative to precede.

هذا اليوم	*hāδā l-yawmu*	this day
فى هذه المدينة	*fī hāδihi l-madīnati*	in this city
تلك الآيات	*tilka l-'āyātu*	those signs
لهؤلاء الرجال	*li-hā'ulā'i r-rijāli*	for these men

As the demonstrative is the only thing that can intervene in the construct, it may be helpful to think of the demonstrative as actually an extension of the definite article.

مدينة هؤلاء الرجال	*madīnatu hā'ulā'i r-rijāli*	the city of these men

17.4 When a noun modified by a demonstrative is the first member of a construct or has a pronominal enclitic ending, by virtue of which it cannot have the definite article, the demonstrative follows the whole construct, agreeing with the noun it modifies as an appositive.

فى مدينة النبى هذه	*fī madīnati n-nabīyi hāδihi*	in this city of the prophet
فى مدينتنا هذه	*fī madīnatinā hāδihi*	in this city of ours

18 The "Hollow" Verb: Perfect Inflection. Verbs whose second radical consonant is *w* or *y* (C_2w/y) have slightly altered base forms in the perfect inflection. For V-endings, C_2 is replaced with *alif*, which lengthens the vowel of C_1 to *ā*. Thus, from √*QWM:*

	SINGULAR	DUAL	PLURAL
3 m	قام *qāma*	قاما *qāmā*	قاموا *qāmū*

f	قامت	*qāmat*	قامتا	*qāmatā*		

and from √*SYR:*

3 m	سار	*sāra*	سارا	*sārā*	ساروا	*sārū*
f	سارت	*sārat*	سارتا	*sāratā*		

When the C-endings are added, the base collapses and the weak radical normally appears as the short vowel associated with the original consonant, i.e., *u* for *w*, and *i* for *y*. From √*QWM* (and so also *qāla*/*qul-* and *kāna*/*kun-*):

3 f					قمن	*qumna*
2 m	قمت	*qumta*	قمتما	*qumtumā*	قمتم	*qumtum*
f	قمت	*qumti*	قمتما	*qumtumā*	قمتن	*qumtunna*
1 c	قمت	*qumtu*			قمنا	*qumnā*

And from √*SYR:*

3 f					سرن	*sirna*
2 m	سرت	*sirta*	سرتما	*sirtumā*	سرتم	*sirtum*
f	سرت	*sirti*	سرتما	*sirtumā*	سرتن	*sirtunna*
1 c	سرت	*sirtu*			سرنا	*sirnā*

There are a few exceptional base formations, notably √*NWM* (*nāma* "to sleep"), √*MWT (māta* "to die"), and √*XWF (xāfa* "to fear"). The underlying forms are **nawima, *mawita* and **xawifa,* as opposed to the underlying forms of *qāma* and *sāra,* which are **qawama* and **sayara.* The bases for C-endings of these verbs are *nim-, mit-* and *xif-*.

The common verb *jā'a* ('to come') is regularly inflected on the model of *sāra;* however, because its third radical is *hamza,* the orthography of which is rather complicated (see Appendix G), the paradigm is given here in full.

3 m	جاء	*jā'a*	جاءا	*jā'ā*	جاءوا	*jā'ū*
f	جاءت	*jā'at*	جاءتا	*jā'atā*	جئن	*ji'na*
2 m	جئت	*ji'ta*	جئتما	*ji'tumā*	جئتم	*ji'tum*
f	جئت	*ji'ti*	جئتما	*ji'tumā*	جئتن	*ji'tunna*

1 c	جئت *ji'tu*			جئنا *ji'nā*

In Koranic orthography the otiose *alif* of the 3rd masc. pl. is regularly omitted.

Note that when the third radical consonant and the consonant of the personal ending coincide, they are written together with *šadda,* as in متّ *mittu* ("I died"), كنّ *kunna* ("they [f] were"), and كنّا *kunnā* ("we were").

19 The Defective Verb *Laysa*. As has been seen, Arabic has no verb "to be" in the present tense. "Not to be" in the negative present is expressed by the defective verb *laysa*. This quasi-verb is inflected on the pattern of the perfect but is *present* in meaning. The inflection is similar to that of hollow verbs.

3 m	ليس *laysa*	ليسا *laysā*	ليسوا *laysū*
f	ليست *laysat*	ليستا *laysatā*	لسن *lasna*
2 m	لست *lasta*	لستما *lastumā*	لستم *lastum*
f	لست *lasti*	لستما *lastumā*	لستن *lastunna*
1 c	لست *lastu*		لسنا *lasnā*

Laysa takes its complement either (1) as a predicative in the accusative case

لست مؤمناً *lasta mu'minan*	You are not a believer.

or (2) as a complement to the preposition *bi-* in the genitive case.

أليس الله بربكم *'a-laysa llāhu bi-rabbikum*	Is not God your lord?

Vocabulary

VERBS

جاء *jā'a (ji'-)* come, come to (+ acc., someone, some place); to bring (*bi-* something) to someone (acc.)

قال *qāla (qul-)* say

قام *qāma (qum-)* rise up, arise (*'ilā* for; *'alā* against); go (*'ilā* to); undertake (*bi-* something); *qāma l-layla* stay up at night (all night)

ليس *laysa (las-)* not to be (conjugated like a perfect verb, meaning present)
مات *māta (mit-)* die

NOUNS AND ADJECTIVES

الآخرة *al-'āxirat-* the next world, the life to come
اولئك *'ulā'ika* those (pl.)
تلك *tilka* that (fem. sing.)
حياة *ḥayāt-* life
الدنيا *ad-dunyā* (f., noun and adj., indeclinable) this world, this life; *al-ḥayātu d-dunyā* this-worldly life, the life of this world
ذلك *ðālika* that (masc. sing.)
صلاة/صلوات *ṣalāt-* pl *ṣalawāt-* prayer, ritual prayer
قليل *qalīl-* little (bit); slight, few
كثير *kaθīr-* many, much
متاع/امتعة *matā'-* pl *'amti'at-* goods, wares, chattel
مقام/ مقامات *maqām-* pl *-āt-* place, location, position
هذا *hāðā* this (masc. sing.)
هذه *hāðihi* this (fem. sing.)
هؤلاء *hā'ulā'i* these (pl.)

Exercises

(a) Give the correct form of both demonstratives with the following words:

١ الروح	٥ الحياة	٩ الجميلان	١٣ البيوت	١٧ الكتب
٢ الكتابان	٦ الدنيا	١٠ الشيخين	١٤ النار	١٨ الاسنان
٣ الملوك	٧ العظيمة	١١ الاذنان	١٥ اللعنة	١٩ النفس
٤ الارباب	٨ الروحان	١٢ الزوجين	١٦ النيران	٢٠ الكبار

(b) Give the form of the verb appropriate to the pronoun in parentheses:

١ قال (انتم)	٢ جاء (انت)	٣ قام (انا)

١٠ قال (انت)	٧ جاء (هو)	٤ مات (انتما)
١١ مات (هما)	٨ قام (هى)	٥ كان (هن)
١٢ قال (هو)	٩ جاء (انتن)	٦ كان (نحن)

(c) Vocalize, read and translate:

١ اذ قاموا فقالوا ربنا رب السموات والارض
٢ قمنا الليل الا قليلاً
٣ فقمن من مقامهن وذهبن الى بيوتهن
٤ ولقد جئناهم بكتاب باسم شيخ تلك المدينة
٥ أجئتنى بشىء عظيم
٦ جعل الله فى ذلك خيراً كثيراً
٧ ان كثيراً من عباد الله المؤمنين قاموا باوامر الله
٨ اولئك اشتروا[1] الحياة الدنيا بالآخرة
٩ متاع الدنيا قليل والآخرة خير
١٠ لكم دينكم ولى دينى
١١ انى وجدت هنا شيخا كبيرا ومعه بنت واحدة
١٢ وجد نفسه فى بيت عظيم فقام الى الصلاة مع رجال البيت

(d) Translate into Arabic:

1. This is not your place.
2. On *(fī)* that day his daughter died.
3. We were few, and the enemy many.
4. When the messenger came I rose from my place.
5. The spirit of every man is at God's command.
6. You put this fire here, and it is a sign for those elders.
7. We cursed ourselves for that.
8. This world is the believer's prison *(sijn-)* and the infidel's paradise.
9. This child wrote his name in this book. Is he your son?
10. They cursed the king for his disbelief in God.

---

[1] *Ištaraw* "they purchased X (dir. obj.) at the price of *(bi-)*."

Lesson Nine

20 The "Weak-*lâm*" Verb (C_3w/y): Perfect Inflection. Verbs whose third radical is *w* or *y* are known as "weak-*lām*" verbs. They exhibit the following peculiarities in the perfect inflection:

20.1 Verbs with an underlying **fa'awa* base (1) change C_3 to *alif* in the 3rd masc. sing., (2) drop C_3 altogether in the 3rd fem. sing. and dual and in the 3rd masc. pl., where *-ū* is diphthongized as *-w*, and (3) recover the original *w* with C-endings and the 3rd masc. dual. Thus, from √D'W, with underlying perfect **da'awa:*

	SINGULAR		DUAL		PLURAL	
3 m	دعا	*da'ā*	دعوا	*da'awā*	دعوا	*da'aw*
3 f	دعت	*da'at*	دعتا	*da'atā*	دعون	*da'awna*
2 m	دعوت	*da'awta*	دعوتما	*da'awtumā*	دعوتم	*da'awtum*
2 f	دعوت	*da'awti*	دعوتما	*da'awtumā*	دعوتن	*da'awtunna*
1 c	دعوت	*da'awtu*	—	—	دعونا	*da'awnā*

20.2 Verbs with an underlying **fa'aya* base (1) change C_3 to *alif maqṣūra* in the 3rd masc. sing., (2) drop C_3 altogether in the 3rd fem. sing. and dual and 3rd masc. pl., and (3) recover the original *y* with C-endings and the 3rd masc. dual. Thus, from √RMY, with underlying perfect **ramaya:*

3 m	رمى	*ramā*	رميا	*ramayā*	رموا	*ramaw*
3 f	رمت	*ramat*	رمتا	*ramatā*	رمين	*ramayna*
2 m	رميت	*ramayta*	رميتما	*ramaytumā*	رميتم	*ramaytum*

2 f	رميت	*ramayti*	رميتما	*ramaytumā*	رميتن	*ramaytunna*
1 c	رميت	*ramaytu*	— —		رمينا	*ramaynā*

Note that throughout the inflection of both **fa'awa* and **fa'aya* base verbs, C_2 has the vowel *a*.

20.3 Verbs with an underlying base **fa'iwa* (as from √RḌW, perfect **raḍiwa)* become *fa'iya,* changing the *w* to *y,* and are thus identical to base *fa'iya* verbs in the perfect inflection. The only peculiarity of this type in the perfect is the 3rd masc. pl., which drops C_3 along with the preceding vowel when the ending -*ū* is added. All other forms are predictable from the regular paradigm. Example, from √*LQY,* base *laqiya:*

3 m	لقى	*laqiya*	لقيا	*laqiyā*	لقوا	*laqū*
3 f	لقيت	*laqiyat*	لقيتا	*laqiyatā*	لقين	*laqiyna*
2 m	لقيت	*laqiyta*	لقيتما	*laqiytumā*	لقيتم	*laqiytum*
2 f	لقيت	*laqiyti*	لقيتما	*laqiytumā*	لقيتن	*laqiytunna*
1 c	لقيت	*laqiytu*	— —		لقينا	*laqiynā*

For purposes of pronunciation, -*iy*- = -*ī*- *(laqiyta* = *laqīta).*

21 Relative Pronouns and Relative Clauses. Arabic distinguishes two types of relative clause, definite and indefinite.

21.1 The definite relative clause, or clause referring to an antecedent that is grammatically or semantically definite, uses the relative pronouns, which are:[1]

	SING		DUAL		PLURAL	
masc. nom.	الّذى	*allaðī*	اللّذان	*allaðāni*	الّذين	*allaðīna*
obl.			اللّذين	*allaðayni*		
fem. nom.	الّتى	*allatī*	اللّتان	*allatāni*	اللاتى	*allātī*[2]
obl.			اللّتين	*allatayni*		

[1]Note that the three most common forms, masc. sing., fem. sing. and masc. pl., are spelled with one *lām;* all other forms have two *lāms.*

[2]The feminine plural relative has alternative forms: اللائى *allā'ī* and اللواتى *allawātī.*

The Arabic relative pronoun always stands at the head of the relative clause and as close as possible to its antecedent. Relative clauses in which the relative pronoun is the subject of the clause pose no special problem. The verb must of course agree in number and gender with the relative pronoun and its antecedent.

اين الرجل الذى كان هنا	*'ayna r-rajulu llaðī kāna hunā*	Where is the man who was here?
هى المرأة التى جاءت اليوم	*hiya l-mar'atu llatī jā'ati l-yawma*	She is the woman who came today.
هم الرجال الذين سمعوا قولنا	*humu r-rijālu llaðīna sami'ū qawlanā*	They are the men who heard our words.
أهؤلاء هن النساء اللاتى ذهبن	*'a-hā'ulā'i hunna n-nisā'u llātī ðahabna*	Are these the women who went?

When the relative pronoun is the logical direct object of the verb in the relative clause, it *may be* so indicated by a resumptive pronoun. This is not obligatory.

هذا هو النبى الذى وجدوا (وجدوه) فى كتابهم	*hāðā huwa n-nabīyu llaðī wajadū(hu) fī kitābihim*	This is the prophet whom they found in their book.

The resumptive pronoun is often omitted in the direct object position in the relative clause. It cannot be omitted, however, when the relative is the complement of a preposition ("with whom, from which," etc.) or possessive ("whose").

النساء اللاتى دخلت عليهن	*an-nisā'u llātī daxalta 'alayhinna*	The women to whom you went
ما هذه الاشياء التى جاءوا بها	*mā hāðihi l-'ašyā'u llatī jā'ū bihā*	What are these things which they have brought?[1]
المقام الذى كان فيه	*al-maqāmu llaðī kāna fīhi*	the place in which he was

[1]Lit., "things *with which* they came."

الرجل الذى دخلوا بيته	*al-rajulu llaðī daxalū baytahu*	the man whose house they entered

21.2 Nominalization of the relative pronouns ("he who, the one which") is very common.

سجد الذى سمع الامر	*sajada llaðī sami'a l-'amra*	He who (the one who) heard the command bowed down.
ان الذين سمعوا قول النبى هم الصالحون	*'inna llaðīna sami'ū qawla n-nabīyi humu ṣ-ṣāliḥūna*	Those (the ones) who heard the prophet's words are the pious.

21.3 The second type of relative clause, the indefinite or asyndetic, the type which has an indefinite antecedent, is unmarked by a relative pronoun. Asyndetic relative clauses look exactly like independent sentences; and in the absence of punctuation, confusion can arise, but context usually makes it clear that it is a relative clause.

قد جاء رسل منكم دعونا الى الله	*qad jā'a rusulun minkum da'awnā 'ilā llāhi*	There came from among you apostles who summoned us to God.
لى ولد اسمه موسى	*lī waladun*^{i} *smuhu mūsā*	I have a child whose name is Musa.
فى المدينة حديقة فيها عين	*fi l-madīnati ḥadīqatun fīhā 'aynun*	There is a garden in the city in which there is a spring.

Vocabulary

VERBS

اتى *'atā* come (+ acc., to someone or someplace); bring (*bi-* something) to (someone/someplace, acc.)

دعا *da'ā* call, call upon, call out to, summon (*'ilā* to)

رمى *ramā* pelt (someone, acc., *bi-* with something); cast (*bi-* something) at (acc.)

راى *ra'ā* see, consider

عفا *'afā* pardon (*'an* someone or something)

NOUN

قوم/اقوام *qawm-* pl *'aqwām-* people, nation, tribe

OTHERS

الّتى *allatī* fem. sing. relative pronoun

الّذى *allaðī* masc. sing. relative pronoun

الّذين *allaðīna* masc. pl. relative pronoun

كـ *ka-* (proclitic + noun in the gen.; does not take pronominal enclitics) like

كذلك *ka-ðālika* thus, likewise

ما *mā* (invariable) what? (interrogative pronoun)

ولكن *wa-lākinna* (+ noun in acc. or enclitic pronoun) but, rather; (when followed by a verb, *wa-lākin)*

يا *yā* O (vocative particle followed by the nominative case of noun without nunation, as *yā rasūlu* "O apostle"; followed by accusative if in construct, as *yā rasūla llāhi* "O Apostle of God")

PROPER NAMES

عيسى *'īsā* (invariable) Jesus

مريم *maryamu* Mary, Miriam

Exercises

(a) Give the Arabic:

1. the two women who came
2. a man you saw
3. the girl who called me
4. the king for whom you rose
5. you (m pl) who have died
6. the sign that I saw
7. the place from which you (f s) arose
8. you (f pl) who have heard
9. the thing they brought
10. (some) things they brought
11. those who saw
12. I who called them
13. words [indef.] you (m pl) heard
14. the women whom you saw

(b) Vocalize, read and translate:

١ لقد عفا الله عن ذلك

٢ فأتت مريم قومها بابنها عيسى فقالوا يا مريم ما هذا الذى جئت به

٣ ان الذين اتوا بالآيات دعوا الله

٤ راى قلبى ربى[1]

٥ يا قوم ان هذه الحياة الدنيا شىء قليل

٦ المؤمنون كنفس واحدة

٧ وما رميت اذ رميت ولكن الله رمى

٨ الشيخ فى بيته كالنبى فى قومه

٩ هذه الحياة الدنيا التى نحن فيها أرأيتموها خيراً لكم

١٠ ان الذين كفروا وماتوا اولئك عليهم لعنة الله

١١ فالذين كفروا من قومه رموه بالرماح[2]

١٢ هو كالرجل الذى اتانا فقال اننا رأينا آيات النبى

١٣ لما رأى الملك المرأة الفقيرة قام ودعاها اليه

١٤ دعوهم الى آخر ايام حياتهم ولكنهم ما سمعوا قولهم

(c) Translate into Arabic:

1. The slave called his master and said, "We who have come here are not many."

2. The old man arose for the prayer and then died devoted[3] to God.

3. I put these (two) hands of mine over my eyes, and so I did not see anything.

4. Thus I said to the child who brought me these two books.

5. O people, did you see when the angels brought God's signs to us from heaven?

6. What did you say to the king's servant when he summoned you?

7. He has two sons he has pardoned and another son he has not.[4]

---

[1]Assume normal word order.

[2]*Rimāḥ*- pl. of *rumḥ*- spear.

[3]Use indefinite accusative.

[4]In Arabic the full verb must be used.

Lesson Ten

22 Geminate (Doubled) Verbs: Perfect Inflection. Verbs whose second and third radical consonants are identical are known as "doubled" or "geminate" verbs. They exhibit the following peculiarity in conjugation: with the V-endings the second and third radicals fall together as a doubled consonant. Otherwise the inflection of the perfect is regular. An example, from √DLL, underlying perfect **dalala > dalla* ("to guide"):

	SINGULAR		DUAL		PLURAL	
3 m	دل	*dalla*	دلا	*dallā*	دلوا	*dallū*
3 f	دلت	*dallat*	دلتا	*dallatā*	دللن	*dalalna*
2 m	دللت	*dalalta*	دللتما	*dalaltumā*	دللتم	*dalaltum*
2 f	دللت	*dalalti*	دللتما	*dalaltumā*	دللتن	*dalaltunna*
1 c	دللت	*dalaltu*	—	—	دللنا	*dalalnā*

23 Active Participles. The active participle, which can be formed from all verbs, transitive and intransitive, is made on the pattern FĀʻIL-, which makes its feminine, dual and plurals with regular adjectival endings. An example, from *daxala:*

	SINGULAR		DUAL		PLURAL	
masc.	داخل	*dāxilun*	داخلان	*dāxilāni*	داخلون	*dāxilūna*
fem.	داخلة	*dāxilatun*	داخلتان	*dāxilatāni*	داخلات	*dāxilātun*

The active participle often functions, like the English present active participle in "-ing," as a verbal adjective for on-going action, or the durative aspect.

هو ساجد لله	*huwa sājidun li-llāhi*	He is bowing down to God.

The active participle as complement to *kāna* in the perfect gives the past progressive:

كان ساجداً لله	*kāna sājidan li-llāhi*	He was bowing down to God.

Contrast this use of the durative participle with the finite perfect, *sajada,* which is temporal and may mean, according to context, "he bowed down, he did bow down, he had bowed down, he will bow down."

The active participle is also substantivized and used as an agent noun, so that *kātib-* (from *kataba* "to write") may mean not only "writing, going to write, one who is writing," but also, as a noun, "writer, scribe."

كان احمد كاتباً	*kāna 'aḥmadu kātiban*	Ahmad was writing *or* Ahmad was a scribe.
الله خالقُ كل شيء	*allāhu xāliqu kulli šay'in*	God is the creator of everything.

However, when the participle retains verbal force, the participial object is in the accusative.

الله خالقٌ بشراً	*allāhu xāliqun bašar<u>an</u>*	God is going to create a human being.
انى باعثٌ من بعدك نبيًّا	*'innī bā'iθun min ba'dika nabīy<u>an</u>*	I am going to send, after you, a prophet.

Note, as in the above examples, that the active participle in the predicate position very often has a future signification ("going to...") when it is not substantivized. When a transitive active participle has its object in the accusative, it is clear that the participle is used verbally, and it almost always has a future sense; when the participle is in construct, it is generally substantivized. Otherwise, as in the first example above, *huwa sājidun,* only context can determine whether the meaning is present progressive ("he is bowing down") or future ("he is going to bow down").

24 The Passive Participle. The passive participle of all transitive verbs is formed on the pattern MAF'ŪL-. Feminines, duals and plurals are formed like regular adjectives, as from *wajada* ("to find"):

	SINGULAR		DUAL		PLURAL	
masc.	موجود	*mawjūdun*	موجودان	*mawjūdāni*	موجودون	*mawjūdūna*
fem.	موجودة	*mawjūdatun*	موجودتان	*mawjūdatāni*	موجودات	*mawjūdātun*

The passive participle is used in the following ways:

(1) purely adjectivally, like the English past passive participle:

شيء مخلوق	*šay'un maxlūqun*	a created thing
الرجل ملعون	*ar-rajulu mal'ūnun*	The man is cursed.
كان الكتاب مكتوباً	*kāna l-kitābu maktūban*	The book was written.

(2) that which can be, ought to be, is worth doing or liable to be:

شيء مذكور	*šay'un maδkūrun*	a thing worth mentioning / a mentionable thing
قول مسموع	*qawlun masmū'un*	words that are/ought to be heard

(3) substantively:

الملعونون	*al-mal'ūnūna*	those who are cursed, accursed ones
المذكور من قبل	*al-maδkūru min qablu*	that which has been mentioned before

25 Cognate Subjects. The active participle is often used as a cognate subject (i.e., the active participle of a given verb as subject of that same verb) in the indeterminate sense of "someone, some people, somebody or other."

قال قائل	*qāla qā'ilun*	Somebody has said…
قال قائلون	*qāla qā'ilūna*	Some people have said…

The definite cognate subject necessarily refers to a subject already introduced.

فقال القائل	*fa-qāla l-qā'ilu*	and then the one who was speaking went on to say…

26 Circumstantial Constructions. Circumstantial constructions indicate circumstances contemporaneous with or prior to the action/state of the verb.

26.1 The indefinite accusative of nouns, adjectives and especially participles occurs in an adverbial sense to modify the circumstance or to indicate the manner of the verb.

مات مخلصاً لربه	*māta <u>muxlisan</u> li-rabbihi*	He died devoted ("as a devoted one") to his lord.
خرج على النبى كافراً	*xaraja 'alā n-nabīyi <u>kāfiran</u>*	He went out against the prophet as an infidel ("in the manner of an infidel").

This construction rarely poses any special difficulty for comprehension or translation. It should be noted that the word in the accusative may modify the object as well as the subject of the verb (gender/number considerations usually eliminate confusion).

رايتهم خارجين من البيت	*ra'aytuhum <u>xārijīna</u> min l-bayti*	I saw them leaving the house.

This last construction is really an objective complement where, as expected, an adjective or participle modifying the direct object is in the accusative case.

وجدناهم ساجدين لربهم	*wajadnāhum <u>sājidīna</u> li-rabbihim*	We found them bowing down to their master.

26.2 The circumstantial *wa-*. The use of a parallel clause introduced by *wa* + pronoun (or noun) indicates circumstantiality, or what pertains concurrently to the action/state of the verb.

رايته وهو نازل من المدينة	*ra'aytuhu <u>wa-huwa</u> nāzilun mina l-madīnati*	I saw him as he was coming down from the city.
دعوتك وانت خارج من بيتك	*da'awtuka <u>wa-'anta</u> xārijun min baytika*	I called out to you as you were coming out of your house.
دعوتك وانا خارج من بيتى	*da'awtuka <u>wa-'ana</u> xārijun min baytī*	I called out to you as I was coming out of my house.

Circumstantial *wa-* + *qad* + a perfect verb indicates circumstantiality prior to the main verb.

رآنى وقد خرج من بيته	*ra'ānī <u>wa</u>-qad xaraja min baytihi*	He saw me after he had come out of his house.

Vocabulary

VERBS

بعث *ba'aθa* send, send forth; resurrect

ذكر *ðakara* mention, make mention of, recollect

ضل *ḍalla (*ḍalala)* go astray, get lost

فعل *fa'ala* do

هدى *hadā* lead, lead aright

NOUNS

بشر *bašar-* human being, mankind

ماء/مياه *mā'-* pl *miyāh-* water

OTHERS

بعد *ba'da* (+ gen., temporal preposition) after; also *min ba'di* + gen.; note especially the adverbial *min ba'du* afterwards

عند *'inda* (+ gen.) with, in the possession of, in the opinion of, in the presence of, in/at the house of (like the French *chez,* Latin *apud); min 'indi* (+ gen.) from among, from the presence/possession of

قبل *qabla* (+ gen., temporal preposition) before; also *min qabli* + gen.; (adverbial) *min qablu* beforehand

ل *la-* (proclitic) "really," an emphasizing particle that affects no case; it often marks the predicate of an *'inna*-clause and is usually best left untranslated

ما *mā* (negative particle) not, takes its complement in the nominative or, like *laysa,* with *bi-*

PROPER NAMES

الانجيل *al-'injīlu* the Gospel, the Evangel

التوراة *at-tawrātu* the Torah, the Pentateuch

Exercises

(a) Give the active and passive (if possible) participles:

١ امر	٥ خلق	٩ سمع	١٣ لعن
٢ بعث	٦ دخل	١٠ فعل	١٤ منع
٣ جعل	٧ ذكر	١١ كتب	١٥ نزل
٤ خرج	٨ ذهب	١٢ كفر	١٦ وجد

(b) Vocalize, read and translate:

١ دخلوا النار بامر الله وما هم بخارجين منها

٢ قال النبى انى كنت نبياً وآدم بين الماء والطين

٣ وكان امر الله مفعولاً

٤ والذى كفر بعد ذلك بالله وملائكته وكتبه ورسله واليوم الآخر فقد ضلّ

٥ هذا هو الرسول النبى الذى وجدوه مكتوباً عندهم فى التوراة والانجيل

٦ قال ربك للملائكة انى خالق بشراً من طين

٧ ان الله فى قلوب عباده المخلصين

٨ انى ذاهب الى ربى

٩ ولما كان الملائكة ساجدين لآدم قال ابليس أخلقتنى لهذا انى له لعدو

١٠ المؤمنون كرجل واحد

١١ كان الرجل نازلاً الى العدو فأتاه رسول باوامر الشيخ

١٢ ليس هذا مذكوراً فى الكتب التى رايتها

١٣ بعثه عند الكفار فهداهم

١٤ اولئك هم الرجال الذين هدونا الى الماء ونحن قد ضللنا

١٥ والله هو الذى خلق من الماء بشراً

(c) Translate into Arabic:

1. We were sent, and so we have come to you.

2. Thus it was written in the Torah of Moses and the Gospel of Jesus.

3. The words of mankind are heard in God's presence.

4. You brought the king's orders, but the men of the city left before you.

5. After that, they saw a woman going down to the spring for water.

6. Was it mentioned thus in the books that are in your possession?

7. I saw him with[1] his finger over his heart, and that was for me like the king's command.

8. You saw all my children except for Muhammad, who[2] was not near our house on *(fī)* that day.

---

[1]Use circumstantial *wa-*.

[2]Because proper names are semantically definite, they require the relative pronoun.

Lesson Eleven

27 Active and Passive Participles (cont.).

27.1 For hollow verbs (C_2w/y), the active participial pattern is FĀ'IL-, with *hamza* taking the place of C_2 in all cases.

قائم < قام *qāma* (√QWM) > *qā'im-*
سائر < سار *sāra* (√SYR) > *sā'ir-*

27.2 For weak-*lām* verbs (C_3w/y) the pattern is FĀ'IN, the inflection of which demands special treatment. An example is *hādin*, from √HDY:

	INDEFINITE	DEFINITE
nom. & gen.	هادٍ *hādin*	الهادي *al-hādī*
acc.	هادياً *hādiyan*	الهادي *al-hādiya*

In both the definite and indefinite states, the nominative and genitive cases are identical. Only the accusative case actually shows its case ending. This results from an internal collapse due to weakness: **hādiyun* → *hādin* and **hādiyin* → *hādin*, where the "weak" vowels *u* and *i* cannot maintain a weak consonant between them; the "strong" vowel *a* does support a weak consonant, so *hādiyan* and *al-hādiya* do not suffer collapse.

The feminines are regularly formed, with *-y-* for C_3w as well as for C_3y roots: *hādiyat-* pl *hādiyāt-*.

The masculine plurals suffer the same collapse as the singular: **hādiyūna* → *hādūna* and **hādiyīna* → *hādīna*.

The inflectional patterns of *hādin* are not limited to active participles but occur with many broken plurals of C_2w/y roots and also certain anomalous plurals such as ارض *'arḍ-* pl اراض *'arāḍin,* اسم *ism-* pl اسام *'asāmin,* and يد *yad-* pl ايد *'aydin* and اياد *'ayādin.*[1]

27.3 Doubled verbs undergo the same loss of weak vowel as in the verbal inflection. The pattern for the active participle is FĀLL- (< **fālil-).*

دلّ *dalla* > **dālil-* > دالّ *dāll-*

27.4 Passive participles of hollow, weak-*lām* and doubled verbs.

(1) The contracted pattern MAFŪL- is used for C_2w roots *(*mafwūl- → mafūl-).*

قال *qāla (√QWL)* > **maqwūl-* → مقول *maqūl-*

لام *lāma (√LWM)* > **malwūm-* → ملوم *malūm-*

The patterns MAFĪL- and MAFYŪL- (regular) are attested for most C_2y roots.

باع *bā'a* ('sell') *(√BY')* > مبيع ، مبيوع *mabyū'-/mabī'-*

كال *kāla* ('measure') *(√KYL)* > مكيل ، مكيول *makyūl-/makīl-*

(2a) Weak-*lām* roots: C_3w produces a regular passive participle on the pattern MAF'ŪW-.

دعا *da'ā (√D'W)* > مدعوّ *mad'ūw-*

(2b) C_3y roots give a passive participle on the pattern MAF'ĪY-.

هدى *hadā (√HDY)* > مهديّ *mahdīy-*

(3) The formation of passive participles from doubled roots is perfectly regular.

دلّ *dalla (√DLL)* > مدلول *madlūl-*

---

[1]The indefinite accusative of *'arāḍin, 'asāmin,* and *'ayādin* are without nunation: *'arāḍiya, 'asāmiya* and *'ayādiya* (see Appendix A §10e). The indefinite accusative of *'aydin* has nunation: *'aydiyan* (see Appendix A §1d).

28 Verbal Nouns. Every verb in Arabic has at least one verbal noun, known as a *maṣdar-*, the usage of which is roughly equivalent to the English infinitive or gerund in '-ing.' Many verbal nouns have a concrete meaning as a noun as well as the verbal sense, as *xalq- (< xalaqa),* which means "creation" as well as "(the act of) creating." Verbal nouns of the base form of the verb (the only one introduced so far) are not predictable and must be learned as a "principal part" for each and every verb.

28.1 Following are the verbal nouns, by pattern, for the verbs that have been seen so far (note that some verbs have more than one verbal noun in common use, often reflecting different senses of the verb).

(1) FA'L-, the most common pattern for verbal nouns, generally for transitive verbs of the *fa'ala* and *fa'ila* types.

أمر	*'amr-*	رأى	*ra'y-*[1]	قول	*qawl-*
بعث	*ba'θ-*	رمى	*ramy-*	لعن	*la'n-*
جعل	*ja'l-*	عفو	*'afw-*	منع	*man'-*
خلق	*xalq-*	فعل	*fa'l-*	موت	*mawt-*

(2) FU'ŪL-, mainly for intransitive *fa'ala* verbs.

خروج	*xurūj-*	سجود	*sujūd-*	وجود	*wujūd-*
دخول	*duxūl-*	نزول	*nuzūl-*		

(3) FI'L-,

ذكر	*ðikr-*	فعل	*fi'l-*

(4) FU'L(AT)-

رؤية	*ru'yat-*	كفر	*kufr-*

(5) FA'ĀL(AT)-

ذهاب	*ðahāb-*	سماع	*samā'-*	ضلال/ضلالة	*ḍalāl(at)-*

[1]Of the two senses of *ra'ā*, "to see" and "to consider," *ra'y-* is the verbal noun for "considering, notion, view" and *ru'yat-* is the verbal noun for "seeing, vision."

(6) FI'ĀL(AT)-

قيام *qiyām-* كتابة *kitābat-* هداية *hidāyat-*

The verbal noun is extensively used as a verbal complement, especially with verbs that take their complements through prepositions, for example:

منعه من الدخول	*mana'ahu mina d-duxūli*	He prevented him from entering
دعوناهم الى الخروج	*da'awnāhum 'ilā l-xurūji*	We called upon them to leave.
امرونا بالسماع	*'amarūnā bis-samā'i*	They ordered us to hear.

Where the Arabic verbal noun corresponds to an English infinitive or gerund, it is almost always definite (as in the above examples).

28.2 Subjective and Objective Genitives. When only the doer of the action (subject) occurs with a verbal noun, it is put into construct with the noun as a **subjective genitive.**

خلق الله	*xalqu llāhi*	God's creating (creation)
دخول الرجال	*duxūlu r-rijāli*	the men's entering
بعث الملك	*ba'θu l-maliki*	the king's sending

When only the object of a verbal noun occurs, it is in construct as an **objective genitive.**

خلق الارض	*xalqu l-'arḍi*	creating the earth
دخول البيت	*duxūlu l-bayti*	entering the house
بعث رسول	*ba'θu rasūlin*	sending a messenger

When both the subject and the object occur with a verbal noun, the subject is in construct in the **genitive** and the object follows in the **accusative**.

خلق الله الارض	*xalqu llāhi l-'arḍa*	God's creating the earth

دخول الرجال البيت	*duxūlu r-rijāli l-bayta*	the men's entering the house
بعث الملك رسولاً	*ba'θu l-maliki rasūlan*	the king's sending a messenger

29 The Cognate Accusative. One of the most common uses of the verbal noun is as a cognate accusative. This typically Semitic construction gives added emphasis to the verb.

ذكروا الله ذكراً	*ðakarū llāha ðikran*	They recollected God.[1]

When the cognate accusative is modified, it usually translates adverbially.

ذكروا الله ذكراً كثيراً	*ðakarū llāha ðikran kaθīran*	They recollected God much/ often.
خرج خروج عبد	*xaraja xurūja 'abdin*	He went out servilely.[2]

Vocabulary

VERBS

أخذ *'axaða 'axð-*[3] take, seize; take hold (*bi-* of)

سأل *sa'ala su'āl-* ask (*'an* about)

عبد *'abada 'ibādat-* worship

NOUNS/ADJECTIVES

اثنان/اثنتان *iθnāni* (m), *iθnatāni* (f) two; *yawmu l-iθnayni* Monday

آخر/أخرى/أخر *'āxaru* (m), *'uxrā* (f), *'uxaru* (pl) other

أحد/إحدى *'aḥad-* (m), *'iḥdā* (f) one (pronoun, used either with partitive *min* or with construct, e.g., *'aḥadun minhum* or *'aḥaduhum* 'one of them'); (+ neg.) no one, nobody; *yawmu l-'aḥadi* Sunday

---

[1]Lit., "they recollected God a recollecting."

[2]Lit., "he went out the going out of a slave, as a slave would."

[3]The verbal noun will be so listed with every new verb henceforth.

تربة ، تراب *turbat-* and *turāb-* dust, earth, ground

جبل/جبال *jabal-* pl *jibāl-* mountain

جديد/جدد *jadīd-* pl *judud-* new

خلق *xalq-* creation, created beings, people

رحمة *raḥmat-* mercy

رحيم *raḥīm-* merciful, compassionate

سبت *sabt-* Sabbath; *yawmu s-sabti* Saturday[1]

يهود ، يهودى *yahūd-* (collective) Jews; *yahūdiyy-* (sing.)[2] Jew, Jewish

OTHERS

ما *mā* that which, what (relative); *kullu mā* everything that, all that which

من *man(i)* who? (interrogative pronoun); he who, whoever (relative pronoun); *kullu man* everyone who, all who

مما *mimmā* = *min* + *mā*

ممن *mimman* = *min* + *man*

Exercises

(a) Give the active participle, masc. and fem. sing., def. and indef.:

١ اتى   ٣ نام   ٥ رأى   ٧ خاف   ٩ قال   ١١ رمى

٢ دعا   ٤ سأل   ٦ كان   ٨ أمر   ١٠ قام   ١٢ أكل

(b) Give the passive participle of as many verbs as possible from the list in (a).

(c) Read and translate:

١ ان اليهود أتت النبى فسألته عن خلق السموات والارض فقال خلق الله

---

[1]For the other days of the week, see Appendix H.

[2]This represents a large class of words for peoples, nations and groups, where the unit singular is formed by adding *-iyy-* to the collective, e.g., افرنج *'ifranj-* 'Franks, Europeans,' روم *rūm-* 'Greek Orthodox, Byzantines,' زنج *zanj-* 'Blacks, Ethiopians,' عجم *'ajam-* 'Persians,' عرب *'arab-* 'Arabs,' يونان *yūnān-* 'Greeks, Hellenes.'

الارض يوم الاحد والاثنين.
٢ وقال قائل آخر أخذ رسول الله بيدى فقال خلق الله التربة يوم السبت وخلق
الجبال يوم الاحد.
٣ يا نساء النبى، لستن كاحد من النساء.
٤ أمرنى بعبادة الله مخلصاً له.
٥ قال النبى لست كاحدكم.
٦ قد فعل الصالحون ما امرهم الله به.
٧ الدنيا ملعونة وملعون ما فيها الا ذكر الله.
٨ هداكم وكنتم من قبله لمن الضالين وكنتم بعبادتكم كافرين.
٩ وجدته ضالا فهديته وانك لكل قوم هاد.
١٠ انا باعث لكم كتاباً قد كتبت فيه كل ما ذكر لى الرجل الذى كان عندى.

(d) Translate into Arabic:

1. He who heard Gabriel's voice was a leader for humankind.

2. I prevented him from going against his people and from sending the messenger to them.

3. On the last day the rich will be *(kāna)* poor because of their disbelief.

4. She is sending to us one of her sons with his daughter.

5. The last of the infidels said to me, "Your religion is not better than our religion, but it is not forbidden here."

6. Did you hear the summoner who called the nation and said, "The day of judgment is coming"?

7. The women are bringing water from the spring.

8. That which they seized was not theirs.

9. This is one of the things seized from the possession of (من عند) the poor.

10. The mountains are created from the dust of the earth.

Lesson Twelve

30 Verbal Inflection: Imperfect Indicative. The Arabic imperfect is basically the imperfective, or durative, aspect of the verb for habitual or on-going action and contrasts with the perfect, the perfective or punctual aspect of the verb, which signals actions and changes of state that happen at one temporal point, usually but not necessarily past.

30.1 The imperfect indicative inflection is formed by adding personal prefixes (preformatives) and suffixes (postformatives) to the imperfect base of the verb. The imperfect base may be on any one of the following patterns: (1) *-f'al-*, (2) *-f'ul-*, or (3) *-f'il-*. Whereas the vowel of C_2 is not predictable, either from the perfect base or from the radicals, and must be learned as a "principal part" of the verb, the following guidelines are offered:

(1) Verbs of the *fa'ala* type generally have an imperfect base in *-f'ul-* or *-f'il-*, except verbs whose second or third radical is guttural *(', ', h, ḥ, x, ğ)*, which tends to produce *-a-* in the imperfect base, as *la'ana* gives an imperfect base of *-l'an-* and *ðahaba* gives an imperfect base of *-ðhab-*.

(2) Verbs of the *fa'ila* type—with very few exceptions—have imperfect bases in *-f'al-*, as *fahima* ('understand') gives an imperfect of *-fham-*.

(3) Verbs of the *fa'ula* type, all of which are stative or qualitative in meaning, have imperfect bases in *-f'ul-*, as *kabura* ('to be/get big') has an imperfect of *-kbur-*.

30.2 The personal prefixes and suffixes added to the imperfect base are as follows:

	SINGULAR	DUAL	PLURAL
3 m	*ya-CCvC-u*	*ya-CCvC-āni*	*ya-CCvC-ūna*
f	*ta-CCvC-u*	*ta-CCvC-āni*	*ya-CCvC-na*
2 m	*ta-CCvC-u*	*ta-CCvC-āni*	*ta-CCvC-ūna*
f	*ta-CCvC-īna*	*ta-CCvC-āni*	*ta-CCvC-na*
1 c	*'a-CCvC-u*	—	*na-CCvC-u*

Example: *kataba* 'write,' imperfect base *-ktub-:*

3 m	يكتب	***yaktubu***	يكتبان	***yaktubāni***	يكتبون	***yaktubūna***
f	تكتب	***taktubu***	تكتبان	***taktubāni***	يكتبن	***yaktubna***
2 m	تكتب	***taktubu***	تكتبان	***taktubāni***	تكتبون	***taktubūna***
f	تكتبين	***taktubīna***	تكتبان	***taktubāni***	تكتبن	***taktubna***
1 c	اكتب	***'aktubu***	—	—	نكتب	***naktubu***

30.3 The negative particle for the imperfect is generally *lā* prefixed to the verb: *lā yaktubu, lā taktubu, &c.*

30.4 Independent uses of the imperfect indicative:

(1) general present: *yadxulu* "he enters/does enter/is entering."

(2) durative (no specific tense): *yaδhabu* "he was/is/will be going"

(3) habitual (no specific tense): *ya'muru* "he orders (as a matter of habit), he will order/will be ordering (habitually)"

(4) simple future: *yaktubu* "he will write/will be writing."

Tense for the durative and habitual aspects of the imperfect is usually gained from context, although it may be made explicit by combination with various verbs, especially the perfect of *kāna* for the past habitual: *kāna yaktubu* "he used to write."

The affirmative future may be made explicit by prefixing the proclitic *sa-* or the separate particle *sawfa: sa-yaktubu* or *sawfa yaktubu* "he will write, he will be writing." These particles do not occur with the negative (for the negative future explicit see §44.2[2]).

30.5 Dependent uses of the imperfect:

(1) as complement to the subject:

جاء اهل المدينة يسألون	*jā'a 'ahlu l-madīnati yas'alūna*	The people of the city came asking.
ذهب يطلبه	*ðahaba yaṭlubuhu*	He went off looking for it.

(2) as complement to the object:

وجدتهم يعبدون الله	*wajadtuhum ya'budūna llāha*	I found them worshipping God (habitually).

(3) as circumstantial, usually with *wa-* + pronoun:

رأيته وهو يلعن عدوه	*ra'aytuhu wa-huwa yal'anu 'adūwahu*	I saw him (while he was) cursing his enemy.

30.6 Imperfect of C_1' verbs. Verbs whose first radical is /'/ are regularly inflected in the imperfect, with the exception of the 1st-person singular, where the expected initial *'a'-* becomes *'ā-* to avoid two adjacent glottal stops.

اخذ > آخذ *'axaða* > **'a'xuðu* → *'āxuðu*

اكل > آكل *'akala* > **'a'kulu* → *'ākulu*

30.7 The following is a list of the sound verbs introduced so far, arranged by the characteristic vowel of the second radical in the imperfect:

(1) imperfect in *-u-*: يأخُذ يخرُج يدخُل يسجُد يكتُب
يأمُر يخلُق يذكُر يعبُد يكفُر

(2) imperfect in *-a-*: يبعَث يسمَع يلعَن يذهَب
يجعَل يفعَل يمنَع يسأل

(3) imperfect in *-i-*: ينزِل

Vocabulary

VERBS

اكل *'akala (u)*[1] *'akl-* eat, consume

شهد *šahida (a) šuhūd-/šahādat-* bear witness, testify (*'alā* against); followed by *'inna* to introduce direct quotation; followed by *'anna* to introduce indirect quotation

صدق *ṣadaqa (u) ṣidq-* tell the truth to (+ acc.), be truthful

علم *'alima (a) 'ilm-* know, learn (*bi-* about); realize

غر *ğarra (u) ğurūr-* delude, deceive

كذب *kaðaba (i) kiðb-/kaðib-* lie, tell a lie (acc. or *'alā*, to someone)

نظر *naẓara (u) naẓar-* look, regard

NOUNS/ADJECTIVES

اهل/اهالٍ *'ahl-* pl *'ahālin/'ahlūna* people; family; *'ahlu madīnatin* the people, inhabitants of a city; *'ahlu l-kitābi* Christians and Jews, people possessed of scripture

شمس *šams-* (f) sun

علم/علوم *'ilm-* pl *'ulūm-* knowledge (*bi-* of), learning

فاكهة/فواكه *fākihat-* pl *fawākihu* fruit

كريم *karīm-* pl *kirām-/kuramā'u* noble, generous, honorable

نبأ/انباء *naba'-* pl *'ambā'-* news

يقين *yaqīn-* certainty; *'ilmu l-yaqīni* certain knowledge

---

[1] The characteristic vowel of the imperfect will be so indicated in the vocabularies.

OTHERS

أن *'anna* (+ acc.) that (subordinating conjunction, follows verbs of perception; like *'inna*, must be followed by noun in the accusative or enclitic pronoun)

سـ *sa*- (proclitic + imperfect) particle for the future explicit

سوف *sawfa* (+ imperfect) particle for the future explicit

لِمَ ، لما ، لماذا *li-ma/li-mā/li-māðā* why?

ماذا *māðā* what?

PROPER NAMES

سبأ *saba'* - Sheba

سليمان *sulaymānu* Solomon

Exercises

(a) Give the imperfect of each of the following (retain the number, gender and person):

١ خرجوا	٥ بعثتَ	٩ دخلا	١٣ سألتم	١٧ عبدنا
٢ كفرتَ	٦ نزلتم	١٠ اخذتُ	١٤ جعلتِ	١٨ ذكرتا
٣ سجدتما	٧ فعلتُ	١١ لعنوا	١٥ امرنا	١٩ خلقتْ
٤ ذهبن	٨ سمعتن	١٢ كتبتِ	١٦ منعا	٢٠ علم

(b) Give the imperfect of each of the following (retain the number, gender and person of the verb; also retain the pronoun object):

١ اخذوكم	٣ منعتمونى	٥ لعنتْهم	٧ عبدناه	٩ فعلنها
٢ سمعتُهما	٤ سألاها	٦ ذكرتِه	٨ دخلتَه	١٠ خلقكم

(c) Read and translate:

١ والله يشهد انهم لكاذبون

٢ يا اهل الكتاب لم تكفرون بآيات الله وانتم تشهدون

٣ اولئك الذين يكذبون على ربهم فمقامهم فى النار

٤ فقال انى لأصدق ولست من الكاذبين وانى أعلم ما لا تعلمون

٥ قالوا شهدنا على انفسنا وغرّتنا الحياة الدنيا وشهدوا على انفسهم أنهم
كانوا كافرين
٦ قد خلقنا جنات لكم فيها فواكه كثيرة منها تاكلون
٧ ليس لنا به علم والله يعلم ونحن لا نعلم
٨ وهؤلاء هم الذين يعلم الله ما فى قلوبهم
٩ سالعنهم لسؤالهم عن ذلك
١٠ لم تعبد ما لا يسمع
١١ كان النبى يأمر أهله بالصلاة
١٢ فهى كذبت وهو من الصادقين

(d) Translate into Arabic:

1. You deceived us with *(bi-)* your lying.
2. On that great day hell will consume them all.
3. I will not testify against her, she being truthful.
4. The inhabitants of the city have certain knowledge that one of them took the fruits from their garden.
5. We asked the other woman from where she heard this news.
6. The angels will seize those who disbelieved and put their souls in hell.
7. I shall write a book for my sons, and in it I shall put all of my knowledge.
8. I do not eat from that which those eat.
9. The king takes everything from his people.
10. We looked and saw him prostrate (use participle) in the dust of the earth.
11. Thus it is written: an eye for an eye, and a tooth for a tooth.

Reading Selection: *Ṣūrat al-Naml (27): 22–30,* with slight modification.

Solomon and Sheba

[قال الهدهد[1] لسليمان] جئتُك من سبأٍ بنبأٍ يقينٍ (٢٢)

إنى وجدتُ امرأةً تملِكُهم[3] ... ولها عَرْشٌ[2] عظيمٌ (٢٣)

وجدتُها وقومَها يسجدون للشمس من دون[4] الله (٢٤)

لا يسجدون لله الذى ... يعلم [كل شىء] (٢٥)

قال [سليمان] سننظر أصدقتَ أم[5] كنت من الكاذبين (٢٧)

اذهب[7] بكتابى هذا ... فانظر[6] ماذا [يفعلون] (٢٨)

قالت يا أيّها[9] الملأ[8] إنى [أتانى] كتابٌ كريمٌ (٢٩)

إنه من سليمان وإنه باسم الله الرحمن الرحيم (٣٠)

---

[1] *Hudhud*- the hoopoe-bird, Solomon's scout.
[2] *'Arš*- throne.
[3] *Malaka (i)* to rule.
[4] *Min dūni* to the exclusion of.
[5] *'Am* or (in an interrogative).
[6] *Fa-nẓur* (imperative) and see!
[7] *Iðhab* (imperative) go!
[8] *Mala'* - council of chieftains.
[9] *Yā 'ayyuhā* (vocative particle + nom.) O.

Lesson Thirteen

31 The Five Nouns. There are five nouns in Arabic that behave in an unusual way when they are first members of a construct. Instead of the normal short case-ending vowel, these five nouns show the case-ending as long. Of the five, *'ab-* ('father'), *'ax-* ('brother'), and *ḥam-* ('father-in-law') behave as regular nouns when not in construct. The fourth, *ðū* ('possessed of/possessing'), occurs only as first member of a construct and has no indefinite form at all. The fifth, *fam-* ('mouth'), is a regular noun when not in construct but becomes *fū-* (nom.) when in construct. The double hyphen (=) indicates forms that occur only as first member of a construct:

	NOMINATIVE	GENITIVE	ACCUSATIVE
اب *'ab-*	ابو *'abū=*	ابى *'abī=*	ابا *'abā=*
اخ *'ax-*	اخو *'axū=*	اخى *'axī=*	اخا *'axā=*
حم *ḥam-*	حمو *ḥamū=*	حمى *ḥamī=*	حما *ḥamā=*
ذو *ðū=*	ذو *ðū=*	ذى *ðī=*	ذا *ðā=*
فم *fam-*	فو *fū=*	فى *fī=*	فا *fā=*

The addition of the 1st-sing. possessive enclitic to the first three nouns results in regular forms based on the indefinite: *'abī* "my father," *'axī* "my brother," &c. With other pronominal enclitics the construct forms given above are used: *'abūhu/'abīhi/'abāhu* "his father," &c. *Fīya* serves as "my mouth" for all cases. The word *ðū* does not take pronominal enclitics. With pronominals both *fam-* and the construct forms are used: فمه *famuhu/famihi/ famahu* and فوه *fūhu,* فيه *fīhi* and فاه *fāhu.*

32 *Imru'un*. The noun *imru'-* ('man, male human being'), like its feminine counterpart *imra'at-*, begins with elidible *alif*. The declensional peculiarity of this noun lies in the fact that the vowel after the *r* harmonizes with the declensional vowel in all three cases. This is turn affects the bearer of the *hamza* (see Appendix G).

	INDEFINITE		DEFINITE	
NOM.	امرؤ	*imru'un*	امرؤ	*imru'u*
GEN.	امرئ	*imri'in*	امرئ	*imri'i*
ACC.	امرأ	*imra'an*	امرأ	*imra'a*

33 Exception. The common particle of exception is *'illā*. When it occurs in a negative clause to mean "(no one, nothing) but/except," it does not affect the case of the following noun. That is, the syntax remains as it would be if both the negative and *'illā* were removed.

ما جاء الا الولد	*mā jā'a 'illā l-waladu*	No one came but the boy (only the boy came).
ما نزل الكتاب الا ذكرا لكم	*mā nazala l-kitābu 'illā ðikran lakum*	The book descended only as a reminder to you.

The particle *'illā* is commonly followed by a purpose clause or prepositional phrase.

ما امرهم الا بعبادة الله	*mā 'amarahum 'illā bi-'ibādati llāhi*	He did not order them (to do anything) except to worship God.[1]

In affirmative sentences, *'illā* takes the accusative.

قام القوم الا رجلاً واحداً	*qāma l-qawmu 'illā **rajulan wāḥidan***	The people stood up—all but one man.

[1]Or, "he ordered them only to worship God."

34 Categoric Negation. The negative particle *lā* followed by an indefinite noun with a definite accusative ending *(-a)* gives the sense of total negation of the category to which the noun belongs.[1] This construction is the negation of the predication of existence (§5).

لا نبا لنا	*lā naba'a lanā*	(There is) no news to us (we have no news).
لا رجال فى المدينة	*lā rijāla fi l-madīnati*	There are no men in the city.

The categoric negative *lā* is often found in combination with *'illā*.

لا اله الا الله	*lā 'ilāha 'illā llāhu*	There is no god but God (the only god there is is God).

Vocabulary

VERB

وهب *wahaba* give

NOUNS

اب/آباء *'ab-* pl *'ābā'-* (construct nom. *'abū=)* father, progenitor; dual *'abawāni* parents

ابتى *'abatī* (anomalous form) "my dear father"

اخ/اخوة ، اخوان *'ax-* pl *'ixwat-/'ixwān-* (construct nom. *'axū=*, dual *'axawāni)* brother

اخت/اخوات *'uxt-* pl *'axawāt-* sister

اله/آلهة *'ilāh-* pl *'ālihat-* god, deity

اولو الامر *'ulū l-'amr* (nom.), *'ulī l-'amr* (obl.) those in authority

امرؤ *imru'-* (no plural) man, male (with the definite article, المرء *al-mar'-*)

---

[1]The categoric negative of the Five Nouns introduced in §31 shows long *-ā*, as in *lā 'axā laka* "you have no brother."

ذو *ðū=*[1] possessor of, owner of

صنم/اصنام *ṣanam-* pl *'aṣnām-* idol

OTHERS

ان *'in* not (invariable negative particle)

الا *'illā* except, except for (particle of exception)

الا *'allā = 'an + lā* that…not, that…no

او *'aw(i)* or

بل *bal(i)* on the contrary, but rather

هل *hal(i)* interrogative particle

PROPER NAMES

هرون *hārūnu* Aaron

فرعون *fir'awnu* Pharaoh

مصر *miṣru* (f) Egypt

Exercises

(a) Read and translate:

١ مات المرء ولا ولد له فأكل اخوته كل ما كان عنده

٢ لقد رأيناهم يعبدون الاصنام هم وآباؤهم واخوانهم واخواتهم

٣ يا اخت هرون ، ما كان ابوك امرأ سوءٍ[2]

---

[1]All forms given here for reference; note especially the suppletion forms for the masc. pl., *'ulū=/'ulī=*, the *wāw* of which is otiose.

	NOMINATIVE		GENITIVE		ACCUSATIVE	
masc. sing.	ذو	*ðū=*	ذي	*ðī=*	ذا	*ðā=*
fem. sing.	ذات	*ðātu*	ذات	*ðāti*	ذات	*ðāta*
masc. dual	ذوا	*ðawā=*	ذوي	*ðaway=*	ذوي	*ðaway=*
fem. dual	ذواتا	*ðawātā=*	ذواتي	*ðawātay=*	ذواتي	*ðawātay=*
masc. pl.	اولو	*'ulū=*	اولي	*'ulī=*	اولي	*'ulī=*
	ذوو	*ðawū=*	ذوي	*ðawī=*	ذوي	*ðawī=*
fem. pl.	ذوات	*ðawātu*	ذوات	*ðawāti*	ذوات	*ðawāti*

[2]*Saw'*- evil (noun, not adjective).

٤ ان هو الا كاذب غرّنا بقوله الكاذب

٥ يا ابانا الذى فى السموات ...

٦ اشهد الا اله الا الله واشهد ان محمداً رسول الله

٧ وهب الله لموسى اخاه هرون نبياً وبعثهما بآياته الى فرعون

٨ هذا النبأ لأولى الامر من قومنا وليس للذين لا علم لهم به

٩ هل علمت لم قام ابوك واخوك من مقامهما وخرجا من مدينة اهلهما

١٠ ان تلك المرأة الجميلة لا تنظر الى الحياة الدنيا بل هى ناظرة الى الآخرة

١١ كان هرون اخا موسى وكان لهما اخت اسمها مريم

١٢ ان امرأة فرعون واسمها آسية بنت مُزاحِم وجدت موسى وهو ولد صغير فاخذته من المياه وكان ابناً لها

(b) Translate into Arabic:

1. After that Moses left the land of Egypt and went to another land.

2. The news has come to us today that many of *(min)* the inhabitants of the city have died.

3. Did you lie to us when you testified against your brother?

4. There is no pious one except him who worships God with *(bi-)* all his heart and with certain knowledge.

5. There is no fruit in my father's garden, so we will eat but little tonight.

6. He, his father and brother all rose for the prayer, and afterwards they came to our house.

Lesson Fourteen

35 Doubled Verbs: Imperfect Indicative. Doubled verbs in the imperfect inflection combine C_2 and C_3, throwing the vowel of C_2 back onto C_1 in all persons except the feminine plural forms, the only imperfect suffixes that begin with consonants. Example: *dalla* "to guide" > **yadlulu* → *yadullu*.

	SINGULAR		DUAL		PLURAL	
3 m	يدلّ	*yadullu*	يدلّان	*yadullāni*	يدلّون	*yadullūna*
f	تدلّ	*tadullu*	تدلّان	*tadullāni*	يدللن	***yadlulna***
2 m	تدلّ	*tadullu*	تدلّان	*tadullāni*	تدلّون	*tadullūna*
f	تدلّين	*tadullīna*	تدلّان	*tadullāni*	تدللن	***tadlulna***
1 c	ادلّ	*'adullu*	—	—	ندلّ	*nadullu*

36 Elative Pattern: 'AF'ALU.

36.1 The patterns for the elatives, which are formed from adjectives and *fā'il-* participles, are as follows:

	SINGULAR		DUAL		PLURAL	
masc.	افعل	*'af'alu*	افعلان	*'af'alāni*	افعلون	*(1) 'af'alūna*
					افاعل	*(2) 'afā'ilu*
fem.	فعلى	*fu'lā*	فعليان	*fu'layāni*	فعليات	*(1) fu'layāt-*
					فعل	*(2) fu'al-*

From an adjective like *kabīr-*, the elatives are:

masc.	اكبر	*'akbaru*	اكبران	*'akbarāni*	اكبرون	*(1) 'akbarūna*
					اكابر	*(2) 'akābiru*
fem.	كبرى	*kubrā*	كبريان	*kubrayāni*	كبريات	*(1) kubrayāt-*
					كبر	*(2) kubar-*

36.2 Patterns for weak radicals.

(1) C_2y roots become *fūlā* in the feminine singular *fu'lā* pattern:

طيّب < طوبى *ṭayyib-* > *ṭūbā* more pleasant

All other C_2y forms are regular. All C_2w forms are perfectly regular.

(2) C_3w/y roots become 'AF'Ā with *alif maqṣūra* in the 'AF'ALU pattern.

عليّ < اعلى *'alīy-* > *'a'lā* higher

The feminine singular FU'LĀ pattern becomes FU'YĀ, with *y* for C_3.

عليّ < عليا *'alīy-* > *'ulyā* higher

دنيّ < دنيا *danīy-* > *dunyā* lower

Note that FU'YĀ is spelled with tall *alif*, not *alif maqṣūra*. The formative principle is that *alif maqṣūra* may not follow the letter *yā'*.

(3) The broken plural patterns 'AFĀ'ILU and FU'AL- become 'AFĀ'IN and FU'Ā with collapse of C_3. Thus, اعلى *'a'lā* > اعالٍ *'a'ālin* (a diptote pattern, see §27.2, note 1 for declension), and عليا *'ulyā* > على *'ulā*.

(4) Doubled roots geminate C_2 and C_3 and throw the vowel back onto C_1 in the 'AF'ALU pattern as 'AFALLU (i.e., **'aflalu* → *'afallu*).

جديد < اجدّ *jadīd-* > *'ajaddu* newer

All other patterns from doubled roots are regularly formed.

36.3 Comparative Usages. As an adjective in the comparative degree, the *masculine singular elative form is used regardless of the gen-*

der and number of the referent. When the preposition for "than," *min,* occurs, the elative is explicitly comparative.

انا اعلم منك	*'ana 'a'lamu minka*	I am more learned than you.
هى اكرم منه	*hiya 'akramu minhu*	She is more generous than he.
هم اقوى منا	*hum 'aqwā minnā*	They are stronger than we.

When the elative form occurs as an indefinite predicate adjective without a *min*-comparison, there is no essential difference between the comparative and superlative degrees. Such an elative should generally be considered emphatic or superlative in meaning.

الله اكبر	*allāhu 'akbaru*	God is greatest/very great.
الله اعلم	*allāhu 'a'lamu*	God knows best/most/is all knowing.

Only when the preposition *min* accompanies the elative is it *explicitly comparative.*

36.4 Superlative Usages. *A definite elative is explicitly superlative.* The superlative may be an attributive or predicative, and in both cases it agrees in number and gender with the noun it modifies.

انا ربكم الاعلى	*'ana rabbukumu l-'a'lā*	I am your highest lord.
لقد راى من آيات ربه الكبرى	*la-qad ra'ā min 'āyāti rabbihi l-kubrā*	He saw some of his lord's greatest signs.
خلق الارض والسموات العلى	*xalaqa l-'arḍa was-samāwāti l-'ulā*	He created the earth and the highest heavens.
كلمة الله هى العليا	*kalimatu llāhi hiya l-'ulyā*	God's word is the highest.
هم الاكرمون	*humu l-'akramūna*	They are the noblest.

The elative, generally the maculine singular form,[1] may also be in construct with a definite plural noun or pronoun (or noun or pronoun that indicates plurality, although the form may not be plural) for a superlative.

اقوى الرجال	*'aqwā r-rijāli*	the strongest of the men
اكرم النساء	*'akramu n-nisā'i*	the noblest of women
اكثرهم	*'akθaruhum*	most of them
اكبر اولاده	*'akbaru 'awlādihi*	the eldest of his children

Superlatives are also made by placing the masculine singular elative in construct with an *indefinite singular* noun.

اقوى رجل	*'aqwā rajulin*	the strongest man
اكرم امراة	*'akramu mra'atin*	the noblest woman
اكبر ولد له	*'akbaru waladin lahu*	his eldest child (the eldest child of his)

Note that the noun in this construction is grammatically indefinite; therefore, when it is the antecedent of a relative clause, the asyndetic-type clause (see §21.3) is used.

اقوى رجل رايته	*'aqwā rajulin ra'aytuhu*	the strongest man I (ever) saw

36.5 Two suppletion forms should be mentioned here: *xayr-* "good" and *šarr-* "evil." These two are nouns, not adjectives, and hence do not agree adjectivally. When followed by *min* they are used for "better" and "worse."

انا خير منه	*'ana xayrun minhu*	I am better than he is.
هم شر منكم	*hum šarrun minkum*	They are worse than you.

When followed in construct by the indefinite singular or the definite plural, *xayr-* and *šarr-* are superlative in meaning.

[1]The feminine singular elative is found, but it is of rare occurrence.

كنتم خير قوم	*kuntum xayra qawmin*	You were the best nation.
هو شر الكافرين	*huwa šarru l-kāfirīna*	He is the worst unbeliever.

36.6 The accusative of respect/specification. A noun in the indefinite accusative case follows the elative form to indicate the basis of comparison, or in what respect a thing is comparative or superlative. This construction is extensively used in combination with the elatives *'ašaddu* ('stronger'), *'akθaru* ('more'), and *'aqallu* ('less') for the comparative and superlative of words that either cannot or idiomatically do not occur in the elative pattern.

كانوا اشدّ منكم قوةً	*kānū <u>'ašadda</u> minkum <u>quwwatan</u>*	They were mightier ("stronger in might") than you were.
انا اكثر منك مالاً	*'ana 'akθaru minka <u>mālan</u>*	I have more wealth ("more with respect to wealth") than you.
هى اكثرهم علماً	*hiya <u>'akθar</u>uhum <u>'ilman</u>*	She is the most knowledgeable ("most in knowledge") of them.
هو اقلّ منها صدقاً	*huwa <u>'aqallu</u> minhā <u>ṣidqan</u>*	He is less truthful ("less with respect to truth") than she.

Vocabulary

VERBS

فر *farra (i) firār-* flee

مر *marra (u) murūr-* pass (*'alā* over), (*bi-* by)

ضل *ḍalla (i) ḍalāl(at)-* go astray, get lost

NOUNS

تقى/اتقياء *taqīy-* pl *'atqiyā'u* devout, God-fearing

شديد/اشدّاء *šadīd-* pl *'ašiddā'u* forceful, violent

شر *šarr-* evil, bad(ness); (+ *min*) worse than; (+ construct) worst
عدد/اعداد *'adad-* pl *'a'dād-* number
قوة/قوى *quwwat-* pl *quwan* strength, force, might
قوى/اقوياء *qawīy-* pl *'aqwiyā'u* strong, powerful
مال/اموال *māl-* pl *'amwāl-* property, possession, wealth
ناس *nās-* (pl, no singular) people

Exercises

(a) Read and translate:

١ اصغر المدن
٢ اقلّهم قوة
٣ اكبر اولادى
٤ الاكثرون مالا
٥ اغنى الاغنياء
٦ هم اكثر منكم علما
٧ بنتنا الكبرى
٨ المرأة العليا مقاما
٩ آية الله العظمى
١٠ هو اكبر منى سنا
١١ الاكثر عبادة لله
١٢ اشدّ قومنا كفرا

(b) Give the Arabic:

1. the most noble kings
2. the nearest city
3. newer than that
4. fewer in number
5. the biggest city
6. the highest heavens
7. the poorest woman
8. the strongest men
9. less strong than them
10. the most devout believer

(c) Read and translate:

١ انه لقول رسول كريم ذى قوة
٢ كانوا اشدّ منكم قوة واكثر اموالا واولادا
٣ لا قوة الا بالله
٤ ان العدو اقلّ منا عدداً
٥ لَخلق السموات والارض اكبر من خلق الناس ولكن اكثر الناس لا يعلمون
٦ ابوكم ذو مال كثير وانه اكرم قومه واصلحهم
٧ قد راينا من آيات الله العظمى فدعونا الناس ولكنهم شر قوم
٨ قال الله لقد خلقنا الانسان ونحن اقرب اليه من حبل الوريد[1]

[1] *Ḥablu l-warīdi* jugular vein.

١ ان اكرمكم عند الله اتقاكم

(d) Translate into Arabic:

1. My daughter is younger than my two sons.
2. Why do you flee from those men, who are ("they being," circumstantial) God's devout servants.
3. My brother is more powerful than those who are possessed of much might.
4. When I passed by his father's house, I saw the two of them bowing down (use participle) before an idol.
5. Moses and his people fled from the land after the passage of the angel of God over the houses of Egypt.
6. His sister is more learned [do two ways] than his brother.
7. My sisters have much property, but my brothers have more than they do.
8. Most of the people will go astray (future explicit), and there is no one for leading them aright.
9. Before today you have not mentioned what you saw in the mountains.
10. Pharaoh considered himself the greatest god of Egypt.

Lesson Fifteen

37 Imperfect Indicative: C2*w/y* Verbs. Verbs whose middle radical is *w* or *y* show the weakness in the imperfect with the long vowel corresponding to the original weak radical, i.e., *-ū-* for *w*, and *-ī-* for *y*. Example: √QWM > **yaqwumu* → *yaqūmu*.

	SINGULAR		DUAL		PLURAL	
3 m	يقوم	*yaqūmu*	يقومان	*yaqūmāni*	يقومون	*yaqūmūna*
f	تقوم	*taqūmu*	تقومان	*taqūmāni*	يقمن	***yaqumna***
2 m	تقوم	*taqūmu*	تقومان	*taqūmāni*	تقومون	*taqūmūna*
f	تقومين	*taqūmīna*	تقومان	*taqūmāni*	تقمن	***taqumna***
1 c	اقوم	*'aqūmu*	—	—	نقوم	*naqūmu*

The only forms that require special attention are the feminine plurals, where the long vowel has been shortened to accommodate the addition of the consonant-initial ending *(*yaqūm+na → yaqumna)*.

37.1 A few C2*w* verbs, such as *nāma* 'to sleep' and *xāfa* 'to fear,' with underlying imperfects in **yafwalu* have *-ā-* as the vowel of the imperfect, shortened to *-a-* in the feminine plurals.

3 m	ينام	*yanāmu*	ينامان	*yanāmāni*	ينامون	*yanāmūna*
f	تنام	*tanāmu*	تنامان	*tanāmāni*	ينمن	***yanamna,***

&c.

37.2 Almost all C2*y* verbs show *-ī-* as the vowel of the imperfect, with shortening to *-i-* in the feminine plurals, as √SYR *sāra:*

3 m	يسير	*yasīru*	يسيران	*yasīrāni*	يسيرون	*yasīrūna*

f	تسير	*tasīru*	تسيران	*tasīrāni*	يسرن	***yasirna***

38 Cardinal Numbers: 1–10. The cardinal numbers from one to ten are:

واحد	*wāḥid-* one	ست	*sitt-* six
اثنان	*iθnāni* two	سبع	*sab'-* seven
(ثلث) ثلاث	*θalāθ-* three	ثمانٍ	*θamānin* eight
اربع	*'arba'-* four	تسع	*tis'-* nine
خمس	*xams-* five	عشر	*'ašr-* ten

REMARKS:

(1) The number 'one,' *wāḥid(at)-*, functions as a regular adjective:

ولد واحد	*waladun wāḥidun*	one child
بنت واحدة	*bintun wāḥidatun*	one girl

(2) The number 'two,' as a pronoun or when needed to emphasize the dual—which is all that is normally necessary for 'two'—also functions as a regular dual adjective.

ولدان اثنان	*waladāni θnāni*	two children (nom.)
ولدين اثنين	*waladayni θnayni*	two children (obl.)
بنتان اثنتان	*bintāni θnatāni*	two girls (nom.)
بنتين اثنتين	*bintayni θnatayni*	two girls (obl.)

(3) The number 'eight,' *θamānin*, is inflected like *hādin* (see §27.2).

(4) The numbers from three through ten exhibit a phenomenon called *chiastic concord:* if the singular of the noun being counted is masculine, the number appears feminine with *tā' marbūṭa;* if the singular is feminine, the number appears masculine with no *tā' marbūṭa.* The numbers from three through ten form *constructs* with the *genitive plural* of the noun counted.

ثلاثة بيوت	*θalāθatu buyūtin*	three houses

The singular of *buyūt-*, *bayt-*, is masculine, hence a feminine-appearing number with the plural.

ثلاث مدن *θalāθu mudunin* three cities

The singular of *mudun-*, *madīnat-*, is feminine, hence a masculine-appearing number.

The following chart gives the numbers from one through ten using the examples *walad-* for a masculine singular and *bint-* for a feminine singular.

SINGULAR MASCULINE		SINGULAR FEMININE	
ولد واحد	*walad- wāḥid-*	بنت واحدة	*bint- wāḥidat-*
ولدان اثنان	*waladāni θnāni* (nom)	بنتان اثنتان	*bintāni θnatāni*
ثلاثة اولاد	*θalāθatu 'awlādin*	ثلاث بنات	*θalāθu banātin*
اربعة اولاد	*'arba'atu 'awlādin*	اربع بنات	*'arba'u banātin*
خمسة اولاد	*xamsatu 'awlādin*	خمس بنات	*xamsu banātin*
ستة اولاد	*sittatu 'awlādin*	ست بنات	*sittu banātin*
سبعة اولاد	*sab'atu 'awlādin*	سبع بنات	*sab'u banātin*
ثمانية اولاد	*θamāniyatu 'awlādin*	ثمانى بنات	*θamānī banātin*
تسعة اولاد	*tis'atu 'awlādin*	تسع بنات	*tis'u banātin*
عشرة اولاد	*'ašaratu 'awlādin*	عشر بنات	*'ašru banātin*

Note especially the masculine and feminine forms of 'ten.'

38.1 For the definite, (1) the number may follow the definite noun adjectivally but still with chiastic agreement, or (2) the article may be put on the noun, or (3) the article may be on both the noun and the number.

المدن الست *al-mudunu s-sittu*
ست المدن *sittu l-muduni* the six cities
الست المدن *as-sittu l-muduni*

Vocabulary

VERBS

خاف *xāfa (xif-) (ā) xawf-* fear, be afraid (+ acc. or *min* of), (*'alā* for, on behalf of)

سار *sāra (ī) sayr-* travel, set out, depart
ظلم *ẓalama (i) ẓulm-* wrong, treat unjustly, oppress
عمل *'amila (a) 'amal-* do, perform
نام *nāma (nim-) (ā) nawm-* sleep

NOUNS

صالحات *ṣāliḥāt-* good works, good deeds
ظلم *ẓulm-* injustice, tyranny
عالم/عوالم ، عالمون *'ālam-* pl *'awālimu/-ūna* world, pl. universe
عذاب/اعذبة *'aðāb-* pl *'a'ðibat-* torment
عمل/اعمال *'amal-* pl *'a'māl-* deed, job, chore, work
مثل/امثال *miθl-* pl *'amθāl-* likeness, similarity; *miθla* (+ gen.) like (preposition)

CONJUNCTION

يوم *yawma* (+ verb) on the day when

Exercises

(a) Give the Arabic for the following:

1. in five cities
2. eight men
3. from two gardens
4. one woman
5. in two houses
6. three prophets
7. six days
8. for eight girls
9. ten books
10. one son
11. seven heavens
12. ten fingers

(b) Read and translate:

١ ان النوم اخو الموت ولا يموت اهل الجنة
٢ يوم تسير الجبال سيراً ليخافون كلهم
٣ ان نساء قومنا لا يخفن من العدو شيئاً
٤ بعثنا اليكم اثنين يقومان بمنعكم من الظلم
٥ لابينا اربعة ابناء وثلاث بنات وله كذلك اخوان واخت واحدة
٦ ساقوم للسير الى اهلي ولا اخاف من احد وهم معي
٧ انكم لتقولون قولا عظيما

٨ ولا أقول لكم عندى خزائن[2] الله ولا أعلم الغيب[1] ولا أقول لكم انى ملَك
٩ انى اخاف عليكم عذاب يوم عظيم[3]
١٠ ومن يعمل من الصالحات وهو مؤمن فلا يخاف ظلماً
١١ الله الذى خلق سبع سموات ومن الارض مثلهن
١٢ ان الله لا يظلم الناس شيئاً ولكن الناس انفسهم يظلمون

(c) Translate into Arabic:

1. On that nearby day (the) man will flee from his brother and father.

2. The angel of death, from whom you (m pl) flee, will pass over those who are more powerful than you.

3. God made only one heart in the children of Adam, and in it he placed the spirit.

4. When I called them, they put their fingers in their ears, for they were not God-fearing.

5. Humankind is a noble creation.

6. We mentioned to the king that the enemy sent a large number of *(min)* their violent ones, who seized our possessions.

7. When you went astray I sent a messenger to you, and he led you aright.

8. Is one religion better than two?

9. I ordered him to depart, but he did nothing.

---

[1]*al-ğaybu* the unseen (realm).

[2]*Xazīnat-/xazā'inu* treasury, storehouse.

[3]*Yawmun 'aẓīmun* "a great day" is often used in the Koran to refer to Doomsday.

Lesson Sixteen

39 Imperfect Indicative Inflection: C3*w/y* Verbs. Weakness (*w* or *y*) in the third radical consonant (C3) appears in the imperfect indicative as (1) *-ā*, (2) *-ī*, or (3) *-ū*. In no case does the normal *-u* ending of the indicative show up.

39.1 Imperfect in *-ā*. Example *laqiya* (√LQY) > imperfect *yalqā:*

	SINGULAR		DUAL		PLURAL	
3 m	يلقى	*yalqā*	يلقيان	*yalqayāni*	يلقون	*yalqawna*
f	تلقى	*talqā*	تلقيان	*talqayāni*	يلقين	*yalqayna*
2 m	تلقى	*talqā*	تلقيان	*talqayāni*	تلقون	*talqawna*
f	تلقين	*talqayna*	تلقيان	*talqayāni*	تلقين	*talqayna*
1 c	القى	*'alqā*	—	—	نلقى	*nalqā*

REMARKS:

(1) The *alif maqṣūra* becomes consonantal *-y-* in the dual and feminine plurals.

(2) The masc. pl. ending *-ūna* becomes *-wna* to form a diphthong *(*-ayūna* [= *ayuwna*] → *-awna,* with loss of weak *-yu-).*

(3) The 2rd fem. sing. undergoes a similar diphthongization *(*-ayīna* [= *ayiyna*] → *-ayna,* with loss of weak *-yi-).*

(4) The *-a-* vowel of C2 remains stable throughout.

39.2 Imperfect in *-ī*. Example *ramā* (√RMY) > imperfect *yarmī:*

3 m	يرمى	*yarmī*	يرميان	*yarmiyāni*	يرمون	*yarmūna*
f	ترمى	*tarmī*	ترميان	*tarmiyāni*	يرمين	*yarmīna*
2 m	ترمى	*tarmī*	ترميان	*tarmiyāni*	ترمون	*tarmūna*
f	ترمين	*tarmīna*	ترميان	*tarmiyāni*	ترمين	*tarmīna*
1 c	ارمى	*'armī*	— —		نرمى	*narmī*

REMARKS:

(1) The vowel *-ī-* splits into its component parts as *-iy-* with the dual endings.

(2) The 2nd fem. sing. **-iyīna* becomes *-īna* with internal collapse *(*-iyīna* [= *-iyiyna*] → *-iyna, -īna).*

(3) Masc. pl. forms in **-iyūna* suffer a familiar collapse to *-ūna* (see §27.2).

Inflected like *ramā* are *'atā/ya'tī* and *hadā/yahdī.*

39.3 Imperfect in *-ū*. Example *da'ā* (√D'W) > imperfect *yad'ū:*

3 m	يدعو	*yad'ū*	يدعوان	*yad'uwāni*	يدعون	*yad'ūna*
f	تدعو	*tad'ū*	تدعوان	*tad'uwāni*	يدعون	*yad'ūna*
2 m	تدعو	*tad'ū*	تدعوان	*tad'uwāni*	تدعون	*tad'ūna*
f	تدعين	*tad'īna*	تدعوان	*tad'uwāni*	تدعون	*tad'ūna*
1 c	ادعو	*'ad'ū*	— —		ندعو	*nad'ū*

REMARKS:

(1) The vowel *-ū-* splits into *-uw-* with the dual endings.

(2) The 2nd fem. sing. **-uwīna* collapses to *-īna*.

(3) The masc. pl. **-uwūna* collapses to *-ūna*.

Inflected like *da'ā* is *'afā/ya'fū.*

40 Common Broken Plural Patterns. Although no hard and fast rules can be given for what broken plural pattern or patterns will emerge from a given singular, a few general observations can be made on the FA'ĪL- and FĀ'IL- patterns.

40.1 The FA'ĪL- pattern:

(1) FA'ĪL- as a *noun pattern* (not adjectival) generally produces a diptote plural pattern FU'ALĀ'U:

شريك > شركاء	*šarīk- > šurakā'u*	partner
عليم > علماء	*'alīm- > 'ulamā'u*	learned (person)
فقير > فقراء	*faqīr- > fuqarā'u*	poor (person)
كريم > كرماء	*karīm- > kuramā'u*	noble (person)

(2) FA'ĪL- as an *adjectival pattern* usually gives a plural on the pattern FI'ĀL-:

كبير > كبار	*kabīr- > kibār-*	big, great
كريم > كرام	*karīm- > kirām-*	noble
صغير > صغار	*ṣağīr- > ṣiğār-*	small

(2a) The subgroup of FA'ĪL- for C3*w/y* nouns and adjectives (FA'ĪY-) gives a diptote plural on the pattern 'AF'IYĀ'U:

نبى > انبياء	*nabīy- > 'ambiyā'u*	prophet
غنى > اغنياء	*ğanīy- > 'ağniyā'u*	rich
قوى > اقوياء	*qawīy- > 'aqwiyā'u*	strong

(2b) The subgroup of FA'ĪL- for doubled roots (FALĪL-) gives a diptote plural on the pattern 'AFILLĀ'U:

شديد > اشداء	*šadīd- > 'ašiddā'u*	mighty
حبيب > احباء	*ḥabīb- > 'aḥibbā'u*	beloved

40.2 FĀ'IL- as a *concrete noun*—not with participial force—commonly gives a plural on the pattern FU''ĀL-, with an alternate on FA'ALAT-. Although both plurals are potential, only one of the two may be in actual or common use.

SINGULAR	PLURAL I	PLURAL II
كاتب *kātib-* 'scribe' >	كتاب *kuttāb-*	كتبة *katabat-*
حاكم *ḥākim-* 'ruler' >	حكام *ḥukkām-*	(حكمة *ḥakamat-*)
ظالم *ẓālim-* 'tyrant' >	ظلام *ẓullām-*	ظلمة *ẓalamat-*
كافر *kāfir-* 'infidel' >	كفار *kuffār-*	كفرة *kafarat-*

وارث *wāriθ-* 'heir' >	(وراث *wurrāθ-*)	ورثة *waraθat-*
عامل *'āmil-* 'agent' >	عمال *'ummāl-*	عملة *'amalat-*

An important subgroup of this type for C3*w*/*y* nouns is FĀ'IN (see §27.2 for inflection), with a plural on the pattern FU'ĀT-.

رماة > رامٍ	√*RMY* > *rāmin* pl *rumāt-*	archer, bowman
دعاة > داعٍ	√*D'W* > *dā'in* pl *du'āt-*	summoner
قضاة > قاضٍ	√*QḌY* > *qāḍin* pl *quḍāt-*	judge

See Appendix A for all plural patterns that occur in this book.

Vocabulary

VERBS

بنى *banā (ī) binā'-/bunyān-* build

درى *darā (ī) dirāyat-* know, comprehend something (acc.); be aware (*bi-* of)

رضى *raḍiya (ā) riḍwān-/riḍan (√RḌW)* find something (acc.) acceptable; be pleased/content (*'an* with)

شاء/يشاء *šā'a (ši'-) (ā) maši'at-* will, want

ضر *ḍarra (u) ḍarar-* injure, harm

عصى *'aṣā (ī) ma'ṣiyat-/'iṣyān-* disobey

لقى *laqiya (ā) liqā'-* meet, encounter

نسى *nasiya (ā) nisyān-/nasy-* forget

NOUNS

ايمان *'īmān-* faith, believing (*bi-* in)

زكاة *zakāt-* alms, almsgiving

نور/انوار *nūr-* pl *'anwār-* light

OTHERS

اذا *'iδā* (+ perfect verb) when

ان *'in* if

اى *'ayy-* (+ construct with indef. sing. or def. pl.) which?, what kind of?

PROPER NAMES

اسرئيل *'isrā'īlu* Israel

اسمعيل *'ismā'īlu* Ishmael

Exercises

(a) Vocalize, read and translate:

١ ادرى	٤ ينسون	٧ يبنون	١٠ ياتون
٢ يرضون	٥ تأتين	٨ ترمين	١١ ترضين
٣ يعصين	٦ يدعون	٩ تهدون	١٢ تنسيان

(b) Read and translate, then give the imperfect in the same person and number:

١ اتيتُ	٤ هدينا	٧ نسيتَ	١٠ عصيتِ
٢ رضى	٥ رميا	٨ اتى	١١ رضيتم
٣ عصين	٦ دريتم	٩ دعونا	١٢ درت

(c) Read and translate:

١ ان اسمعيل مذكور فى الكتاب وكان رسولاً نبياً وكان يامر اهله بالصلاة

٢ ما كنت تدرى ما الكتاب ولا الايمان ولكنا جعلنا نوراً نهدى به من نشاء

٣ وما تدرى نفس بأى ارض تموت

٤ الدنيا والآخرة ضرتان[3] فبقدر ما[2] ترضى احداهما تسخط[1] الاخرى

٥ ان سالتم من خلق السموات والارض ليقولون خلقهن الله

٦ تنام عيناى ولا ينام قلبى

٧ ولقد جاءهم رسول منهم فكذّبوه[4] فاخذهم العذاب وهم ظالمون

٨ واذ جعل السامرى عجلاً[5] لبنى اسرئيل قال هذا الهكم واله موسى فعبدوه ونسوا الله

---

[1]*Saxiṭa (a)* be angry.

[2]*Bi-qadri mā* "to the extent that."

[3]*Ḍarrat-* wife (the relationship wives in a polygamous relationship have one to the other).

[4]*Kaððaba* call (acc., someone) a liar.

[5]*Sāmiriyy-* Samaritan; *'ijl-* calf.

٩ فاذا جاء موسى قال يا هرون ما منعك اذ رأيتهم ضلوا الا تتبعنى[1]

١٠ يهدى الله لنوره من يشاء

١١ انى اخاف ، ان عصيت ربى ، عذاب يوم عظيم

(d) Translate into Arabic:

1. We arose and travelled and did not sleep while travelling [use circumstantial + active participle].

2. We are rich, and they are poor; but we have not oppressed them.

3. I saw a light in the house, but when I looked (in) I did not see anyone.

4. They do *('amila)* good works,[2] and that is better for them than tyranny.

5. When the Children of Israel disobeyed Moses and forgot their faith, he cursed them violently (see §29).

6. Have you ever heard the likes of this?

7. I do not know which of the unbelievers is the most disobedient (§36.6).

Reading Selection: *Sūrat al-Shu'arā' (26): 70–78*

Abraham and the Idols

اذ قال ابرهيم لأبيه وقومه ما تعبدون (٧٠)

قالوا نعبد اصناماً (٧١)

قال هل يسمعونكم اذ تدعون (٧٢)

او ينفعونكم[3] او يضرّون (٧٣)

قالوا بل وجدنا آباءنا كذلك يفعلون (٧٤)

قال أفرأيتم ما كنتم تعبدون (٧٥)

[1] *'Allā tattabi'anī* "from following me."

[2] Generic sense. Use definite article.

[3] *Nafa'a (a)* profit.

انتم وآباؤكم الاقدمون[1] (٧٦)

فإنهم عدو لى الا رب العالمين (٧٧)

الذى خلقنى فهو يهدينى (٧٨)

[1] *'Aqdamu* (< *qadim*- ancient, fore-).

Lesson Seventeen

41 Imperfect Indicative: C_1w and C_2wC_3y Verbs.

41.1 C_1w verbs, which exhibit no peculiarity of inflection in the perfect, drop the initial *w* altogether in the imperfect. Otherwise the inflection is absolutely regular. An example is *wajada* (√WJD) > imperfect *yajidu:*

	SINGULAR	DUAL	PLURAL
3 m	يجد *yajidu*	يجدان *yajidāni*	يجدون *yajidūna*
f	تجد *tajidu*	تجدان *tajidāni*	يجدن *yajidna* &c.

The doubled verb *wadda* 'to wish' does not drop the initial *w* in the imperfect but forms a regular paradigm on the pattern of doubled verbs (*yawaddu, tawaddu, &c.*).

A verb like *waqā* (√WQY), imperfect *yaqī* 'ward off' combines the predictable loss of the initial *w*-radical common to C_1w verbs and the inflectional patterns of a C_3y verb:

3 m	يقي *yaqī*	يقيان *yaqiyāni*	يقون *yaqūna*
f	تقي *taqī*	تقيان *taqiyāni*	يقين *yaqīna* &c.

41.1 The so-called doubly weak verbs, i.e., whose second radical is *w* and third *y* (as √RWY), are not doubly weak at all. The C_2w functions throughout the inflection as a regular "sound" consonant, and the inflection follows that of C_3w/y verbs. Example: *rawā* (√RWY) > *yarwī* "to relate, tell."

3 m	يروى *yarwī*	يرويان *yarwiyāni*	يروون *yarwūna*

f	تروى *tarwī*	ترويان *tarwiyāni*	يروين *yarwīna* &c.
active part.		راوٍ *rāwin*	
passive part.		مروى *marwīy-*	

42 *Ra'â*. The common verb *ra'ā* 'to see,' which is regularly inflected as a C3y verb in the perfect, has an anomalous imperfect. From the expected **yar'ā*, the /'/ is dropped, giving *yarā*. Aside from this, the imperfect inflection is like that of *yalqā* (§39.1).

3 m	يرى *yarā*	يريان *yarayāni*	يرون *yarawna*
f	ترى *tarā*	تريان *tarayāni*	يرين *yarayna* &c.

43 The Optative with *Wadda*. The verb *wadda/yawaddu* "to wish" is normally followed by the optative particle *law* and the imperfect indicative (for wishes posterior to the main verb) or the perfect (for unfulfilled wishes anterior to the main verb).

اود لو يموت	*'awaddu <u>law</u> <u>yamūtu</u>*	I wish he would die.
يود الذين كفروا لو كانوا مسلمين	*yawaddu llaðīna kafarū <u>law</u> <u>kānū</u> muslimīna*	Those who disbelieved wish they had been Muslims.

For non-verbal complements to *wadda, law 'anna* is used.

تود لو أن بينها وبينه امدا بعيدا	*tawaddu <u>law</u> <u>'anna</u> baynahā wa-baynahu 'amadan ba'īdan*	She wishes there were a great distance between her and him.

Vocabulary

VERBS

رد *radda (u) radd-* make...again; send/bring/take back; reply (*'alā* to)

صبر *ṣabara (i) ṣabr-* be patient, have patience

وجد *wajada (i) wujūd-* find

ود *wadda (*wadida) (a) wudd-/mawaddat-* wish

ورث *wariθa (i) 'irθ-/wirāθat-* inherit from (acc.), be the heir of (acc.)

وسع *wasi'a (a) sa'at-* contain, hold, have the capacity for (acc.)

وعد *wa'ada (i) wa'd-* promise someone (acc.) something (acc. or *bi-*); threaten someone (acc.) with (*bi-*)

ولد *walada (i) wilādat-* give birth to, beget

وهب *wahaba (a) wahb-* give, bestow

NOUNS

بعض *ba'ḍ-* (+ construct) some of; *ba'ḍu* (+ noun/pronoun in construct)... *ba'ḍ-an/-in* (indef., appropriate case) each other, as in *ra'aw ba'ḍuhum ba'ḍan* "they saw each other"

بينة *bayyinat-* pl *-āt-* indisputable evidence, proof

والد *wālid-* pl *-ūna* father, progenitor; *wālidat-* pl *-āt-* mother; *wālidāni* (dual) parents

OTHERS

ام *'am(i)* or? (continues alternatives in an interrogative)

دون *dūna, min dūni* (+ construct) below; to the exclusion of, disregarding, up to but not including

Exercises

(a) Read and translate:

١ قال الله لا يسعنى سمائى ولا ارضى ووسعنى قلب عبدى المؤمن

٢ سيرى الله عملكم ورسولُه ويرى الذين ظلموا ، اذ يرون العذاب ، أن القوة لله

٣ ود كثير من اهل الكتاب لو يردونكم من بعد ايمانكم كفاراً

٤ انا نحن نرث الارض ومن عليها وقال الله ان الارض يرثها عبادى الصالحون

٥ أرأيتم شركاءكم الذين تدعون من دون الله؟ ماذا خلقوا من الارض؟ ام لهم شرك[1] فى السموات؟ ام اتاهم كتاب...؟ بل إن يعد الظالمون بعضهم بعضاً الا غروراً

٦ ويبسطون[2] اليكم ايديهم ويودون لو تكفرون

٧ فللنبى قال الذين كفروا من قومنا ما نراك الا بشراً مثلنا

٨ قال ستجدنى ان شاء الله صابراً ولا اعصى لك امراً

[1]*Širk-* portion.

[2]*Basaṭa (u)* spread.

٩ جعل نوح فى فلكه[1] من كلٍّ زوجين اثنين

١٠ واذا سألوه عن الروح قال ان الروح من امر ربى

١١ أتأمرون الناس بالخير وتنسون انفسكم

(b) Translate into Arabic:

1. Witnesses will testify (see §25) against you, and hell will consume you all.
2. When you disobeyed his orders, he was not pleased with you.
3. I do not know which fruit is best for eating.
4. The alms they brought were more than the alms prescribed for them.
5. She looked and saw that he had told the truth.
6. They lied to each other when they said they would be their fathers' heirs.
7. Have you forgotten that the light of faith is from the heart?
8. I am not aware of anyone more truthful than him.
9. They are deluded in that which they say, and we see them lying.
10. I wish we were mightier than our enemy.

[1]*Fulk*- ark.

Lesson Eighteen

44 The Subjunctive. The inflection of the subjunctive is based on that of the indicative with changes in the endings.

44.1 The inflection of the subjunctive is as follows:

	SINGULAR		DUAL		PLURAL	
3 m	يدخل	*yadxula̲*	يدخلا	*yadxulā̲*	يدخلوا	*yadxulū̲*
f	تدخل	*tadxula̲*	تدخلا	*tadxulā̲*	يدخلن	*yadxulna*
2 m	تدخل	*tadxula̲*	تدخلا	*tadxulā̲*	تدخلوا	*tadxulū̲*
f	تدخلى	*tadxulī̲*	تدخلا	*tadxulā̲*	تدخلن	*tadxulna*
1 c	ادخل	*'adxula̲*	—	—	ندخل	*nadxula̲*

REMARKS:

(1) The short *-u* termination of the indicative is changed to *-a* wherever it occurs.

(2) The *-na*/*-ni* termination of indicative forms are dropped: the 2nd fem. sing. thus ends in *-ī;* the 3rd and 2nd masc. plurals end in *-ū,* to which otiose *alif* is added, as in the perfect; the duals all end in *-ā*.

(3) The feminine plural forms remain unchanged from the indicative.

44.2 Uses of the subjunctive. The subjunctive must be preceded by a subjunctivizing particle; there is no "free" occurrence of the subjunctive in Arabic. It occurs

(1) after any of the particles of purpose, *li-*, *kay*, *li-kay*, or *ḥattā*, which have no marked distinction in meaning among them.

قالوا أجئتنا لنعبد الله	*qālū 'a-ji'tanā li-na'buda llāha*	They said, "Have you come to us that we should worship God?"

(2) after the particle *lan* to express explicit negative future.

لن يدخل الجنة	*lan yadxula l-jannata*	He will not enter paradise.

(3) after *ḥattā* when it means "until" with reference to the future.

انّا لن ندخلها حتى يخرجوا منها	*'innā lan nadxulahā ḥattā yaxrujū minhā*	We shall not enter it until they leave.

(4) after complementary constructions with *'an* ('that') or any of its variants (*li-an* 'in order that,' *'allā* [for *'an lā*] 'that...not,' and *li'allā* 'in order that...not').

نخاف ان يفرّ	*naxāfu 'an yafirra*	We fear that he may flee.
امروك الا تقول شيئاً	*'amarūka 'allā taqūla šay'an*	They ordered you not to say ("that you not say") anything.

(5) after the hypothetical consequential *fa-* preceded by a prohibition, negative command, wish, hope (or something to this effect, provided it have a negative import), which means "as a consequence of which" or "lest" (this should not be confused with the consecutive *fa-*, which does not affect verbal moods or cases).

نهاني عن ذلك فاكون ظالماً	*nahānī 'an ðālika fa-'akūna ẓāliman*	He forbade me that lest I be unjust.
لا تفعل فتندم	*lā taf'al fa-tandama*	Do not do it lest you regret.

45 The Subjunctive of Weak-*Lam* Verbs. Since weak-*lām* verbs do not have the *-u* termination of the indicative, their subjunctive forms differ only slightly from the regular paradigm.

45.1 For verbs that end in *-ā* in the indicative, the only change for the subjunctive is the dropping of the *-na*/*-ni* terminations of the 2nd fem. sing., duals and masc. plurals. All other forms are identical to the indicative.

	SINGULAR		DUAL		PLURAL	
3 m	يلقى	*yalqā*	يلقيا	*yalqayā*	يلقوا	*yalqaw*
f	تلقى	*talqā*	تلقيا	*talqayā*	يلقين	*yalqayna*
2 m	تلقى	*talqā*	تلقيا	*talqayā*	تلقوا	*talqaw*
f	تلقى	*talqay*	تلقيا	*talqayā*	تلقين	*talqayna*
1 c	القى	*'alqā*	—	—	نلقى	*nalqā*

45.2 Verbs that end in *-ī* and *-ū* in the indicative drop the *-na*/*-ni* terminations and also add the subjunctive *-a* to the remaining indicative forms.

3 m	يرمى	*yarmiya*	يرميا	*yarmiyā*	يرموا	*yarmū*
f	ترمى	*tarmiya*	ترميا	*tarmiyā*	يرمين	*yarmīna*
2 m	ترمى	*tarmiya*	ترميا	*tarmiyā*	ترموا	*tarmū*
f	ترمى	*tarmī*	ترميا	*tarmiyā*	ترمين	*tarmīna*
1 c	ارمى	*'armiya*	—	—	نرمى	*narmiya*
3 m	يدعو	*yad'uwa*	يدعوا	*yad'uwā*	يدعوا	*yad'ū*
f	تدعو	*tad'uwa*	تدعوا	*tad'uwā*	يدعون	*yad'ūna* &c.

Vocabulary

VERBS

قرب *qariba (a) qurb-* draw near to, approach

نهى *nahā (ā) nahy-* forbid someone (acc.) (*'an* something)

NOUNS

اذن *'iðn-* permission

شجر/اشجار *šajar-* (collective) pl *'ašjār-*; شجرة/شجرات *šajarat-* (unit) pl *-āt-* tree

شيطان/شياطين *šayṭān-* pl *šayāṭīnu* demon, devil

OTHERS

حتى *ḥattā* (+ subj.) so that, in order that; (+ subj. with reference to the future; + perfect with reference to the past) until

قبل أن *qabla 'an* (+ subj. with reference to the future; + perfect with reference to the past) before (conjunction)

IDIOM

ما كان لـ أن *mā kāna li- 'an* it was not possible *(li-* for someone) (*'an* + subj., to do something)

SUBJUNCTIVIZING PARTICLES

الا *'allā* that...not

ان *'an* that

حتى *ḥattā* in order that, until

كي/لكي *kay/li-kay* in order that

لـ *li-* in order that

لن *lan* "will not" (negative future)

Exercises

(a) Give the subjunctive of the following verb forms:

١ ياتى	٦ تبعثين	١١ يجدون	١٦ ينهى	٢١ ناكل
٢ يخلقن	٧ تذكرون	١٢ يخافان	١٧ ندرى	٢٢ ارى
٣ تسير	٨ تكونين	١٣ يضل	١٨ اموت	٢٣ تهدى
٤ آخذ	٩ تجعلون	١٤ يامرون	١٩ تخرج	٢٤ يدعو
٥ تدخلن	١٠ تذهبان	١٥ يرضى	٢٠ تعصى	٢٥ ينسون

(b) Read and translate:

١ قال له انى آتيك بما امرتنى به قبل ان تقوم من مقامك

٢ ما كان لنفس ان تموت الا باذن الله

٣ فقال الملك لمريم انا رسول ربك لأهب لك ولداً

٤ أيودّ احدكم ان تكون له جنة من نخيل واعناب[1]
٥ اعبد ربى حتى يأتينى اليقين
٦ يا ربنا وسعت كل شيء رحمة وعلما
٧ ما يكون لنا ان نعدكم بذلك
٨ فإن الاخوين جاءا ليرثا اباهما
٩ امرنى الشيطان ان اقرب الكفار
١٠ قالت بنو اسرئيل يا موسى لن نصبر على طعام[2] واحد
١١ امرنى ان اكون من المؤمنين
١٢ أتنهانا ان نعبد ما يعبد آباؤنا
١٣ قال الله لابليس ما منعك الا تسجد لما خلقت بيدى
١٤ نهونا ان ناكل من فواكه اشجار حدائقهم فنكون من الظالمين

(c) Translate into Arabic.

1. I have brought proof (of the fact) that[3] I am my father's son in order that I may be his heir.
2. The people of this city will never know why the demons did not approach them.
3. It was not possible for you (f s) to summon your brother.
4. We approached the man in order to hear his words.
5. I wish they were here to guide us, for we are lost.
6. He forbids you to enter his house.
7. Will you eat something before you leave?

---

[1]*Naxīl-* dates; *'a'nāb-* grapes.
[2]*Ṭa'ām-* food.
[3]The *'anna* clause will be in construct with the noun, *bi-bayyinati 'annī...*

Lesson Nineteen

46 The Jussive. Like the subjunctive, the jussive mood is based on the indicative with changes in the terminations.

46.1 The inflection of the jussive is as follows:

	SINGULAR		DUAL		PLURAL	
3 m	يدخل	*yadxul*	يدخلا	*yadxulā*	يدخلوا	*yadxulū*
f	تدخل	*tadxul*	تدخلا	*tadxulā*	يدخلن	*yadxulna*
2 m	تدخل	*tadxul*	تدخلا	*tadxulā*	تدخلوا	*tadxulū*
f	تدخلي	*tadxulī*	تدخلا	*tadxulā*	تدخلن	*tadxulna*
1 c	ادخل	*'adxul*	—	—	ندخل	*nadxul*

REMARKS:

(1) The short *-u* termination of the indicative is dropped and replaced by *sukūn* wherever it occurs.

(2) Feminine plurals remain unchanged from the indicative; all other forms ending in *-na/-ni* drop that termination, resulting in forms identical to those of the subjunctive.

(3) When the jussive forms that end in an unvocalized consonant are followed by elidible *alif,* they are given a prosthetic vowel *-i (*yadxul l-bayta → yadxuli̱ l-bayta).*

46.2 Uses of the jussive:

(1) following proclitic *li-* in the 1st and 3rd persons as a cohortative/hortatory ("let me/us/ him/her/them"[1]):

لناخذها	*li-na'xuðhā*	Let's take it.
ليشهد عذابهم	*li-yašhad 'aðābahum*	Let him witness their torment.

When this *li-* is preceded by *wa-* or *fa-*, it loses its vowel and becomes *wa-l-* and *fa-l-*.

فلناخذها	*fa-l-na'xuðhā*	So let's take it.
وليشهد عذابهم	*wa-l-yašhad 'aðābahum*	And let him witness their torment.

(2) with *lā* as negative imperative in all persons:

لا تكفروا	*lā takfurū*	Be not ungrateful!
لا اظلمهم	*lā 'aẓlimhum*	May I not oppress them!
لا يخرج	*lā yaxruj*	May he not go out. / Let him not go out.

(3) preceded by *lam* to indicate negative past definite.

لم ادخل	*lam 'adxul*	I did not enter
الم تامرني	*'a-lam ta'murnī*	Didn't you command me?

(4) in conditionals of all types (conditionals will be discussed in §54).

ان يدخل يجدني	*'in yadxul, yajidnī*	If he enters, he will find me.

47 The Imperative. The imperative occurs in the affirmative second persons only. It is formed by removing the personal prefixes from the jussives. In sound verbs of the *fa'ala* type, this results in an initial cluster of two consonants (e.g., jussive *tadxul* > *-dxul).* When the imperative is not preceded by a vowel, a prosthetic vowel must be supplied: if the stem vowel is *-a-* or *-i-*, prosthetic *i-* is added. If the stem

[1]Not "let him" in the sense of "allow him," but in the sense of "may he."

vowel is *-u-*, prosthetic *u-* is added. Orthographically an elidible *alif* is written in all cases.

INDICATIVE		JUSSIVE		IMPERATIVE	
تكتب	*taktubu* >	*taktub* >	*-ktub* >	اكتب	*uktub*
تذهب	*taðhabu* >	*taðhab* >	*-ðhab* >	اذهب	*iðhab*
تنزل	*tanzilu* >	*tanzil* >	*-nzil* >	انزل	*inzil*

The imperative occurs in all the second persons; the endings are like those of the jussive.

	SINGULAR		DUAL		PLURAL	
m	ادخل	*udxul*	ادخلا	*udxulā*	ادخلوا	*udxulū*
f	ادخلى	*udxulī*	ادخلا	*udxulā*	ادخلن	*udxulna*

For the negative imperative, the jussive is used, see §46.2(2).

48 Imperative and Jussive of Doubled Verbs. In doubled verbs the removal of the *-u* termination of the indicative would result in the impossible form **yafill* (a doubled consonant may not be unvocalized). Such forms are therefore either given an ancillary vowel, *-a* or *-i*, or else replaced by a regular formation, *yaflil*. Although both the doubled and regular forms occur in more or less free variation, the latter is slightly more common with enclitic pronouns.

The jussive forms of *dalla/yadullu* 'to guide' are:

	SINGULAR		DUAL		PLURAL	
3 m	يدل	*yadulla(i)*	يدلا	*yadullā*	يدلوا	*yadullū*
	يدلل	*yadlul*				
3 f	تدل	*tadulla(i)*	تدلا	*tadullā*	يدللن	*yadlulna*
	تدلل	*tadlul*				
2 m	تدل	*tadulla(i)*	تدلا	*tadullā*	تدلوا	*tadullū*
	تدلل	*tadlul*				
2 f	تدلى	*tadullī*	تدلا	*tadullā*	تدللن	*tadlulna*
1 c	ادل	*'adulla(i)*	—	—	ندل	*nadulla(i)*
	ادلل	*'adlul*			ندلل	*nadlul*

The only form affected in the imperative is the masc. sing., which is formed on the same principles:

2 m	دل *dulla(i)* ادلل *udlul*	دلا *dullā*	دلوا *dullū*
2 f	دلى *dullī*	دلا *dullā*	ادللن *udlulna*

49 Imperative of *Hamza*-Initial Verbs. In the imperative of three common C₁' verbs, the glottal stop is dropped:

اخذ > خذ	*'axaða > xuð*	Take!
اكل > كل	*'akala > kul*	Eat!
امر > مر	*'amara > mur*	Command!

Alone of the three, *mur* may regain its glottal stop when preceded by *wa-* or *fa-*.

اذهب وأمرهم	*iðhab wa-'murhum*	Go and command them!
خذو وكلوا	*xuðū wa-kulū*	Take and eat!

Other C₁ imperatives are regularly formed.

اذن > ائذن	*'aðina > i'ðan*	Permit!
اتى > ائت به	*'atā > i'ti bihi*	Bring it!

Proclitic *fa-* or *wa-* will change the seat of the *hamza* (see Appendix G), although the form is quite regular.[1]

فأت بها	*fa-'ti bihā*	...so bring it!
وأذن لهم	*wa-'ðan lahum*	...and permit them!

50 The Vocative. Direct address is indicated by the use of the vocative particles *yā* and *yā 'ayyuhā*.

[1]In the rare instance when such forms stand first in a sentence, the prosthetic *i-* is given a glottal stop and the glottal stop of the verb is changed to *-y-* to avoid two adjacent *hamzas* (**'i'ðan* → إيذن *'īðan* "Permit!" and **'i'ti* → إيت *'īti*, as in *'īti bihi* "Bring it!").

50.1 *Yā* is **never followed by the definite article.** When the noun following *yā* is **not** in construct, it takes the *nominative case without nunation*, regardless of whether the noun is diptote or triptote.

يا محمد	*yā muḥammadu*	O Muhammad!
يا رسول	*yā rasūlu*	O apostle!

But if the noun following *yā* **is** the first member of a construct, it is in the *accusative*.

يا رسول الله	*yā rasūla llāhi*	O Apostle of God!
يا اهل العراق	*yā 'ahla l-'irāqi*	O people of Iraq!
يا الهنا	*yā 'ilāhanā*	O our God!

In the construction *yā rabbī* "O my lord," the *ī* is usually written defectively (يا ربِّ).

50.2 The other vocative particle, *yā 'ayyuhā* (optional feminine *yā 'ayyatuhā)* **must be followed by the definite article**, and the noun is in the nominative case.

يا ايها الرسول	*yā 'ayyuhā r-rasūlu*	O Apostle!
يا ايها الناس	*yā 'ayyuhā n-nāsu*	O people!
يا ايـ(تـ)ها المرأة	*yā ayy(at)uhā l-mar'atu*	O woman!

Vocabulary

VERBS

دل *dalla (u) dalālat-* lead, guide, show (*'ilā / 'alā* to)

رحم *raḥima (a) raḥmat-/marḥamat-* be merciful toward, have mercy on (acc.)

سكن *sakana (u) sakan-/suknā* inhabit, dwell in

غفر *ğafara (i) mağfirat-/ğufrān-* forgive (*li-* somebody) something (acc.)

نصح *naṣaḥa (a) nuṣḥ-/naṣāḥat-* advise, give good advice to; take good care of

NOUNS AND ADJECTIVES

حين/احيان *ḥīn-* pl *'aḥyān-* time; *ḥīna* (+ imperfect) at the time when, (+ gen.) at the time of

قرية/قرى *qaryat-* pl *quran* village

مبين *mubīn-* clear, obvious

ورق/اوراق *waraq-* (collective) pl *'awrāq-;* ورقة *waraqat-* (unit) pl *-āt-* leaf (of a tree), folio, sheet (of paper)

OTHERS

حيث *ḥayθu* (invariable) where, wherever (conjunction commonly followed by perf. or imperf. ind.)

لم *lam* (+ jussive) negative past definite particle

PROPER NAMES

زليخا *zulayxā* Zuleikha, wife of the Biblical Potiphar, Pharaoh's officer who bought Joseph from the Ishmaelites

يوسف *yūsufu* Joseph

Exercises

(a) Give the jussive of the following verb forms:

١ ياخذ	٦ أجعل	١١ يدللن	١٦ يسال	٢١ أشهد
٢ تعبدون	٧ تاكل	١٢ يخرجان	١٧ تذكرون	٢٢ تفر
٣ يصدقان	٨ تعلمن	١٣ تأمر	١٨ تخلقان	٢٣ تجدن
٤ تسكن	٩ يضلون	١٤ نعمل	١٩ تبعثين	٢٤ يدخلون
٥ نرحم	١٠ تسمعين	١٥ يظلمن	٢٠ يغر	٢٥ تنظر

(b) Give the imperatives of the following verbs:

١ اخذ	٣ عبد	٥ رحم	٧ اكل	٩ سأل
٢ فر	٤ سمع	٦ نظر	٨ بعث	١٠ دل

(c) Read and translate:

١ وقلنا لهم آسكنوا هذه القرية وكلوا منها حيث شئتم

٢ ففروا الى الله! انى لكم منه نذير[1] مبين

٣ ما تسقط[2] من ورق الا يعلمها

٤ لا تبعث مالك اليهم حتى تعلم اهم اتقياء ام لا

٥ فقالت نساء مصر انا لنرى زليخا فى ضلال مبين فلما سمعت بقولهن دعتهن وقالت ليوسف اخرجْ عليهن فلما راينه قلن ليس هذا بشراً ان هذا الا ملَك كريم

٦ سوف يعلمون ، حين يرون العذاب ، من اضل

٧ يا ربنا اغفر لنا وارحمنا وانت ارحم الراحمين

٨ يا ايها الناس اذكروا الله ذكراً كثيراً

٩ هو الله احد لم يلد

١٠ فعلمنا منه ما لم نعلم

١١ فخذها بالقوة وأمر قومكَ ان ياخذوا اموال الناس

١٢ اولم تنصحنا الا نقرب الذين هم اشد منا وهم مارّون على مدينتنا

(d) Translate into Arabic:

1. The enemy has drawn near, so let us flee.
2. They forbade me to guide you to the garden in which they are.
3. I have no strength to lead you (m pl) aright when you are lost.
4. He will advise her to invite ("that she invite") all those who inhabit the city, and their number is great.
5. It was not possible for me to forgive them, so I had no mercy (past definite) on them.
6. Dwell (m s) here and eat of the fruits of these trees, but *(wa-)* do not approach that nation lest hell-fire consume you.
7. O my son, take this property of mine and be merciful toward those who have less wealth than you.

---

[1]*Naðir-* warner.

[2]*Saqaṭa (u)* fall.

Lesson Twenty

51 The Jussive of Hollow and Weak-*Lâm* Verbs.

51.1 Hollow verbs in the jussive. When the *-u* termination of the indicative is dropped for the jussive of a hollow verb like *yaqūmu,* the impossible form **yaqūm* results. Since the phonetic laws of Arabic do not allow a long vowel to be followed by an unvocalized consonant, the anomalous form is resolved by shortening the long vowel, as was done in the feminine plural forms of the indicative (see §37). Persons that have vowel-initial suffixes (2nd fem. sing., all duals, masc. plurals) do not require shortening of the imperfect vowel for obvious reasons.

	SINGULAR		DUAL		PLURAL	
3 m	يقم	***yaqum***	يقوما	*yaqūmā*	يقوموا	*yaqūmū*
f	تقم	***taqum***	تقوما	*taqūmā*	يقمن	*yaqumna*
2 m	تقم	***taqum***	تقوما	*taqūmā*	تقوموا	*taqūmū*
f	تقومى	*taqūmī*	تقوما	*taqūmā*	تقمن	*taqumna*
1 c	اقم	***'aqum***	—	—	نقم	***naqum***

All C_2*w*/*y* verbs behave in a similar fashion.

3 m	يسر	***yasir***	يسيرا	*yasīrā*	يسيروا	*yasīrū*
f	تسر	***tasir***	تسيرا	*tasīrā*	يسرن	*yasirna,* &c.
3 m	ينم	***yanam***	يناما	*yanāmā*	يناموا	*yanāmū*
f	تنم	***tanam***	تناما	*tanāmā*	ينمن	*yanamna,* &c.

51.2 Weak-*lām* verbs in the jussive: apocopated forms. All weak-*lām* verbs end in a long vowel in the indicative (see §39). The jussive is formed by shortening the long vowel of the indicative. Orthographically this results in dropping the *alif-maqṣūra, yā'* or *wāw* of the indicative. Forms with *-na*/*-ni* terminations in the indicative have jussive forms identical to the subjunctive (see §45).

3 m	يلق	***yalqa***	يلقيا	*yalqayā*	يلقوا	*yalqaw*
f	تلق	***talqa***	تلقيا	*talqayā*	يلقين	*yalqayna*
3 m	يرم	***yarmi***	يرميا	*yarmiyā*	يرموا	*yarmū*
f	ترم	***tarmi***	ترميا	*tarmiyā*	يرمين	*yarmīna*
3 m	يدع	***yad'u***	يدعوا	*yad'uwā*	يدعوا	*yad'ū*
f	تدع	***tad'u***	تدعوا	*tad'uwā*	يدعون	*yad'ūna*

52 The Imperative of Hollow and Weak-*Lâm* Verbs.

52.1 When the personal prefix is dropped from the jussive of hollow verbs, an initial consonant cluster does *not* result; therefore the prosthetic vowel and *alif* of the imperative of sound verbs are not necessary

m	قم	*qum*	قوما	*qūmā*	قوموا	*qūmū*
f	قومى	*qūmī*	قوما	*qūmā*	قمن	*qumna*

52.2 Weak-*lām* verbs form the imperative quite regularly from the jussive.

m	الق	*ilqa*	القيا	*ilqayā*	القوا	*ilqaw*
f	القى	*ilqay*	القيا	*ilqayā*	القين	*ilqayna*
m	ارم	*irmi*	ارميا	*irmiyā*	ارموا	*irmū*
f	ارمى	*irmī*	ارميا	*irmiyā*	ارمين	*irmīna*
m	ادع	*ud'u*	ادعوا	*ud'uwā*	ادعوا	*ud'ū*
f	ادعى	*ud'ī*	ادعوا	*ud'uwā*	ادعون	*ud'ūna*

Vocabulary

VERBS

بدا *badā (ū) budūw-* seem, appear

خسر *xasira (a) xasār-/xusrān-* lose, suffer loss, forfeit; go astray, perish

خلد *xalada (u) xulūd-* last forever, be immortal

ذاق *ðāqa (ðuq-) (ū) ðawq-* taste

قص *qaṣṣa (u) qaṣaṣ-* narrate, tell (*'alā* to)

هبط *habaṭa (i) hubūṭ-* go down, descend, collapse

NOUNS

امة/امم *'ummat-* pl *'umam-* community (usually in the sense of a religious community, community of the faithful)

حديث/احاديث *ḥadīθ-* pl *'ahādīθu* talk, conversation; report, account; حديث نبوى *ḥadīθ- nabawīy-* narrative relating an utterance of the Prophet Muhammad; حديث قدسى *ḥadīθ- qudsīy-* a narrative in which God speaks in the first person

خلد *xuld-* eternity, immortality

عداوة *'adāwat-* pl *-āt-* enmity, hostility

قيامة *qiyāmat-* pl *-āt-* resurrection

نبوى *nabawīy-* (adj) prophetic, relating to a prophet

OTHERS

انما *'innamā* (conj.) only, specifically; (after a negative clause) however, rather

كأن *ka-'anna* (+ acc. or pron. encl.) as though

كيف *kayfa* how?

فوق *fawqa* above, over

PROPER NAME

يعقوب *ya'qūbu* Jacob

Exercises

(a) Vocalize, read and translate:

١ ليأت	٥ لا يخف	٩ لم ار	١٣ ليمت	١٧ لم يقل
٢ لم يبد	٦ لا تدع	١٠ ليرم	١٤ لم تقم	١٨ لم ننم
٣ لم آت	٧ لم نذق	١١ لأسر	١٥ لم اكن	١٩ لا ينه
٤ ليهد	٨ لم ندر	١٢ لا تنس	١٦ لم يشأ	٢٠ ليرض

(b) Vocalize, read and translate; then give the masc. pl. imperatives:

١ نم	٣ اهد	٥ قم	٧ مت	٩ ارم	١١ قل
٢ ادع	٤ كن	٦ ذق	٨ خف	١٠ سر	١٢ ائت

(c) Read and translate:

١ قال ابليس يا آدم هل ادلك على شجرة الخلد

٢ فليقم من مقامه وليدع الظالمين لينصحوه

٣ اعبد الله كانك تراه

٤ يا ابتى انى قد جاءنى من العلم ما لم ياتك

٥ ان امتى امة مرحومة ليس عليها فى الآخرة عذاب انما عذابها فى الدنيا (حديث نبوى)

٦ الم ياتهم نبا الذين من قبلهم من قوم نوح

٧ يا ربى اهد قومى فانهم لا يعلمون

٨ لما لم تدللهم ولم تهدهم اذ بدا لك انهم قد ضلوا

٩ فلما جاءه وقص عليه القصص قال لا تخف

١٠ لم نكن من الذين خسروا متاع الدنيا

١١ كفرنا بكم وبدا بيننا وبينكم العداوة

١٢ فقال يعقوب ليوسف قال يا ابنى لا تقصص رؤياك[1] على اخوتك

١٣ الم تر كيف فعل ربك بذلك القوم

١٤ اولم يسيروا فى الارض فينظروا كيف كان عاقبة[2] الذين من قبلهم وكانوا اشد منهم قوة

١٥ لا تدع مع الله الهاً آخر فتكون من الكافرين

١٦ الم ينظروا الى السماء فوقهم كيف بنيناها

---

[1] *Ru'yā* vision.

[2] *'Āqibat-* end.

١٧ ان الخاسرين الذين خسروا انفسهم واهليهم يوم القيامة. الا ذلك هو الخسران المبين

(d) Translate into Arabic

1. Let him taste the fruits of his good deeds.
2. Let us not fear those who travel on the earth oppressing the people.
3. It appears to me as though you did not sleep.
4. Do not be unjust and be not ungrateful lest you be among those who perish.
5. Do you know the number of the leaves of the trees?
6. Did the prophet not bring you clear signs from his Lord?
7. Let him call upon me at the time when he has gone astray; I shall not come to him, and I shall not guide him aright.

Lesson Twenty-One

53 The Passive Voice: Perfect. The passive voice of the perfect is formed by replacing the internal vowels of the active inflection with the invariable pattern FU'ILA, i.e., *-u-* on C_1 and *-i-* on C_2. Generally speaking, only transitive verbs can be made passive (an important exception for impersonal passives will be treated in §88); intransitives such as *ḍalla* 'go astray' and *kabura* 'get big' have no passive forms.

Arabic has no device for expressing personal passive agents. In English we have both the active "he found you" and the passive "you were found by him," but in Arabic the passive verb cannot be used with agents, i.e., *wujidta* "you were found" is a viable passive form, but the agent "by him" cannot be expressed. Passive constructions with agents must be rendered in the active voice, i.e., *wajadaka* "he found you / you were found by him."

53.1 As the third radical of sound verbs is not affected by the vocalic pattern of the passive, the inflection is unchanged.

	SINGULAR	DUAL	PLURAL
3 m	خلق *xuliqa*	خلقا *xuliqā*	خلقوا *xuliqū*
f	خلقت *xuliqat*	خلقتا *xuliqatā*	خلقن *xuliqna,*

&c.

53.2 The passive of the few transitive hollow verbs is on the pattern FĪLA *(fīl-)*.

اما قيل لكم *'a-mā qīla lakum* — Was it not said to you?

53.3 All weak-*lām* verbs become FU'IYA in the passive, with all weak C_3 changed to *-y-* by the preceding *-i-*. The inflection follows the model of *laqiya* (§20.3).

دعا > دعى	*da'ā > du'iya*	he was summoned/called
نهى > نهى	*nahā > nuhiya*	he was forbidden

53.4 Doubled verbs drop the vowel of C_2 with V-endings, giving a base FULL-. The inflection is regular with C-endings.

دل	*dalla > dulla*	he was guided
دللت	*dalalta > dulilta*	you were guided

53.5 Verbs that are doubly transitive, or that take a complement in the accusative in addition to a direct object, retain the accusative second object or complement in the passive voice.

جعل الله الارض مسكناً لآدم	*ja'ala llāhu l-'arḍa maskanan li-'ādama*	God made the earth a habitation for Adam.
جعلت الارض مسكناً لآدم	*ju'ilati l-'arḍu maskanan li-'ādama*	The earth was made a habitation for Adam.
راوا الملك ظالماً لقومه	*ra'aw l-malika ẓāliman li-qawmihi*	They considered the king a tyrant of his people.
رئى الملك ظالماً لقومه	*ru'iya*[1] *l-maliku ẓāliman li-qawmihi*	The king was considered a tyrant of his people.

54 Conditional Sentences. Arabic conditionals are divided into (1) real and (2) impossible conditionals.

54.1 Real conditionals, or those that are fulfillable, are introduced in the protasis (the "if" clause) by *'in*. The verb of an affirmative protasis introduced by *'in* may be either perfect or jussive; *lam* + jussive is almost always used for the negative. If there was ever a meaningful distinction between the perfect and the jussive in the conditional, it was ob-

---

[1]Note the change in *hamza*-seat for the passive vocalic pattern.

scured by the time of Koranic Arabic, for the two appear to occur with no significant distinction in meaning. The verb of the apodosis (the result clause) is also commonly perfect or jussive but may also be imperfect, imperative or non-verbal (see below). A negative apodosis is usually *lam* + the jussive. Since the verbs of the Arabic conditional are dictated by the form, they are basically "tenseless." The proper tense for translation can be gained only from context.

ان فعلوا (يفعلوا) ذلك ظلموا (يظلموا)	*'in faʻalū / yafʻalū ðālika, ẓalamū / yaẓlimū*	If they did / do that, they were / are / will be unjust.
ان لم يفعلوا ذلك...	*'in lam yafʻalū ðālika…*	If they did not / do not do that…

54.2 Real conditionals are also introduced in the protasis by ***'iðā,*** which may mean 'if' or 'when.' (This is the conditional, hypothetical 'if and when,' not the temporal 'when' of *lammā* and *'ið.*) The verb of an affirmative protasis introduced by *'iðā* is commonly perfect, almost never jussive, though a negative protasis may be jussive. As in the ***'in***-conditional, proper tense for translation depends upon context and/or sense.

اذا متنا وكنّا تراباً وعظاماً أئنا لمبعوثون	*'iðā mitnā wa-kunnā turāban wa-ʻiẓāman 'a-'innā la-mabʻūθūna?*	When we are dead and dust and bones, are we really going to be resurrected?
اذا راوهم قالوا إن هؤلاء لضالّون	*'iðā ra'awhum, qālū 'inna hā'ulā'i la-ḍāllūna*	If/when they saw them, they said, "These are gone astray."
اذا قال العبد الحمد لله ملأ نوره الارض	*'iðā qāla l-ʻabdu l-ḥamdu lillāhi, mala'a nūruhu l-'arḍa*	If/when a worshipper says, "Praise God," his light fills the earth.
اذا مات ابن آدم ينقطع عمله	*'iðā māta bnu 'ādama, yanqaṭiʻ ʻamaluhu*	When a human being dies, his labor is finished.
اذا بلغ الماء قلّتين لم يحمل الخبث	*'iðā balağa l-mā'u qullatayn, lam yaḥmili l-xabaθa*	If/when water amounts to two jugfuls, it does not carry filth.

54.3 Another, very common and important type of conditional consists of an imperative in the protasis followed by the jussive in the apodosis. Since English has no exact parallel, translations will vary.

ارحم ترحم	*irḥam, turḥam*	Have mercy, and you will be shown mercy.
اذكرونى أذكركم	*uðkurūnī, 'aðkurkum*	(If you) remember me, I will remember you.

54.4 The apodosis is introduced by *fa-* under the following conditions:

(1) when the apodosis is a nominal sentence:

ان فعلت ذلك فانت ظالم	*'in fa'alta ðālika, fa-'anta ẓālimun*	If you do that, you are unjust.

(2) when the apodosis is imperative or hortatory:

ان تفعل ذلك فاخرج من المدينة	*'in taf'al ðālika, fa-xruj mina l-madīnati*	If you do / have done that, then leave the city.
ان يفعل ذلك فليخرج من المدينة	*'in yaf'al ðālika, fa-l-yaxruj mina l-madīnati*	If he does / has done that, then let him leave the city.

(3) when an initial verb in the apodosis is preceded by *sa-*, *sawfa*, *qad*, or any negative particle other than *lam* and *mā*. Verbs preceded by *sa-*, *sawfa* and *lan* of course have explicitly future signification, and verbs preceded by *qad* have explicitly past signification.

ان تكفروا فستاكلكم النار	*'in takfurū, fa-sa-ta'kulukumu n-nāru*	If you disbelieve, hell-fire will consume you.
ان تفعل ذلك فلن يغفر الله لك	*'in taf'al ðālika, fa-lan yağfira llāhu laka*	If you do that, God will never forgive you.
ان لم يكن صالحاً فقد كان ابوه ظالماً من قبله	*'in lam yakun ṣāliḥan, fa-qad kāna 'abūhu ẓāliman min qablihi*	If he is not pious, (it is because) his father was a tyrant before him.

(4) when a perfect in the apodosis is meant explicitly to retain the past signification of the perfect. Here the perfect of *kāna* is used as an auxiliary to the perfect of the protasis, often with *qad*. The construction occurs often enough in the Koran, but in post-Koranic classical Arabic the apodosis too is usually marked with *qad*, in which case it falls into category (3) above.

ان كنت قد فعلت ذلك فظلمت	*'in kunta qad fa'alta ðālika, fa-ẓalamta*	If you did do that, you were unjust (unambiguously past).
ان كان قميصه قدّ من قبل فصدقت	*'in kāna qamīṣuhu qudda min qubulin fa-ṣadaqat*	If his shirt has been torn from the front, then she has told the truth.

Real conditional types can be summarized as follows:

PROTASIS		APODOSIS
'in/'iðā +	perfect →	perfect
	jussive →	jussive

PROTASIS			APODOSIS
'in/'iðā +	perfect or jussive	*fa-* +	nominal clause, imperative, *l-* + jussive, *sa-*, *sawfa*, *qad*, or *lan*

54.5 The verbs in sentences with *man* ('whoever, anyone who'[1]) follow all the principles of the conditional, though the perfect tends to predominate in affirmative clauses and *lam* + jussive in negative clauses.

من كان لله كان الله له	*man kāna li-llāhi, kāna llāhu lahu*	Whoever is for God, God is for him.

[1]This use of *man* contrasts with the non-conditional use as 'he who, the one who' with no special verb tense or mood.

من قال لا اله الا الله دخل الجنة	*man qāla lā 'ilāha 'illā llāhu, daxala l-jannata*	Anyone who says, "There is no god but God," will enter paradise.
من لم يكن له شيخ فشيخه الشيطان	*man lam yakun lahu šayxun fa-šayxuhu š-šayṭānu*	Whoever has no master, his master is the devil.
من بدّل دينه فاقتلوه	*man baddala dīnahu, fa-qtulūhu*	Anyone who changes his religion—kill him!
من اراد ان ينظر الى يمشي ميت على الارض فلينظر الى ابن ابى قحافة	*man 'arāda 'an yanẓura 'ilā mayyitin yamšī 'alā l-'arḍi, fa-l-yanẓur 'ilā bni 'abī quḥāfata*	Let anyone who wants to gaze upon a dead man walking upon the earth look at Ibn Abi-Quhafa.
من آمن بالنجوم فقد كفر	*man 'āmana bin-nujūmi fa-qad kafara*	Whoever believes in the stars has become an infidel.

54.6 Impossible, or irrealis/contrafactual, conditionals are introduced by *law*. The apodosis is commonly but not consistently introduced by *la-*. Verbs in both parts of the conditional are perfect (even the negative, with *mā)*. Again, correct tense for translation can be gained only from context.

لو فعلوا ذلك لكانوا من الظالمين	*law fa'alū ðālika, la-kānū mina ẓ-ẓālimīna*	If they had done / were to do that, they would have been / would be unjust.
لو شاء ربنا لما خلقنا	*law šā'a rabbunā, la-mā xalaqanā*	If our Lord had so willed, he would not have created us.
لو كنا نسمع ما كنا كذلك	*law kunnā nasma'u, mā kunnā ka-ðālika*	If we had listened, we wouldn't be like this.

Vocabulary

بكى *bakā (ī) bukā'* - cry, weep (*'alā* over)

حكم *ḥakama (u) ḥukm*- pass judgment (*bi-* of) (*'alā* on)

ضحك *ḍaḥika (a) ḍaḥk-* laugh (*li-*, *bi-*, *'alā* at)

عاد *'āda (ū) 'iyādat-* visit the sick

عاد *'āda (ū) 'awd-/ma'ād-* return

مرض *mariḍa (a) maraḍ-* fall ill, be sick

NOUNS AND ADJECTIVES

اول ، اولى *'awwalu* (masc.), *'ūlā* (fem.) first (occurs either as a regular attributive adjective or as first member of construct, like the superlative, see §36.4[2])

برىء/ابرياء *barī'-* pl *'abriyā'u* free (*min* of blemish, guilt, &c.)

فلان ، فلانة *fulān-* (masc.), *fulānatu* (fem.) so-and-so (dummy name)

مريض/مرضى *marīḍ-* pl *marḍā* sick, ill

OTHERS

اذا *'iðā* (+ perf. or jussive) if (possible conditional), when

لو *law* (+ perf.) if (contrary to fact)

لولا *law-lā* (+ noun in nom., pron. encl. or independent pron.) were it not for

كما *kamā* as, just as (conj.)

Exercises

(a) Give the passive (e.g., *katabahā* "he wrote it (f)" > *kutibat* "it (f) was written")

١ اخذَنا	٦ جعلكم	١١ دللتُهم	١٦ سألناهن	٢١ غرّتنى
٢ نسيناها	٧ اكلتها	١٢ خفتَه	١٧ ذقته	٢٢ سمعتموه
٣ قلتُه	٨ نهاهم	١٣ امرتنى	١٨ خلقتك	٢٣ بعثوك
٤ ذكرنى	٩ عبدتُك	١٤ كتبوه	١٩ وجدتها	٢٤ دعانا
٥ رآها	١٠ عصيتُهم	١٥ منعك	٢٠ وعدته	٢٥ عدتُهم

(b) Read and translate (beginning here, punctuation is given in the Arabic):

١ «يا ابن آدم ، مرضت فلم تعدنى.» قال «يا رب كيف اعودك وانت رب

العالمين؟» قال «أما علمت ان عبدى فلاناً مرض فلم تعده؟ أما علمت انك لو عدته لوجدتنى عنده؟» (حديث قدسى)

٢ اما قيل لكم انى كنت اول النبيين فى الخلق وآخرهم فى البعث (حديث نبوى)

٣ خُلقت من نور الله وخُلق اهل بيتى من نورى (حديث نبوى)

٤ ان ابن آدم لحريص[1] على ما مُنع.

٥ ان يعلم الله فى قلوبكم خيراً يؤتكم[2] خيراً مما أخذ منكم ويغفر لكم.

٦ انكم تسالون رسولكم كما سئل موسى من قبل.

٧ اذا دعيتم فادخلوا.

٨ انما كان قول المؤمنين، اذا دعوا الى الله ورسوله ليحكم بينهم، أن يقولوا «سمعنا».

٩ لو علمتم ما اعلم لضحكتم قليلاً وبكيتم كثيراً.

١٠ لما قيل لامرأة ابرهيم انها ستلد وهى كبيرة بالسن، ضحكت.

١١ كلوا مما ذكر اسمُ الله عليه ان كنتم بآياته مؤمنين.

١٢ قل أذلك خير أم جنة الخلد التى وُعد الاتقياءُ؟

١٣ ان عصوك فقل انى برىء مما تعملون.

١٤ لو شئنا لبعثنا نور الايمان لخلق آخر.

١٥ ان عصيت امر الملك حكم عليك بالموت.

١٦ قال الله للنبى «لولاك لما خلقت الافلاك[3]».

١٧ قالت امرأة فرعون قبل موتها «ربى، ابن لى عندك بيتاً فى الجنة».

(c) Translate into Arabic:

1. Before the prophet other deities were worshipped.
2. If you disbelieve after (having) faith, you will taste the torment.
3. When judgment was passed on her, she wept.
4. I was told ("it was said to me") if I brought the alms they would forgive me.
5. If you were pleased with the goods, why did not not say (so)?
6. If you fall ill I will visit you.

---

[1]*Ḥarīṣ- 'alā* greedy for.
[2]*Yu' tikum* "he will give you" (juss.).
[3]*Falak-/' aflāk-* celestial sphere.

7. If you had been invited, you would not have been questioned.
8. If they know what we know, let them laugh little and weep much.

Reading Selection: *Sūrat al-A'rāf (7): 19–25.*

Adam and Eve

«يا آدم اسكن انت وزوجك الجنة ، فكلا من حيث شئتما ولا تقربا هذه

الشجرة فتكونا من الظالمين» (١٩)

فوسوس لهما الشيطان لِيُبْدِيَ لهما ما وُورِيَ عنهما من سوءاتهما

وقال «ما نهاكما ربكما عن هذه الشجرة إلا أن تكونا مَلَكين

او تكونا من الخالدين» (٢٠)[1]

وقاسمهما «إني لكما لمن الناصحين» (٢١)[2]

فدلّاهما بغرورٍ فلما ذاقا الشجرة بدت لهما سوءاتهما وطَفِقا

يَخْصَفان عليهما من ورق الجنة وناداهما ربهما «ألم أنهكما عن تلكما[3]

الشجرة وأقل لكما إن الشيطان لكما عدوّ مبين؟» (٢٢)[4]

قالا «ربّنا ظلمنا أنفسنا وإن لم تغفر لنا وترحمنا لنكوننّ من

الخاسرين» (٢٣)[5]

قال «اهبطوا بعضكم لبعضٍ عدو ولكم في الأرض مستقر ومتاع

---

[1]*Waswasa* whisper; *li-yubdiya* "in order that he reveal; *wūriya* "was kept secret"; *saw'āt*- shame, private parts

[2]*Qāsama* swear to.

[3]The pronouns *ðālika* and *tilka* are sometimes attracted into a curious accord with the 2nd persons addressed: fem. sing. *ðāliki & tilki;* dual *ðālikumā & tilkumā;* plural *ðālikum/ðālikunna & tilkum/tilkunna*. I.e., the *-ka* ending of *ðālika* and *tilka* are construed as the 2nd-person masculine enclitic.

[4]*Dallā* lead on; *ṭafiqā yaxṣafāni* "they began to pile on"; *nādā* call out to.

[5]*Nakūnanna* "we shall surely be."

الى حين» (٢٤)[1]

قال «فيها تحيَون وفيها تموتون ومنها تُخرَجون» (٢٥)[2]

[1]*Mustaqarr*- habitation, resting-place.
[2]*Taḥyawna* "you will live"; *tuxrajūna* "you will be taken out."

Lesson Twenty-Two

55 The Passive Voice: Imperfect. Like the perfect passive, the imperfect passive is formed through internal vocalic change. The pattern for the imperfect passive is YUF'ALU, with *-u-* on the prefix consonant and *-a-* on the middle radical.

55.1 The personal and modal inflection of sound verbs is unaffected by the passive vocalization.

	SINGULAR		DUAL		PLURAL	
INDICATIVE						
3 m	يقتل	*yuqtalu*	يقتلان	*yuqtalāni*	يقتلون	*yuqtalūna*
f	تقتل	*tuqtalu*	تقتلان	*tuqtalāni*	يقتلن	*yuqtalna*
SUBJUNCTIVE						
3 m	يقتل	*yuqtala*	يقتلا	*yuqtalā*	يقتلوا	*yuqtalū*
f	تقتل	*tuqtala*	تقتلا	*tuqtalā*	يقتلن	*yuqtalna*
JUSSIVE						
3 m	يقتل	*yuqtal*	يقتلا	*yuqtalā*	يقتلوا	*yuqtalū*
f	تقتل	*tuqtal*	تقتلا	*tuqtalā*	يقتلن	*yuqtalna*

55.2 With C_1w verbs the initial radical *w* is restored in the passive (YUW'ALU).

PERFECT		IMPERF. ACTIVE		IMPERF. PASSIVE	
وجد	*wajada* >	يجد	*yajidu*	يوجد	*yūjadu*
ولد	*walada* >	يلد	*yalidu*	يولد	*yūladu*

55.3 In hollow verbs the middle radical appears as long *alif* in all cases (YUFĀLU).

PERFECT	IMPERF. ACTIVE	IMPERF. PASSIVE
قال *qāla*	يقول *yaqūlu*	يقال *yuqālu*
باع *bā'a*	يبيع *yabī'u*	يباع *yubā'u*

55.4 In weak-*lām* verbs the vocalic pattern of the passive takes precedence over the original weak letter, which becomes *alif maqṣūra* in all cases (pattern: YUF'Ā). The inflection is identical to that of *yalqā* (see §39.1 for the indicative, §45.1 for the subjunctive, §51.2 for the jussive).

رمى *ramā*	يرمي *yarmī*	يرمى *yurmā*
نهى *nahā*	ينهى *yanhā*	ينهى *yunhā*
دعا *da'ā*	يدعو *yad'ū*	يدعى *yud'ā*

55.5 The inflection of doubled roots is unaffected by the passive.

صب *ṣabba*	يصب *yaṣubbu*	يصب *yuṣabbu*

The jussive passive is *yuṣabba, yuṣabbi* or *yuṣbab.*

55.6 Like the passive participle, the imperfect passive is often used in the sense of what "can be, should be, might be, is to be done."

أجعلنا من دون الرحمن آلهة يعبدون	*'a-ja'alnā min dūni r-raḥmāni 'ālihatan* <u>*yu'badūna*</u>	Have we made, other than the Merciful, gods to be worshipped?
لا يقال ذلك	*lā* <u>*yuqālu*</u> *ðālika*	That is not said / should not be said / is not to be said / cannot be said.

56 The Energetic Mood. The energetic mood, used for emotionally charged and rhetorical statements, is formed by suffixing *-nna* to the subjunctive forms that end in *-a*. The *-ī* of the 2nd fem. sing. is shortened to *-inna;* the dual forms become *-ānni;* masc. plurals shorten the *-ū* of the jussive to *-unna;* feminine plurals in *-na* become *-nānni*.

	SINGULAR	DUAL	PLURAL
3 m	يقتلَن *yaqtulanna*	يقتلانِّ *yaqtulānni*	يقتلُن *yaqtulunna*
f	تقتلَن *taqtulanna*	تقتلانِّ *taqtulānni*	يقتلنانِّ *yaqtulnānni*
2 m	تقتلَن *taqtulanna*	تقتلانِّ *taqtulānni*	تقتلُن *taqtulunna*
f	تقتلِن *taqtulinna*	تقتلانِّ *taqtulānni*	تقتلنانِّ *taqtulnānni*
1 c	اقتلَن *'aqtulanna*		نقتلَن *naqtulanna*

The most common uses of the energetic mood are (1) with *la-* to indicate absolute determination

لأقتلنّك	*la-'aqtulannaka*	I shall kill you!!

and (2) with *lā* to indicate a forceful negative jussive.

لا يغرنّكم الشيطان	*lā yağurrannakumu š-šayṭānu*	By no means let the devil deceive you!

56.1 The apocopated form of the energetic is formed by deleting the final *-na* syllable from the energetic. The inflection is defective in that forms ending in *-ānni* in the regular paradigm are not apocopated.

3 m	يقتلن *yaqtulan*	— —	يقتلن *yaqtulun*
f	تقتلن *taqtulan*	— —	— —
2 m	تقتلن *taqtulan*	— —	تقتلن *taqtulun*
f	تقتلن *taqtulin*	— —	— —
1 c	اقتلن *'aqtulan*	— —	نقتلن *naqtulan*

Koranic orthography sometimes writes the apocopated energetic as though it were the indefinite accusative ending.

ليكوناً كذلك	*la-yakūnan ka-ðālika*	It will surely be thus.

Vocabulary

بدأ *bada'a (a) bad'* - begin, start (*bi-* with)

خفى *xafā (ī) xafā'* - hide, conceal (*'alā* from)

عاش *'āša (ī) 'ayš*- live

عرف *'arafa (i) ma'rifat-* know *(connaître)*, recognize

قتل *qatala (u) qatl-* kill

ورد *warada (i) wurūd-* reach, arrive at (+ acc.); appear, show up

NOUNS AND ADJECTIVES

باب/ابواب *bāb-* pl *'abwāb-* gate, door

بعيد *ba'īd-* far, distant

سبيل/سبل *sabīl-* (masc. & fem.) pl *subul-* way, path; *fī sabīli llāhi* in God's cause

كنز/كنوز *kanz-* pl *kunūz-* treasure

مثل/امثال *maθal-* pl *'amθāl-* likeness, parable, simile; *maθalu X ka-maθali Y* "X is like Y"

مطر/امطار *maṭar-* pl *'amṭār-* rain

ميّت/اموات ،موتى *mayyit-* pl *-ūna/'amwāt-/mawtā* dead

OTHER

على ما...عليه *'alā mā...'alayhi* according to how

Exercises

(a) Give the passive of the following verb forms:

١ يأخذ	٦ تجعل	١١ تدلين	١٦ تسال	٢١ اغر
٢ ينسيان	٧ تاكلان	١٢ يخفون	١٧ يقتلن	٢٢ تسمعون
٣ تخلقن	٨ يقول	١٣ تنهى	١٨ تامر	٢٣ تذكرين
٤ أعبد	٩ يكتبان	١٤ تجدان	١٩ يبعثون	٢٤ يدعون
٥ ترون	١٠ تمنعن	١٥ يعد	٢٠ نعصى	٢٥ يحكم

(b) Read and translate:

١ يُبعث كل عبد على ما مات عليه.

٢ ياتى اقوام ابواب الجنة فيقولون «الم يعدنا ربنا ان نرد النار؟» فيقال

«مررتم عليها وهى خامدة[1]».
٣ مثل امتى كمثل المطر - لا يُدرى اولُه خير ام آخره.
٤ كما تعيشون فكذلك تموتون فكذلك تُحشرون[2].
٥ قال كذلك اتتك آياتنا فنسيتها وكذلك اليوم تُنسى.
٦ كنت كنزاً مخفياً واحببتُ[3] ان أعرف فخلقت الخلق لكى أعرف (حديث قدسى).
٧ من عرف نفسه فقد عرف ربه.
٨ لا تقولوا لمن يقتل فى سبيل الله اموات.
٩ إن ادرى اقريب أم بعيد ما توعدون.
١٠ فلا تغرنّكم الحياة الدنيا ولا يغرنّكم بالله الغرور.
١١ ان الملائكة لا يعصون الله ما امرهم ويفعلون ما يؤمرون.
١٢ من يفعل ذلك فقد ظلم نفسه.
١٣ بنى الاسلامُ على خمس[4].
١٤ وكان رسول الله اذا ذكر احداً بدعائه بدأ بنفسه.

(c) Translate into Arabic:

1. It cannot be concealed from us that judgment was passed upon the innocent.
2. When we visited the sick, we wept over them.
3. Can the knowledge of the prophets be inherited?
4. If the lying infidel had come in God's cause, he would wish to be recognized.
5. If the people of the city are deceived, will they testify truthfully?
6. The first one who *('awwalu man)* laughed was Adam.
7. I shall most certainly bring indisputable evidence, and I shall assuredly testify that you killed your brother.

---

[1]*Xamada* go out, die down (fire).

[2]*Ḥašara (u) ḥašr-* resurrect.

[3]*'Aḥbabtu* "I wanted."

[4]This refers to the five fundamental principals of Islam: profession of faith, prayer, alms, fasting, pilgrimage to Mecca.

Lesson Twenty-Three

57 A Preface to the Increased Forms of the Verb. All verbs introduced so far belong to the unaugmented, or base, form of the Arabic conjugational system. That is, each consists of a simple stem with personal prefixes and/or suffixes in conformity with the inflectional patterns. According to set patterns, other verbs can be made from the simple stem, or radical, by means of prefixes, infixes and changes in the radical itself. The verbs so produced are known as the increased conjugational forms, of which there are nine in common use. Few base radicals are actually increased to more than a few of the potentially available forms.

The nine increased forms were named by Arabic grammarians after the patterns that would be assumed by the root √F'L; western lexicographers of Arabic have numbered these forms according to the traditional order (not the order in which they will be introduced in this book), which is:

I	فعل	FA'ALA	VI	تفاعل	TAFĀ'ALA
II	فعّل	FA''ALA	VII	انفعل	INFA'ALA
III	فاعل	FĀ'ALA	VIII	افتعل	IFTA'ALA
IV	افعل	'AF'ALA	IX	افعلّ	IF'ALLA
V	تفعّل	TAFA''ALA	X	استفعل	ISTAF'ALA

Form I is the base, or ground, form of the verb and will be referred to henceforth as the "G-form," the Semitic designation, from *Grundstamm* ('base stem').

Most if not all verbs of the G-form are also found in at least one of the increased types, but no radical is attested in all ten forms. There are also a good many radicals that occur in several of the increased forms for which there is no known G-form, although in nouns and adjectives the radical may be well represented.

58 Medio-Passive Verbs: Form VII. Characteristic of the medio-passive Form VII is the prefix *n* to the radical consonants. The base form is INFA'ALA.

58.1 Synopsis of Form VII, with example from √QṬ':

PERFECT	انفعل	*infa'ala*	انقطع	*inqaṭa'a*
IMPERFECT	ينفعل	*yanfa'ilu*	ينقطع	*yanqaṭi'u*
SUBJUNCTIVE	ينفعل	*yanfa'ila*	ينقطع	*yanqaṭi'a*
JUSSIVE	ينفعل	*yanfa'il*	ينقطع	*yanqaṭi'*
PARTICIPLE	منفعل	*munfa'il-*	منقطع	*munqaṭi'-*
VERBAL NOUN	انفعال	*infi'āl-*	انقطاع	*inqiṭā'-*

Since the intrinsic meaning of Form VII is the medio-passive of the G-form, there are no passive forms within the class. All patterns are *active in form but middle, or medio-passive, in meaning*. The medio-passive Form VII differs in signification from the true passive (FU'ILA/YUF'ALU) in that the agency of the action is completely disregarded in the medio-passive. It is true that personal agents cannot be expressed in the true passive—nor, for that matter, with Form VII; nonetheless, the fact of there being an agent is inherent in the true passive. In a sentence such as

قطع راسه *quṭi'a ra'suhu* His head was cut off.

the agency of an executioner—or at least an instrument such as a sword—is very much in the mind of the speaker, while in the medio-passive construction

انقطع راسه *inqaṭa'a ra'suhu* His head got cut off.

the activity/passivity of the verbal notion does not pertain. What is of importance is the result, the fact that a head was severed from a body. Another illustration of the distinction between the G-form passive and the Form VII medio-passive is in the two senses of the English verb "to break," which functions as both active ("to break something") and middle ("for something to break"). The G-form active construction

كسر الكاس	*kasara l-ka'sa*	He broke the goblet.

gives a G-form passive of

كسر الكاس	*kusira l-ka'su*	The goblet was broken.

implying that it was broken by somebody. The Form-VII construction

انكسر الكاس	*inkasara l-ka'su*	The goblet broke.

implies that the goblet got broken somehow, regardless of agency, at some point in the past and is still broken, so a translation of "the goblet is broken" would fit some contexts better than "the goblet broke" or "the goblet was broken."

SUMMARY OF PASSIVE FORMS:

G-FORM PERFECT PASSIVE

kusira l-ka'su	The goblet was broken (by someone at some point in the past)

MEDIO-PASSIVE PERFECT

inkasara l-ka'su	The goblet broke / got broken (at some point in the past, agency irrelevant) / is (now in a state of having been) broken.

G-FORM IMPERFECT PASSIVE

yuksaru l-ka'su	The goblet can be broken.

MEDIO-PASSIVE IMPERFECT

yankasiru l-ka'su	(As a general rule,) the goblet will break (if you drop it).

G-FORM PASSIVE PARTICIPLE

'inna l-ka'sa maksūrun	The goblet is broken (it was broken by someone in the past and it is now broken).

MEDIO-PASSIVE PARTICIPLE

'inna l-ka'sa munkasirun	The goblet is breakable / is liable to be broken.

A significant distinction between the G-form and Form VII lies in the verbal noun. The verbal noun of the G-form can be either active or passive in signification, depending upon the sense and context, while the verbal noun of Form VII is passive only. For example, *hazmuhu* (< *hazama* 'to rout, defeat') can mean either "his defeat (of someone else)" or "his defeat (by someone else)"; the Form VII verbal noun, *inhizāmuhu* can only mean "his defeat" in the passive sense of "his having been defeated" by someone.

58.2 Form VII: Doubled Verbs. The second and third radicals of doubled verbs fall together in what should be a familiar pattern. Example from √ŠQQ 'to split':

PERFECT	انفلّ	*infalla*	انشقّ	*inšaqqa*
IMPERFECT	ينفلّ	*yanfallu*	ينشقّ	*yanšaqqu*
SUBJUNCTIVE	ينفلّ	*yanfalla*	ينشقّ	*yanšaqqa*
JUSSIVE	ينفلّ	*yanfalla/i*	ينشقّ	*yanšaqqa/i*
	ينفلل	*yanfalil*	ينشقق	*yanšaqiq*
PARTICIPLE	منفلّ	*munfall-*	منشقّ	*munšaqq-*
VERBAL NOUN	انفلال	*infilāl-*	انشقاق	*inšiqāq-*

Vocabulary

طلق VII *inṭalaqa* depart, go on, proceed on one's way, move freely

شق *šaqqa (u) šaqq-* split, cleave; VII *inšaqqa* be split apart, cloven asunder

غفل *ğafala (u) ğaflat-* neglect, be unmindful (*'an* of)

قطع *qaṭa'a (a) qaṭ'-* cut; VII *inqaṭa'a* get cut off

قلب *qalaba (i) qalb-* turn around, turn upside down; VII *inqalaba* return, turn back, be changed

وضع *waḍa'a (a) waḍ'-* put down, lay aside

NOUNS

جناح *junāḥ-* a sin *('alā)* for someone *('an* + subj.) to do something

حذر *ḥiðr-* precaution; *'axaða ḥiðrahu* take one's precaution

سلاح/اسلحة *silāḥ-* pl *'asliḥat-* arms, weapon

طائفة/طوائف *ṭā'ifat-* pl *ṭawā'ifu* group, band, party

عقب/اعقاب *'aqib-* pl *'a'qāb-* heel

مكان/امكنة *makān-* pl *'amkinat-* place

OTHERS

لعلّ *la'alla* (+ noun in the acc. or encl. pron.) perhaps

وراء *warā'a* and *min warā'i* (+ gen.) behind, beyond, the other (far) side of

IDIOM

انقلب على عقبيه *inqalaba 'alā 'aqibayhi* he turned back on his heels, retraced his steps, went back to where he came from

Exercises

(a) Give the perfect and imperfect (3rd masc. sing.), participle and verbal noun of Form VII for the following roots. Also give the meaning of each.

1. قطع 'cut'	4. دفع 'push'	7. عقد 'tie up'
2. كسر 'break'	5. شقّ 'split'	8. بسط 'spread'
3. قلع 'uproot'	6. حطّ 'lower'	9. فجر 'burst'

(b) Read and translate:

١ وما محمد الا رسول قد ماتت من قبله الرسل. أفإن مات او قتل انقلبتم على اعقابكم؟

٢ واذا كنت في الكافرين فقمت الى الصلاة فلتقم طائفة من المؤمنين معك وليأخذوا اسلحتهم. فاذا سجدوا فليكونوا من ورائكم ولتأت طائفة اخرى

وليأخذوا حذرهم واسلحتهم. ودّ الذين كفروا لو تغفلون عن اسلحتكم وامتعتكم. ولا جناح عليكم، إن كان بكم اذى[1] من المطر او كنتم مرضى، أن تضعوا اسلحتكم وخذوا حذركم.

٣ قال النبى انى خائف ان اموت فينقطع منكم هذا العلم.

٤ قد انطلق المرء واخوه حتى قربا شجرة وضعا متاعهما قريباً منها.

٥ اذا انشقّت السماء كان اليوم الآخر قريباً.

٦ ان الذى فى النار ياتيه الموت من كل مكان، وما هو بميت، ومن ورائه عذاب عظيم.

٧ والذين اتاهم الكتاب يعرفونه كما يعرفون ابناءهم.

٨ قال يوسف لرجاله «اجعلوا بضاعة[3] اخوتى فى رحالهم[2]. لعلهم يعرفونها اذا انقلبوا الى اهلهم.»

٩ الملائكة فى الجنة يدخلون على الصالحين من كل باب.

١٠ من يعمل مثقال ذرّة[4] خيراً يره، ومن يعمل مثقال ذرّة شراً يره.

(c) Translate into Arabic:

1. When they recognized him they forbade him to proceed on his way to the distant city of his brothers.

2. It was not possible for me to retrace my steps, so I laid down my arms until they should come to me.

3. The idol your fathers worshipped does not harm anyone, but if you do not put it aside you will be among the cursed.

4. If a band of the enemy approaches us, let us kill them.

5. If you do not depart, you will be cut off from *('an)* the land of your people.

6. Let them live in a distant land, and let them not come to our gates.

---

[1] *'Aðan* annoyance.

[2] *Riḥāl-* saddlebags.

[3] *Biḍā'at-* merchandise.

[4] *Miθqālu ðarratin* + acc. "an atom's weight of."

Lesson Twenty-Four

59 Reflexive/Medio-Passive Verbs: Form VIII. Characteristic of the reflexive/medio-passive Form VIII is the infixation of *-t-* between C_1 and C_2. The base pattern is IFTAʻALA.

Form VIII is properly the reflexive medio-passive of the G-form. In this case the reflexive consonant *t*, which will be met in other reflexive forms, is infixed between C_1 and C_2. Examples of the normal connotive range of this form are: *mala'a* 'fill' (transitive) > *imtala'a* 'fill (middle, intransitive), get filled up'; *nafaʻa* 'avail' (transitive) > *intafaʻa* 'avail oneself' (reflexive). The reflexive sense of Form VIII often results in intransitive verbs that require prepositions for complements, whereas the G-forms take accusative complements, e.g., *samiʻa* 'hear' > *istamaʻa li-l'ilā* 'hear (for oneself), listen to'; *qariba* 'approach' > *iqtaraba 'ilā* 'draw near to.' A good many verbs of this form, especially those with a reflexive connotation, remain transitive and hence may occur in the passive, as *naẓara* 'look' > *intaẓara* 'expect' and *'axaδa* 'take' > *ittaxaδa* 'take unto oneself, adopt.'

59.1 Synopsis of Form VIII.

	ACTIVE		PASSIVE	
PERFECT	افتعل	*iftaʻala*	افتعل	*uftuʻila*
IMPERFECT	يفتعل	*yaftaʻilu*	يفتعل	*yuftaʻalu*
SUBJUNCTIVE	يفتعل	*yaftaʻila*	يفتعل	*yuftaʻala*
JUSSIVE	يفتعل	*yaftaʻil*	يفتعل	*yuftaʻal*
IMPERATIVE	افتعل	*iftaʻil*	—	—
PARTICIPLE	مفتعل	*muftaʻil-*	مفتعل	*muftaʻal-*

VERBAL NOUN		افتعال *ifti'āl*		

Example from √*NẒR:*

PERFECT	انتظر	*intaẓara*	انتظر	*untuẓira*
IMPERFECT	ينتظر	*yantaẓiru*	ينتظر	*yuntaẓaru*
SUBJUNCTIVE	ينتظر	*yantaẓira*	ينتظر	*yuntaẓara*
JUSSIVE	ينتظر	*yantaẓir*	ينتظر	*yuntaẓar*
PARTICIPLE	منتظر	*muntaẓir-*	منتظر	*muntaẓar-*
VERBAL NOUN		انتظار *intiẓār*		

Note that all initial *alifs* produced in this form are elidible.

59.2 Assimilation of C_1 to the *t*-infix. The consonants listed below assimilate or are assimilated to the *t*-infix of Form VIII:

(1) C_1*t* is quite regular in its formation, but the resulting doubled *-tt-* is written with *šadda:*

تبع < اتّبع √*TB'* > *ittaba'a*

(2) C_1*w* assimilates to the *t*-infix, giving *-tt-* in all patterns of the form:

وحد < اتّحد √*WḤD* > *ittaḥada* (for **iwtaḥada*)

(3) C_1*ṭ*, C_1*d* and C_1*ẓ* all assimilate the *t*-infix to themselves:

طلع < اطّلع √*ṬL'* > *iṭṭala'a* (for **iṭtala'a)*
دعو < ادّعى √*D'W* > *idda'ā* (for **idta'ā)*
ظلم < اظّلم √*ẒLM* > *iẓẓalama* (for **iẓtalama)*

(4) C_1*ð* is changed to *d*, which then assimilates the *t*-infix:

ذكر < ادّكر √*ðKR* > *iddakara* (for **iðtakara)*
ذخر < ادّخر √*ðXR* > *iddaxara* (for **iðtaxara)*

(5) C_1*ṣ* and *ḍ* velarize the *t*-infix to *ṭ:*

صحب < اصطحب √*ṢḤB* > *iṣṭahaba* (for **iṣtaḥaba)*
ضر < اضطر √*ḌRR* > *iḍṭarra* (for **iḍtarra)*

(6) C_1*z* voices the *t*-infix to *d:*

زهر > ازدهر √*ZHR* > *izdahara* (for **iztahara)*

59.3 A few C_1' roots behave as though they were C_1w in the production of Form VIII, notably

اخذ > اتّخذ √'*Xð* > *ittaxaða* (for **i'taxaða)*

Most C_1' roots give quite regular forms, as

امر > ائتمر √'*MR* > *i'tamara*
الف > ائتلف √'*LF* > *i'talafa*

Vocabulary

أخذ VIII *ittaxaða* adopt

تبع *tabi'a (a) taba'-/tabā'at-* follow; VIII *ittaba'a* follow, heed, pursue

ترك *taraka (u) tark-* leave, abandon

قرب VIII *iqtaraba* draw near (*'ilā* to)

مشى *mašā (ī) mašy-* walk, go on foot

ملأ *mala'a (a) mal'-* fill; VIII *imtala'a* be filled, full (*min* or *bi-* of)

نفع *nafa'a (a) naf'-* be of benefit to (acc.), avail; VIII *intafa'a* make use, avail oneself (*min* or *bi-* of)

NOUNS

جميع *jamī'-* total, whole, entirety

سلام *salām-* peace, well-being

عجل/عجول، عجلة *'ijl-* pl *'ujūl-/'ijalat-* calf

ملأ/املاء *mala'-* pl *'amlā'-* crowd, assembly, council of notables

نهار *nahār-* day (as contrasted to night)

OTHERS

اذاً، اذن *'iðan* then, therefore

عسى أن *'asā 'an* (+ subj.) perhaps

PROPER NAME

جهنم *jahannamu* (fem) Gehenna, Hell

Exercises

(a) Produce the forms requested for Form VIII:

ROOT	FORM VIII MEANING	FORM TO PRODUCE
ذكر	'remember'	verbal noun
عرف	'confess'	act. part.
نظر	'expect'	3 masc. pl. imperf. act.
وسع	'expand'	2 masc. sing. juss. act.
أخذ	'adopt'	pass. part.
ضرّ	'compel'	1 sing. perf. pass.
تبع	'follow'	act. part.
جمع	'be gathered'	verbal noun
قرب	'draw near'	3 fem. sing. perf. act.
سمع	'listen'	3 masc. sing. imperf. act.
نفع	'make use'	verbal noun
منع	'refrain'	1 pl. perf. act.
صحب	'accompany'	masc. pl. imperative
أمر	'conspire'	act. part.[1]
زحم	'be crowded'	verbal noun

(b) Read and translate:

١ انا مع عبدى حين يذكرنى فان ذكرنى فى نفسه ذكرته فى نفسى وان ذكرنى فى ملأ ذكرته فى ملأ هم خير منهم وان اقترب الىّ شبراً اقتربت اليه ذراعاً وان اقترب الىّ ذراعاً اقتربت اليه باعاً فان اتانى يمشى اتيته هرولةً.[2]

[1]For the seat of the *hamza* see Appendix G.

[2]*Šibr-* span; *ðirā'-* cubit; *bā'-* fathom; *harwalat-* running.

٢ اذ قال موسى يا قوم انكم ظلمتم انفسكم باتخاذكم العجل معبوداً.
٣ وقالت امرأة فرعون «لا تقتلوه. عسى ان ينفعنا او نتّخذه ولداً».
٤ قال الله لابليس «اخرج من الجنة ولَمن تبعك منهم لأملأنّ جهنم منكم اجمعين[1]».
٥ يا اهل الكتاب قد جاءكم من الله نور وكتاب مبين يهدى به الله من اتّبع رضوانه سبلَ السلام[2].
٦ قالوا أبشراً[3] واحداً نتّبعه؟ إنا اذاً لفى ضلال.
٧ قال نوح «يا رب، انى دعوت قومى ليلاً ونهاراً وانى كلما دعوتهم لتغفر لهم جعلوا اصابعهم فى آذانهم».[4]
٨ اولم يروا ان الله الذى خلقهم هو اشد منهم قوة؟
٩ لن ينفعكم الفرار إن فررتم من الموت او القتل.
١٠ أيأمر الهك ان نترك ما يعبد آباؤنا او ان نفعل فى اموالنا ما نشاء؟
١١ اولئك الناس يدعون لمن ضرّه اقرب من نفعه فهم غافلون عن شرّ ما يفعلون.
١٢ اولئك عسى الله ان يعفو عنهم.

---

[1] *'Ajma'īna* "altogether."

[2] *Subula* is a complement of *yahdī*, "he leads…on the paths…"

[3] A preposed accusative direct object is very unusual. The resumptive pronoun -*hu* on the following verb clarifies its function in the sentence.

[4] *Kulla-mā* whenever.

(c) Translate into Arabic:

1. A band of strong nobles passed by a city on the people of which the enemy had had no mercy; and when they looked and saw, they wept.

2. The devout (man)'s house was filled with the light of faith.

3. Be not unmindful of God's mercy lest you dwell in Gehenna until the end of your days.

4. If flight will not avail you, it is no sin for you to lay down your arms.

5. At the time when I advised him, I did not know that he would make use of my words to harm me.

6. Let him turn back on his heels; perhaps we may follow him and find his tribe.

7. Before the prophet, the idols of Mecca had been adopted as gods.

Lesson Twenty-Five

60 Forms VII and VIII: Hollow and Weak-*Lâm* Verbs. In Forms VII and VIII of both hollow and weak-*lām* verbs the distinction between *w* and *y* in the root is obscured in that the two weak letters behave in exactly the same manner. This is the case in almost all increased forms; the few exceptions will be duly noted.

60.1 Synopsis of the hollow verb (C_2w/y), Form VII, example √*SWQ:*

PERFECT	انفال	*infāla*	انساق	*insāqa*
IMPERFECT	ينفال	*yanfālu*	ينساق	*yansāqu*
SUBJUNCTIVE	ينفال	*yanfāla*	ينساق	*yansāqa*
JUSSIVE	ينفل	*yanfal*	ينسق	*yansaq*
IMPERATIVE	انفل	*infal*	انسق	*insaq*
PARTICIPLE	منفال	*munfāl-*	منساق	*munsāq-*
VERBAL NOUN	انفيال	*infiyāl-*	انسياق	*insiyāq-*

60.2 Synopsis of the hollow verb (C_2w/y), Form VIII:

	ACTIVE		PASSIVE	
PERFECT	افتال	*iftāla*	افتيل	*uftīla*
IMPERFECT	يفتال	*yaftālu*	يفتال	*yuftālu*
SUBJUNCTIVE	يفتال	*yaftāla*	يفتال	*yuftāla*
JUSSIVE	يفتل	*yaftal*	يفتل	*yuftal*
IMPERATIVE	افتل	*iftal*	—	—

PARTICIPLE	مفتال *muftāl-*	مفتال *muftāl-*
VERBAL NOUN	افتيال *iftiyāl*	

Example from √XYR:

PERFECT	اختار *ixtāra*	اختير *uxtīra*
IMPERFECT	يختار *yaxtāru*	يختار *yuxtāru*
SUBJUNCTIVE	يختار *yaxtāra*	يختار *yuxtāra*
JUSSIVE	يختر *yaxtar*	يختر *yuxtar*
IMPERATIVE	اختر *ixtar*	— —
PARTICIPLE	مختار *muxtār-*	مختار *muxtār-*
VERBAL NOUN	اختيار *ixtiyār-*	

REMARKS:

(1) In both the perfect and imperfect of hollow verbs, weakness results in compensatory lengthening to *-ā-* wherever possible. Inflection follows the model of *nāma* (see §18 for the perfect, §37.1 for the imperfect). Note that the perfect stem for C-endings is *infal-* and *iftal-*, with shortening of the perfect vowel—there is no reversion to an "original" vowel in the increased forms as there is in the G-form.

(2) Forms VII and VIII produce only one participle each. Since Form VII is always intransitive, no passive participle can be made. Form VIII is often transitive, but the distinction between the active and passive participles is obscured *(*muftayil → muftāl-; *muftayal- → muftāl-).*

(3) In the verbal noun of both VII and VIII the weak middle radical becomes *y;* original *w* is changed to *y* by the preceding *i*-vowel (VII **infiwāl- → infiyāl-;* VIII **iftiwāl- → iftiyāl-).*

60.3 Synopsis of the weak-*lām* verb, Form VII, example √BĞY:

PERFECT	انفعى *infaʻā*	انبغى *imbağā*
IMPERFECT	ينفعي *yanfaʻī*	ينبغي *yambağī*
SUBJUNCTIVE	ينفعي *yanfaʻiya*	ينبغي *yambağiya*
JUSSIVE	ينفع *yanfaʻi*	ينبغ *yambaği*

IMPERATIVE	انفع	*infa'i*	انبغ	*imbaği*
PARTICIPLE	منفع	*munfa'in*	منبغ	*mumbağin*
VERBAL NOUN	انفعاء	*infi'ā'-*	انبغاء	*imbiğā'-*

60.4 Synopsis of the weak-*lām* verb, Form VIII:

	ACTIVE		PASSIVE	
PERFECT	افتعى	*ifta'ā*	افتعى	*uftu'iya*
IMPERFECT	يفتعى	*yafta'ī*	يفتعى	*yufta'ā*
SUBJUNCTIVE	يفتعى	*yafta'iya*	يفتعى	*yufta'ā*
JUSSIVE	يفتع	*yafta'i*	يفتع	*yufta'a*
IMPERATIVE	افتع	*ifta'i*	—	—
PARTICIPLE	مفتع	*mufta'in*	مفتعًى	*mufta'an*
VERBAL NOUN	افتعاء	*ifti'ā'-*		

Example from √*BĞY*:

PERFECT	ابتغى	*ibtağā*	ابتغى	*ubtuğiya*
IMPERFECT	يبتغى	*yabtağī*	يبتغى	*yubtağā*
SUBJUNCTIVE	يبتغى	*yabtağiya*	يبتغى	*yubtağā*
JUSSIVE	يبتغ	*yabtaği*	يبتغ	*yubtağa*
IMPERATIVE	ابتغ	*ibtaği*	—	—
PARTICIPLE	مبتغ	*mubtağin*	مبتغًى	*mubtağan*
VERBAL NOUN	ابتغاء	*ibtiğā'-*		

REMARKS:

(1) The inflection of VII and VIII weak-*lām* verbs in both the perfect and imperfect follows the model of *ramā* (see Appendix B).

(2) The active participles in *-in* are inflected on the model of *hādin* (see §27.2).

(3) The passive participles are inflected as follows:

	SINGULAR		DUAL		PLURAL	
MASCULINE indefinite	مفتعًى	*mufta'an*	مفتعيان	*mufta'ayāni*	مفتعون	*mufta'awna*

definite	مفتعى	*mufta'ā*				
oblique			مفتعيين	*mufta'ayayni*	مفتعين	*mufta'ayna*
FEMININE	مفتعاة	*mufta'āt-*	مفتعاتان	*mufta'ātāni*	مفتعيات	*mufta'ayāt-*

(4) In the verbal noun the weakness of the third radical shows up as glottal stop *(hamza)*; otherwise formation is regular.

(5) The passive inflection, both perfect and imperfect, follows the model of *laqiya* (see Appendix B).

Vocabulary

بغى VII *imbağā* be proper, seemly (*li-* for), be necessary (*li-/'alā* for); VIII *ibtağā* (+ acc.) strive for, aspire to, desire

جهل *jahila (a) jahl-* be ignorant, not know, be foolish

خير VIII *ixtāra* choose, select (something, acc., *'alā* over something else)

هدى VIII *ihtadā* be rightly guided, be shown the right way

وقى *waqā (yaqī) wiqāyat-* ward off, protect, guard someone/thing (acc.) from someone/thing (acc.); VIII *ittaqā* beware, be on one's guard, fear (God)

NOUNS

صاحب/اصحاب *ṣāḥib-* pl *'aṣḥāb-* companion, friend; master

نجم/نجوم *najm-* pl *nujūm-* star

هوًى/اهواء *hawan* pl *'ahwā'-* lust, passion

OTHERS

بعدما *ba'da-mā (min ba'di-mā)* after (conj.)

غير *ğayr-* (+ construct) other than, non-, un-

PROPER NAMES

كنانة *kinānatu* the Kinana tribe, which, together with Tamīm and Qays, formed Muḍar, one of the two great divisions of the northern Arabs

قريش *qurayš-* the Quraysh, the leading tribe of Mecca and subgroup of Kinana

هاشم *hāšim-* Hashim (ibn 'Abd-Manāf, great-grandfather of Muhammad)

Exercises

(a) Produce the forms requested for Forms VII or VIII:

ROOT	FORM	MEANING	FORM TO PRODUCE
دعو	VIII	'claim'	act. part.
شوق	VIII	'yearn'	act. part.
نهى	VIII	'be finished'	pass. part.
قدو	VIII	'emulate'	verbal noun
ميز	VIII	'excel'	act. part.
شرى	VIII	'buy'	1st sing. subj.
قضى	VII	'cease'	3 masc. pl. juss.
صفو	VIII	'choose'	pass. part.
عود	VIII	'be accustomed'	3 masc. sing. juss.
خفى	VIII	'vanish'	masc. sing. imperative
حنى	VII	'be bent'	act. part.
رضو	VIII	'be pleased with'	pass. part.
وقى	VIII	'be devout'	act. part.
سوق	VII	'be driven'	1 pl. perfect

(b) Read and translate:

١ اصحابى كالنجوم فبأيهم اقتديتم[1] اهتديتم (حديث نبوى).

٢ ان الله اصطفى من ولد[2] آدم ابرهيم واصطفى من ولد ابرهيم اسمعيل واصطفى من ولد اسمعيل بنى كنانة واصطفى من بنى كنانة قريشاً واصطفى من قريش بنى هاشم واصطفانى من بنى هاشم (حديث نبوى).

[1]√*QDW VIII iqtadā bi-* emulate.

[2]*Wuld-* progeny.

٣ انما يتّبعون اهواءهم، ومن اضل ممن اتبع هواه غير هدى من الله؟ ان الله لا يهدى القوم الظالمين.

٤ يا رب اغفر للذين اتّبعوا سبيلك وقهم عذاب اليوم العظيم.

٥ فقالوا «لنا اعمالنا ولكم اعمالكم. سلام عليكم لا نبتغى الجاهلين».

٦ يا ايها الناس اتقوا ربكم الذى خلقكم من نفس واحدة وابتغوا اليه السبيل.

٧ قالوا سبحانك[1] ما كان ينبغى لنا ان نتخذ من دونك من آلهة.

٨ يا ايها المؤمنون اتقوا الله يجعل لكم نوراً تمشون به ويغفر لكم.

٩ يقال لهم «ذلك هو العذاب فذوقوه فادخلوا ابواب جهنم خالدين فيها».

١٠ اتخذوا العجل معبوداً من بعدما جاءتهم البيّنات فعفونا عن ذلك.

(c) Translate into Arabic:

1. We shall relate to you the news of those who travelled the earth.

2. I am not afraid of suffering loss when my companions are with me.

3. O oppressors who do not fear the torment, hell will be filled with the likes of you.

4. It is necessary that we not sleep in order to be on our guard.

5. When they drew near me I feared they would seize my goods and then (consequential) I would be among the losers.

6. If they had followed the way of the rightly-guided (one), they would have been shown the right way; but his words availed them not, and so they descended into the fire.

Reading Selection: *Sūrat Maryam (19):85–96.*

Doomsday

يوم نحشر المتّقين الى الرحمن وفداً (٨٥)[2]

ونسوق المجرمين الى جهنم ورداً (٨٦)[3]

---

[1]*Subḥāna* glory be to.

[2]*Ḥašara (u/i)* gather; *wafd-* herd.

[3]*Sāqa (ū)* drive; *mujrim-* criminal; *wird-* thirsty herd.

لا يملكون الشفاعة الا من اتخذ عند الرحمن عهداً (٨٧)[1]

وقالوا اتخذ الرحمن ولداً (٨٨)

لقد جئتم شيئاً اداً (٨٩)[2]

تكاد السموات يتفطرن منه وتنشقّ الارض وتخرّ الجبال هداً (٩٠)[3]

أن دعوا للرحمن ولداً (٩١)

وما ينبغى للرحمن أن يتخذ ولداً (٩٢)

إنْ كل من فى السموات والارض الا آتى الرحمن عبداً (٩٣)

لقد أحصاهم وعدّهم عداً (٩٤)[4]

وكلّهم آتيه يوم القيامة فرداً (٩٥)[5]

ان الذين آمنوا وعملوا الصالحات سيجعل لهم الرحمن وداً (٩٦)[6]

---

[1] *Malaka (i)* possess; *šafāʿat-* intercession; *ʿahd-* covenant.

[2] *ʾIdd-* disastrous.

[3] *Kāda (ā)* be on the verge of; *tafaṭṭara/yatafaṭṭaru* be torn; *xarra (i)* fall down; *hadd-* ruins.

[4] *ʾAḥṣā* "he enumerated"; *ʿadda (u) ʿadd-* count.

[5] *Fard-* individual.

[6] *ʾĀmana* believe; *wudd-* affection.

Lesson Twenty-Six

61 Optative Constructions. Wishes contrary to fact are normally expressed by *(yā) layta,* which is followed by the pronominal enclitics (first person singular takes *-nī)* or a noun in the accusative. In verbal clauses the verb is generally in the perfect for the affirmative and *lam* + jussive for the negative.

ليتنى كنت طيرا فأطير	*laytanī kuntu ṭayran fa-'aṭīra*	I wish I were a bird so that I could fly.
يا ليت ربه لم يخلقه	*yā layta rabbahu lam yaxluqhu*	Would that his Lord had not created him!

62 Diminutive Pattern: FU'AYL-. The diminutive pattern to which every triliteral noun is theoretically susceptible is FU'AYL-. Feminine nouns add the feminine ending (FU'AYLAT-) even when the base noun does not have the *-at-* ending. The diminutive pattern is used for endearment as well as for denigration.

جبل > جبيل	*jabal- > jubayl-*	little mountain, hillock
عبد > عبيد	*'abd- > 'ubayd-*	little / dear servant
قبل > قبيل	*qabla > qubayla*	a little before (prep.)

C3*w/y* and biliteral roots substitute *y* for the third consonant of the pattern.

ابن > بنى	*ibn- > bunayy-*	dear / little son
اب > ابى	*'ab- > 'ubayy-*	dear father

With the addition of the first-person singular enclitic, these words become *bunayya* and *'ubayya;* otherwise they are regular *('ubayyuka, bunayyuhu, &c.).*

Other, less common diminutive patterns are *fu'ayyil-* and *fuway'il-*.

63 Cardinal Numbers: 11–19. Review the numbers from 1–10 in §38. In the numbers from 11 through 19, the units of 11 and 12 continue to be regular adjectives, while the units from 3 through 9 conform to the rule of chiastic concord given in §38(4). The tens do *not* exhibit chiastic concord. With the exception of the dual ending in 12, *all numbers from 11 through 19 are indeclinable in -a*. Things numbered are in the *accusative singular* following the number.

SINGULAR MASCULINE		SINGULAR FEMININE	
احد عشر بيتاً	*'aḥada 'ašara baytan*	احدى عشرة بنتاً	*'iḥdā 'ašrata bintan*
اثنا عشر بيتاً	*iθnā 'ašara baytan* (nom.)	اثنتا عشرة بنتاً	*iθnatā 'ašrata bintan*
اثنى عشر بيتاً	*iθnay 'ašara baytan* (obl.)	اثنتى عشرة بنتاً	*iθnatay 'ašrata bintan*
ثلاثة عشر بيتاً	*θalāθata 'ašara baytan*	ثلاث عشرة بنتاً	*θalāθa 'ašrata bintan*
اربعة عشر بيتاً	*'arba'ata 'ašara baytan*	اربع عشرة بنتاً	*'arba'a 'ašrata bintan*
خمسة عشر بيتاً	*xamsata 'ašara baytan*	خمس عشرة بنتاً	*xamsa 'ašrata bintan*
ستة عشر بيتاً	*sittata 'ašara baytan*	ست عشرة بنتاً	*sitta 'ašrata bintan*
سبعة عشر بيتاً	*sab'ata 'ašara baytan*	سبع عشرة بنتاً	*sab'a 'ašrata bintan*
ثمانية عشر بيتاً	*θamāniyata 'ašara baytan*	ثماني عشرة بنتاً	*θamāniya 'ašrata bintan*
تسعة عشر بيتاً	*tis'ata 'ašara baytan*	تسع عشرة بنتاً	*tis'a 'ašrata bintan*

For the definite, either (1) the article precedes the entire construction

الاحد عشر ولداً *al-'aḥada 'ašara waladan* the eleven boys

or (2) the indeclinable number follows the plural.

الاولاد الاحد عشر *al-'awlād- l-'aḥada 'ašara* the eleven boys

Vocabulary

جرى *jarā (ī) jary-/jarayān-* flow (water), blow (wind); happen, come to pass

ضرب *ḍaraba (i) ḍarb-* strike, hit, smite; VIII *iḍṭaraba* clash, be upset

كاد *kāda (ī) kayd-* plot for the downfall of, conspire (*li-* against)

NOUNS

حجر/احجار، حجارة *ḥajar-* pl *'aḥjār-/ḥijārat-* stone, rock

رؤيا/رؤى *ru'yā* (fem) pl *ru'an* vision

طير/طيور *ṭayr-* pl *ṭuyūr-* bird (singular sometimes used as collective)

عصا/عصى *'aṣan* (fem) pl *'uṣīy-/'iṣīy-* rod, staff

عقبى *'uqbā* end, final outcome

قمر/اقمار *qamar-* pl *'aqmār-* moon

كوكب/كواكب *kawkab-* pl *kawākibu* heavenly body, star

نهر/انهار، انهر *nahr-* pl *'anhār-/'anhur-* river, stream

OTHER

تحت *taḥta, min taḥti* (+ gen.) beneath, below

اذا *'iðā* (+ noun or pronoun) lo and behold

IDIOM

ضرب مثلاً *ḍaraba maθalan* he gave as an example

Exercises

(a) Give the Arabic:

1. 11 stars
2. 16 other mountains
3. 19 rich (men)
4. 15 sick women
5. 18 new houses
6. 14 worshipped idols

(b) Give the Arabic:

1. would that we had heard
2. I wish I hadn't said that
3. would that he had chosen me
4. would that she had protected me
5. would that he hadn't forgotten
6. would that they (f pl) had not prevented us

(c) Read and translate:

(c) Read and translate:

١ اذ قال يوسف لأبيه «يا ابتى ، اني رأيت احد عشر كوكباً والشمس والقمر
رأيتهم لى ساجدين». قال «يا بنيّ ، لا تقصص رؤياك على اخوتك
فيكيدوا لك كيداً. ان الشيطان للانسان عدو مبين».
٢ فقلنا لموسى «اضرب بعصاك الحجر» فانفجرت[1] منه اثنتا عشرة عيناً.
٣ من ضل فما له من هاد. لهم عذاب فى الحياة الدنيا ولعذاب الآخرة اشقّ[2]،
وما لهم من الله من واق. مثل الجنة التى وُعد المتّقون تجرى من تحتها
الانهار. تلك عقبى الذين اتقوا ، وعقبى الكافرين النار.
٤ يا ليتنى متّ قبل هذا وكنت منسياً.
٥ ضرب الله مثلاً للذين كفروا امرأة نوح وامرأة لوط. كانتا تحت عبدين من
عبادنا صالحين فخانتاهما[3].
٦ الله يصطفى من الملائكة رسلاً ومن الناس ويعلم ما بين ايديهم.
٧ قل انى نُهيت أن أعبد الذين تدعون من دون الله. قل لا أتّبع اهواءكم ، قد
ضللت اذاً وما انا من المهتدين.
٨ فلما جاء موسى فرعون وقومه بآياتنا اذا هم منها يضحكون.
٩ انتم بريئون مما اعمل وانا برىء مما تعملون.
١٠ يا مريم ان الله اصطفاك على نساء العالمين.
١١ اعبد الله كانك تراه فإن لم تكن تراه فإنه يراك.
١٢ واذا سألوه عن الروح قال ان الروح من امر ربى.

(d) Translate into Arabic:

1. The people of the city called upon the pious (men) to pass judgment between them and the unbelievers.

2. Oh, would that we had not been foolish and struck our friend with a stone!

3. God was pleased with the alms of the poor.

4. Whoever disobeys will see his deeds on the day of judgment.

5. It came to pass just as they had said.

---

[1] *Infajara* gush forth.
[2] *Šāqq-* harsh.
[3] *Xāna (ū)* betray.

6. Would that I had chosen a guide other than you, for then I would be on the right track.

7. Had I followed the stars and the sun and moon and not followed you, we would have found a river in which there flows much water.

Lesson Twenty-Seven

64 Factitive Verbs: Form II. Characteristic of the factitive Form II is the doubling of the second radical consonant. The base pattern is FA‘‘ALA.

64.1 The normal connotive range of meaning of Form II falls into three broad categories:

(1) The increase of a stative or intransitive G-form into Form II gives the verb a factitive sense, as *kabura* ‘to get big / great’ > II *kabbara* ‘to make great, magnify’; *nazala* ‘to go down’ > II *nazzala* ‘to make (someone / something) go down, send / bring / take down.’

(2) For G-form verbs that are transitive, Form II makes factitive, intensifies, or specializes the meaning, as *ðakara* ‘to recall’ > II *ðakkara* ‘to make (someone) recall, remind’; *kaðaba* ‘to lie’ > II *kaððaba* ‘to call (someone) a liar), consider (something) false.’ Transitive G-forms may also become factitive with two objects, as *‘alima* ‘to know’ > II *‘allama* ‘to make (someone) know (something), to teach.’

(3) Many denominative verbs, or verbs derived from nouns, do not have G-forms. Instead, they enter the verbal system as transitive at Form II, as *‘aðāb-* ‘torment’ > II *‘aððaba* ‘to torment’ and *nūr-* ‘light’ > II *nawwara* ‘to make light, illuminate.’ Other denominatives have G-forms, but Form II has a different signification, as *qiṭ‘at-* ‘piece, fragment’ > II *qaṭṭa‘a* ‘to cut to pieces, hack off / up’ (cf. G-form *qaṭa‘a* ‘to cut’).

64.2 Synopsis of Form II:

	ACTIVE	PASSIVE
PERFECT	فعّل *fa''ala*	فعّل *fu''ila*
IMPERFECT	يفعّل *yufa''ilu*	يفعّل *yufa''alu*
SUBJUNCTIVE	يفعّل *yufa''ila*	يفعّل *yufa''ala*
JUSSIVE	يفعّل *yufa''il*	يفعّل *yufa''al*
IMPERATIVE	فعّل *fa''il*	— —
PARTICIPLE	مفعّل *mufa''il-*	مفعّل *mufa''al-*
VERBAL NOUN	تفعيل (1) *taf'īl-*	
	تفعلة (2) *taf'ilat-*	

Example from √*KBR:*

PERFECT	كبّر *kabbara*	كبّر *kubbira*
IMPERFECT	يكبّر *yukabbiru*	يكبّر *yukabbaru*
SUBJUNCTIVE	يكبّر *yukabbira*	يكبّر *yukabbara*
JUSSIVE	يكبّر *yukabbir*	يكبّر *yukabbar*
IMPERATIVE	كبّر *kabbir*	— —
PARTICIPLE	مكبّر *mukabbir-*	مكبّر *mukabbar-*
VERBAL NOUN	تكبير *takbīr-*	

REMARKS:

(1) The characteristic vowel of the personal prefixes in the imperfect and all moods built upon the imperfect for Form II (as well as Forms III and IV, to be introduced later) is *u*, not *a* as in the G-form and Forms VII and VIII.

(2) All passive forms are made in absolute conformity to the rules given in §53 and §55. Since the vowel of the prefixes in the imperfect active of this form is *u*, the only distinction between the active and passive of the imperfect is the vowel on the doubled second radical.

(3) In the imperative there is no necessity for a prosthetic *alif* since the removal of the personal prefix does not result in a consonant cluster.

(4) As in Form VIII—as in all increased forms—the characteristic vowel of participles is *-i-* on the second radical for the active and *-a-* for the passive.

(5) The normal verbal noun of Form II is TAF'IL-. The second verbal noun (TAF'ILAT-) is reserved mainly for weak-*lām* (√*WLY wallā* > *tawliyat-*, §65) and C_3' verbs (√*BR' barra'a* > *tabri'at-);* it is rarely used with other roots.

64.3 Weakness in Form II. The only "weakness" that needs to be treated as such in Form II is the weak-*lām* verb, which will be given in §65. All other "weak" radicals, i.e., C_1*w/y* and C_2*w/y,* are retained in their original form, as √*WS'* > II *wassa'a / yuwassi'u,* √*XWF* > *xawwafa / yuxawwifu,* √*SYR* > *sayyara / yusayyiru.*

64.4 Here follows a selective list of verbs / roots already introduced that commonly produce a factitive Form II verb:

برّأ	make whole, exculpate	قلّب	turn over (trs.)
خوّف	cause to fear, scare	كذّب	call a liar, consider false
سلّم	greet *('alā)*	كبّر	magnify
سيّر	set in motion, make go	كثّر	increase
صدّق	accept / declare as true	كرّم	ennoble
طلّق	divorce	نبّأ	inform (*bi-* of / about)
علّم	teach	نزّل	send / bring / take down
عذّب	torment, punish	نوّر	illuminate, make light
قرّب	allow near, bring / take near	وسّع	expand

Vocabulary

VERBS

أذن *'aδina (a) 'iδn-* permit *(li-)* someone *(bi-)* to do something; II *'aδδana* give the call to prayer

سخر II *saxxara* subjugate

قرأ *qara'a (a) qirā'at-* recite, read aloud *('alā* to)

مس *massa (*masisa) (a) mass-/masīs-* touch

ملك *malaka (i) mulk-* possess, rule, reign; II *mallaka* put in possession of, make king (*'alā* over)

هاد *hāda (ū) hawd-* be Jewish, practice Judaism; II *hawwada* Judaize

NOUNS

حسن *ḥasan-* good, beautiful

حسنة/حسنات *ḥasanat-* pl *-āt-* good deed

حمد *ḥamd-* praise; *al-ḥamdu lillāhi* praise (be to) God

القرآن *al-qur'ān-* the Koran

شريك/شركاء *šarīk-* pl *šurakā'u* partner

ولى/اولياء *walīy-* pl *'awliyā'u* friend, helper, supporter

مجوس ، مجوسى *majūs-* (collective), *majūsiyy-* (sing.) Magian, adherent of Mazdaism

نصرانى/نصارى *naṣrāniyy-* pl *naṣārā* Christian, follower of the Nazarene

Exercises

(a) Vocalize, read and translate:

١ لأقطعنّ ايديكم

٢ المطلّقات

٣ قرّبنى اليه تقريباً

٤ نوّرت البيت

٥ المدن المسخّرة

٦ كثّر العدد

٧ كتاب منزّل من السماء

٨ عشنا مكرّمين

٩ المدينة المنوّرة

١٠ كواكب مسيّرة

(b) Read and translate:

١ ولئن سالتهم من خلق السموات والارض وسخّر الشمس والقمر ليقولنّ «الله».

٢ الم يروا الى الطير مسخّرات فى جوّ السماء؟ ما يمسكهن الا الله.[1]

٣ ذلك يخوّف الله به عباده. يا عبادى ، فاتّقونى.

٤ لا جناح عليكم إن طلّقتم النساء ما[2] لم تمسّوهن.

٥ انه لذو علم لما علّمناه ولكن اكثر الناس لا يعلمون.

---

[1]*Jaww-* air; *yumsiku* "he holds."

[2]*Mā* "so long as."

٦ فان كذّبوك فقد كُذّب رسل من قبلك فقل ربكم ذو رحمة واسعة.

٧ قل ادعوا «الله» او ادعوا «الرحمن». ايّاً ما تدعوا فله الاسماء الحسنى ولا تجهر بصلاتك ولا تخافت بها وابتغ بين ذلك سبيلاً وقل الحمد لله الذى لم يتخذ ولداً ولم يكن له شريك فى الملك ولم يكن له ولى من الذلّ وكبّره تكبيراً.[1]

٨ لا جناح عليهن فى آبائهن ولا ما ملكت ايمانهن[2] واتقين الله. ان الله ليشهد على كل شىء.

٩ انبّئكم بخير من ذلك. للذين اتّقوا عند ربهم جنات تجرى من تحتها الانهر خالدين فيها.

١٠ كل مولود يولد على الفطرة[3] فابواه يهودانه او ينصّرانه او يمجّسانه.

١١ إن نعف عن طائفة منكم نعذب طائفة.

(c) Translate into Arabic:

1. Do you (m pl) worship, to the exclusion of God, a stone that possesses for you neither benefit nor harm?

2. Teach us of that which you have been taught.

3. He who does a good deed, the angels record ("write") for him ten like it.

4. When the messenger took the king's order down to the city, the people conspired against him, struck him and killed him, and he had no helper.

5. He scares us when he recites to us the final end of this world, when God will set the mountains in motion.

6. We have been promised beautiful gardens beneath which flow rivers.

7. I wish your father would allow you near, but he calls you a liar and you will never inherit from him.

---

[1] *'Ayyan-mā* "whichever" (acc.); *lā tajhar* "don't raise your voice"; *lā tuxāfit* "don't mumble"; *ðull-* baseness.

[2] *Yamīn-/'aymān-* right hand; "what their right hands possess" refers to slaves.

[3] *Fiṭrat-* "innate disposition," interpreted as an innate disposition to Islam.

Lesson Twenty-Eight

65 Form II: Weak-*Lâm* Verbs. The weak-*lām* verb (C3*w*/*y*) is the only type to be treated as weak in Form II. The synopsis given below will reveal patterns of weakness familiar from Forms VII and VIII.

	ACTIVE	PASSIVE
PERFECT	فعّى *fa''ā*	فعّي *fu''iya*
IMPERFECT	يفعّي *yufa''ī*	يفعّى *yufa''ā*
SUBJUNCTIVE	يفعّي *yufa''iya*	يفعّى *yufa''ā*
JUSSIVE	يفعّ *yufa''i*	يفعّ *yufa''a*
IMPERATIVE	فعّ *fa''i*	— —
PARTICIPLE	مفعّ *mufa''in*	مفعّى *mufa''an*
VERBAL NOUN	تفعية *taf'iyat-*	

Example from √*WLY:*

PERFECT	ولّى *wallā*	ولّي *wulliya*
IMPERFECT	يولّي *yuwallī*	يولّى *yuwallā*
SUBJUNCTIVE	يولّي *yuwalliya*	يولّى *yuwallā*
JUSSIVE	يولّ *yuwalli*	يولّ *yuwalla*
IMPERATIVE	ولّ *walli*	— —
PARTICIPLE	مولّ *muwallin*	مولّى *muwallan*
VERBAL NOUN	تولية *tawliyat-*	

REMARKS:

(1) The perfect active is inflected like *ramā;* the perfect passive is inflected like *laqiya* (see Appendix B).

(2) The imperfect active is inflected on the model of *yarmī;* the passive on the model of *yalqā* (see Appendix B).

(3) The subjunctive and jussive are formed exactly like those of Form VIII, as are the imperative and participles.

(4) Weak-*lām* verbs use the second verbal noun. Note that the *y* is not doubled.

(5) As in Forms VII and VIII, the distinction between original *y* and *w* in C_3 is entirely obscured.

66 The Pronominal Enclitic Carrier; Double Pronominal Objects.

66.1 Certains verbs, such as "to give" and "to teach," take two objects (in English they are called direct and indrect objects, but in Arabic the distinction is not relevant). In Koranic Arabic, when the two objects are different persons and pronominal, both pronominal enclitic objects may be added to the verb, in which case the first-person pronoun precedes the second, which precedes the third. For example:

علّمكه	*'allama-ka-hu*	he taught it to you
انسانيها	*'ansā-nī-hā*	he made me forget it

In post-Koranic Arabic the use of the double-enclitic object was replaced by and large with the pronominal carrier ايا *'iyyā-*, a particle that supports the second of two pronominal enclitic objects, e.g.

علّمك ايّاه	*'allamaka '<u>iyyā</u>-hu*	he taught it to you
انسانى ايّاها	*'ansānī '<u>iyyā</u>-hā*	he made me forget it

66.2 *'Iyyā-* occurs in Koranic Arabic primarily as a pronominal carrier for pronouns that have been separated from the verb for rhetorical force.

ايّاك نعبد	*'<u>iyyā</u>ka na'budu*	Thee do we worship.

فايّاك لأقتلنّك	*fa-'iyyāka la-'aqtulannaka*	You, then—I shall certainly slay you!

'Iyyā- also supports enclitic pronouns that for some reason cannot be attached to the verb. In the following example the carrier is used because, whereas the independent subject pronouns occur after *'illā,* the enclitic pronouns do not, and the pronoun here is direct object of the verb, hence necessarily enclitic:

ضلّ من تدعون الا ايّاه	*ḍalla man tad'ūna 'illā 'iyyāhu*	All those whom you invoke besides Him are lost.

In the following example the carrier is used because the independent pronoun cannot occur as a complement of *'inna:*

انني وايّاك اولياء بعضنا لبعض	*'innanī wa-'iyyāka 'awliyā'u ba'ḍunā li-ba'ḍin*	You and I are supporters of each other.

Vocabulary

VERBS

- بسط *basaṭa (u) basṭ-* spread, stretch out (trs)
- رجع *raja'a (i) rujū'-* return
- زنى *zanā (ī) zinan/zinā'-* fornicate, commit adultery
- سمى II *sammā* name, stipulate (denominative from *ism-*)
- صلو II *ṣallā* pray (*'alā* for), perform the ritual prayer
- طلع *ṭala'a (u) ṭulū'-* rise (sun, moon, &c.); VIII *iṭṭala'a* be informed (*'alā* of), observe (*'alā*) something closely
- وجه II *wajjaha* make someone/thing (acc.) face/turn (*li-/'ilā* toward); VIII *ittajaha* turn towards, set out (*'ilā* for)
- ولى II *wallā* turn aside/away (*min/'an* from)[1]; put someone (acc.) in charge of (acc.)

NOUNS

- اجل/آجال *'ajal-* pl *'ājāl-* term, appointed time, instant of death

[1]Note that this usage of *wallā* is intransitive, a rare occurrence in Form II.

الاسلام *al-'islām-* Islam

حق / حقوق *ḥaqq-* pl *ḥuqūq-* right, truth

راس/ رؤوس *ra's-* pl *ru'ūs-* head

شمال *šimāl-* north; (fem) left (hand)

غريب/ غرباء *ğarīb-* pl *ğurabā'u* strange, foreign

وجه/ وجوه *wajh-* pl *wujūh-* face

يمين/ ايمان *yamīn-* pl *'aymān-* oath; (fem) right (hand)

OTHERS

اينما *'ayna-mā* (+ perf. or juss. as conditional type) wherever

ثم *θamma* there, in that place

ثم *θumma* then, next, afterwards

طوبى ل *ṭūbā li-* blessed be

Exercises

(a) Produce the following forms for Form II:

1. √*SMY* (1) masc. sing. act. part. (2) verbal noun (3) 1 sing. juss. (4) masc. pl. pass. part.
2. √*WLY* (1) fem. sing. pass. part. (2) 3 fem. pl. imperf. (3) masc. pl. act. part. (4) 3 masc. pl. pass. subj.
3. √*ṢLW* (1) masc. sing. imperative (2) fem. pl. pass. part. (3) fem. sing. act. part. (4) 3 fem. sing. perf.

(b) Read and translate:

١ سخر الشمس والقمر كل يجرى الى اجل مسمّى. كذلك سخّرها لكم لتكبروا الله على ما هداكم.

٢ ونقلّبهم ذات اليمين وذات الشمال وكلبهم باسطٌ ذراعيه بالوصيد. لو اطّلعت عليهم لولّيت منهم فراراً ولملئت منهم رعباً.[1]

٣ ولله المشرق والمغرب فاينما تولوا فثم وجه الله.[2]

---

[1] *ðāta* toward; *kalb-* dog; *ðirā'-* paw; *waṣīd-* threshold; *ru'b-* alarm.

[2] *Mašriq-* the east; *mağrib-* the west.

٤ ان الله وملائكته يصلّون على النبى. يا ايها المؤمنون صلّوا عليه وسلّموا تسليماً.
٥ ما تعبدون من دونه الا اسماء سمّيتموها انتم وآباؤكم.
٦ ويقول الله للملائكة «أهؤلاء اياكم كانوا يعبدون؟»
٧ يا عبادى، ان ارضى واسعة فاياى فاعبدونى.
٨ انطلقوا الى المدينة وان لم تجدوا فيها احداً فلا تدخلوها حتى يؤذن لكم.
٩ لو نزّلنا القرآن على بعض الأعجمين[1] فقرأناه عليهم، ما كانوا به مؤمنين.
١٠ قل لعبادى يقولوا التى هى احسن.
١١ انى وجّهت وجهى للذى يملك الملك كله لا شريك له.
١٢ وليشهد عذاب الزانى والزانية طائفة من المؤمنين.
١٣ حكموا عليه بالموت فانقطع راسه.
١٤ ان الاسلام بدأ غريباً وسيعود غريباً فطوبى للغرباء.[2]

(c) Translate into Arabic:

1. If she turns away from us, we will forbid her to retrace her steps.
2. They departed and turned toward the north, they and their partners, unmindful of the plotting of the devil.
3. It is not for us to draw near or to touch the fruit of that tree, for if you observe closely you will see that there is evil in it.
4. After he had performed the prayer, he spread out his arms and called upon his Lord.
5. He laid down the earth and spread it out for men to dwell on.

Reading Selection: *Sūrat al-Anbiyā' (21):51–70.*

Abraham Overturns His People's Idols

ولقد آتينا ابرهيمَ رُشدَه من قبلُ وكنّا به عالمين (٥١)[3]

إذ قال لأبيه وقومه «ما هذه التماثيل التى انتم لها عاكفون؟» (٥٢)[4]

---

[1] *'A'jamu* non-Arab, usually applied specifically to Persians.

[2] The meaning of this dictum is obscure; however, the grammar and literal meaning should be clear.

[3] *'Ātaynā* "we gave"; *rušd-* guidance.

[4] *Timθāl-* pl *tamāθīlu* image; *'akafa li-* be devoted to.

قالوا «وجدنا آباءنا لها عابدين» (٥٣)

قال «لقد كنتم انتم وآباؤكم فى ضلال مبين» (٥٤)

قالوا «أجئتَنا بالحقّ ام انت من اللاعبين؟» (٥٥)[1]

قال «بل ربكم رب السموات والارض الذى فطرهن، وانا على ذلكم من الشاهدين» (٥٦)[2]

وتالله لاكيدنّ اصنامكم بعد أن تولّوا مدبرين» (٥٧)[3]

فجعلهم جُذاذاً إلاّ كبيراً لهم لعلّهم اليه يرجعون (٥٨)[4]

قالوا «من فعل هذا بآلهتنا؟ انه لمن الظالمين» (٥٩)

قالوا «سمعنا فتًى يذكرهم يقال له ابرهيم» (٦٠)[5]

قالوا «فأتوا به على اعين الناس لعلّهم يشهدون» (٦١)[6]

قالوا «أأنت فعلت هذا بآلهتنا يا ابرهيم؟» (٦٢)

قال «بل فعله كبيرُهم هذا فاسألوهم إن كانوا ينطقون» (٦٣)[7]

فرجعوا الى انفسهم فقالوا «انكم انتم الظالمون» (٦٤)[8]

ثُم نكسوا على رؤوسهم. «لقد علمتَ ما هؤلاء ينطقون»(٦٥)[9]

قال «أفتعبدون من دون الله ما لا ينفعكم ولا يضركم؟ (٦٦)

---

[1]*La'iba (a)* jest.

[2]*Faṭara (u)* create; *ðālikum* see p. 103, note 3.

[3]*Ta-llāhi* "by God"; *mudbir-* turning away.

[4]*Juðāð-* fragments.

[5]*Fatan* youth, lad.

[6]*'A'yun-* pl of *'ayn-* eye.

[7]*Naṭaqa (i)* speak.

[8]*Raja'ū 'ilā 'anfusihim* "they conferred apart."

[9]*Nukisū 'alā ru'ūsihim* "they were confounded."

أفٍّ لكم ولما تعبدون من دون الله. أفلا تعقلون؟» (٦٧)[1]

قالوا «حرّقوه وانصروا آلهتكم إن كنتم فاعلين» (٦٨)[2]

قلنا «يا نار، كوني برداً وسلاماً على ابرهيم» (٦٩)[3]

وأرادوا به كيداً فجعلناهم الأخسرين (٧٠)[4]

---

[1] *'Uffin li-* fie on; *'aqala (i)* be reasonable, have sense.
[2] *Ḥarraqa* burn (trs); *naṣara (u)* support
[3] *Bard-* coolness.
[4] *'Arāda* want.

Lesson Twenty-Nine

67 Reflexive/Medio-Passive Verbs: Form V. Form V is the reflexive/medio-passive of Form II, as Form VIII is of the G-form. Characteristic of Form V is the prefix *ta-* (rather than the infix met in Form VIII). The base form is TAFA''ALA.

	ACTIVE		PASSIVE	
PERFECT	تفعّل	*tafa''ala*	تفعّل	*tufu''ila*
IMPERFECT	يتفعّل	*yatafa''alu*	يتفعّل	*yutafa''alu*
SUBJUNCTIVE	يتفعّل	*yatafa''ala*	يتفعّل	*yutafa''ala*
JUSSIVE	يتفعّل	*yatafa''al*	يتفعّل	*yutafa''al*
IMPERATIVE	تفعّل	*tafa''al*	—	—
PARTICIPLE	متفعّل	*mutafa''il-*	متفعّل	*mutafa''al-*
VERBAL NOUN		تفعّل *tafa''ul-*		

Example from √*'LM:*

PERFECT	تعلّم	*ta'allama*	تعلّم	*tu'ullima*
IMPERFECT	يتعلّم	*yata'allamu*	يتعلّم	*yuta'allamu*
SUBJUNCTIVE	يتعلّم	*yata'allama*	يتعلّم	*yuta'allama*
JUSSIVE	يتعلّم	*yata'allam*	يتعلّم	*yuta'allam*
IMPERATIVE	تعلّم	*ta'allam*	—	—
PARTICIPLE	متعلّم	*muta'allim-*	متعلّم	*muta'allam-*
VERBAL NOUN		تعلّم *ta'allum-*		

REMARKS:

(1) Unlike Form II, the imperfect vowel of C_2 is *-a-*, not *-i-*.

(2) In the perfect passive, the vowel of the *t*-prefix harmonizes with the passive C_1 vowel *-u-*. In the imperfect passive, the personal prefix only, and not the *ta*-prefix, is given the passive vowel *-u-*, according to rule.

(3) As in Forms II and VIII, the distinctive C_2 vowel of the participles is *-i-* for the active and *-a-* for the passive.

(4) Note especially the pattern for the verbal noun, with *-u-* on C_2, *tafa''ul-*.

67.2 As the reflexive/medio-passive of Form II, Form V denotes the state the object of the action of Form II is brought into. Form II verbs that take only one object become intransitive in Form V, as II *nazzala* 'to send / bring / take down' > V *tanazzala* 'to be / get sent / brought / taken down'; II *kabbara* 'to magnify, make great' > V *takabbara* 'to magnify oneself, be proud, haughty.'

Doubly transitive Form II verbs are singly transitive in Form V, as II *'allama* 'to teach (someone something)' > V *ta'allama* 'to get / be taught, learn (something).'

67.3 Occasional assimilations in Form V (and VI, to be introduced in §79). Sporadic assimilation of the *t*-prefix of Form V to an initial C_1 *t/θ/ṭ/d/ḍ/ð/s/ṣ/z/ẓ/š/j* is not uncommon, as in اطّيّر *iṭṭayyara* (for *taṭayyara*) 'augur ill,' اصّدّق *iṣṣaddaqa* (for *taṣaddaqa*) 'give alms,' اثّاقل *iθθāqala* (for VI *taθāqala*) 'be sluggish,' and اذّكّر *iððakkara* (for *taðakkara*) 'remember.' The assimilation may affect any word within the form, e.g., مطّهّر *muṭṭahhir-* (for *mutaṭahhir-*) 'purified'

67.4 Occasional contractions of imperfect forms in *ta-*. Imperfect forms in *ta-*, such as *tatafa''alu*, may contract to *tafa''alu*, as in تنزّل *tanazzalu* (for *tatanazzalu*).

If the initial radical is also *t*, the contraction is almost certain to take place, as in تتبّع *tatabba'u* (for *tatatabba'u*)

68 Adjectival Pattern: FA'ĪL-. When derived from *stative* G-form verbs, the common adjectival pattern FA'ĪL- indicates that which exhibits the quality of the verb.

خفي *xafiya* 'be hidden' > خفيّ *xafīy-* 'hidden'

رحم *raḥima* 'be merciful' > رحيم *raḥīm-* 'merciful'

سوي *sawiya* 'be equal' > سوي *sawīy-* 'equal'

قدر *qadira* 'be powerful' > قدير *qadīr-* 'potent'

قرب *qaruba* 'be near' > قريب *qarīb-* 'near'

مرض *mariḍa* 'fall ill' > مريض *marīḍ-* 'sick, ill'

وسع *wasi'a* 'be vast' > وسيع *wasī'-* 'vast'

Although there are many important exceptions, such as *rāḥim-* and *qādir-*, stative verbs tend on the whole not to form active participles but to form a FA'ĪL- adjective instead.

Some transitive G-form verbs also form FA'ĪL-adjectives to indicate possession of a quality, e.g.:

سمع < سميع *sami'a* > *samī'-* '(all-)hearing'

علم < عليم *'alima* > *'alīm-* '(all-)knowing'

امر < امير *'amara* > *'amīr-* 'commander'

Generally, however, FA'ĪL- words from *transitive* G-forms have a passive-participial sense, as in Aramaeo-Syriac פעיל.

قتل < قتيل *qatala* > *qatīl-* 'slain'

أخذ < أخيذ *'axaδa* > *'axīδ-* 'taken, held (captive)'

Vocabulary

VERBS

تلا *talā (ū) tilāwat-* read, recite (out loud)

سوى *sawiya (ā) siwan/sawā'* - be level, equal, equivalent; II *sawwā* equalize, put on the same level (*bi-* with); make / shape properly; VIII *istawā* be even, on a par; stand upright; sit down (*'alā* on); be done (food), be mature, be ripe (fruit)

قبل V *taqabbala* accept, receive something (acc.)

قدر *qadara (i) qadar-/qudrat-* be capable (*'alā* of); II *qaddara* appoint, determine, foreordain

قرب II *qarraba* sacrifice (denominative from *qurbān-*, see below); allow near (*'ilā* to), let approach; V *taqarraba* approach, get near (*min/'ilā* to)

كلم II *kallama* speak to, address; V *takallama* speak (*ma'a* with)

هيا II *hayya'a* prepare, make ready; V *tahayya'a* be prepared, in readiness, get ready

وجه V *tawajjaha* turn, face (intransitive) (*'ilā/li-* toward)

NOUNS

قبلة *qiblat-* direction of prayer, direction toward Mecca

قربان/قرابين *qurbān-* pl *qarābīnu* sacrifice

كلم ، كلمة *kalim-* (collective), *kalimat-* (unit) pl *-āt-* word

مولًى/موالٍ *mawlan* pl *mawālin* master, patron

هيئة/هيآت *hay'at-* pl *-āt-* form, shape

Exercises

(a) Read and translate:

١ متكلم	٤ تهيّأوا	٧ أتعلّم	١٠ تقبّلت
٢ التكبّر	٥ لم تتكلّمى	٨ آيات متنزّلات	١١ توجّهتم
٣ متعلّمون	٦ يتنزّلون	٩ لا تتقرّبوا	١٢ تهيّأنا

(b) Read and translate:

١ الراحمون يرحمهم الرحمن. ارحموا اهل الارض يرحمكم اهل السماء.

٢ وضرب الله مثلاً رجلين أحدهما أبكم لا يقدر على شىء وهو كلّ على مولاه،

اينما يوجّهه لا يات بخير. هل استوى هو ومن يامر بالعدل؟[1]

٣ واتل عليهم نبأ ابنى آدم بالحق اذ قرّبا قرباناً فتُقبّل من احدهما ولم يتقبّل من الآخر. قال «لأقتلنّك». قال «انما يتقبّل الله من المتّقين. لَئن بسطت يدك الىّ لتقتلنى ما انا بباسط يدى اليك لأقتلك. انى أخاف الله رب العالمين.»

٤ نرى تقلب وجهك فى السماء فلنولّينّك قبلة ترضاها. فولّ وجهك اليها.

٥ قال الله لابليس اذ لم يسجد لآدم قال «فاهبط من الجنة فما يكون لك أن تتكبر فيها فاخرج.»

٦ الله الذى خلق سبع سموات ومن الارض مثلهن يتنزل الامر بينهن لتعلموا ان الله على كل شىء قدير.

٧ إن الله يهيّئ لعباده الصالحين ما لا عين رأت ولا اذن سمعت ولا خطر[2] على قلب بشر.

٨ إن الذين يتكبرون فى الارض يولّون وجوههم عن القبلة ويتّجهون الى جهنم.

(c) Translate into Arabic:

1. Shall we lead you to a man who will inform you of the noble ones who grew haughty and then were overturned?

2. Perhaps the most devout may be the most powerful.

3. The truth has come, so let the violent (ones) of the unbelievers beware!

4. At the time when the sun was rising we got in readiness to go (on foot) and speak with the king's advisors.

5. When the appointed time has come, you will not be capable of fleeing from death.

6. Wherever we faced we saw them following and stretching out their arms to seize us.

7. The parents named their child Ismail and then prayed for him.

---

[1] *'Abkamu* mute; *kall-* burden; *'adl-* justice, equity.

[2] *Xaṭara 'alā* occur to.

Lesson Thirty

69 Form V: Weak-*Lâm* Verbs. As in Form II, the only weakness that needs to be dealt with as such in Form V is the weak-*lām* verb (C3*w/y*).

69.1 Synopsis of Form V weak-*lām* verbs, example from √*WFY:*

	ACTIVE		PASSIVE	
PERFECT	توفى	*tawaffā*	توفى	*tuwuffiya*
IMPERFECT	يتوفى	*yatawaffā*	يتوفى	*yutawaffā*
SUBJUNCTIVE	يتوفى	*yatawaffā*	يتوفى	*yutawaffā*
JUSSIVE	يتوف	*yatawaffa*	يتوف	*yutawaffa*
IMPERATIVE	توف	*tawaffa*	—	—
PARTICIPLE	متوفٍ	*mutawaffin*	متوفًى	*mutawaffan*
VERBAL NOUN	توفٍ	*tawaffin*		

REMARKS:

(1) The perfect active is inflected on the model of *ramā* (see Appendix B); the perfect passive is inflected on the model of *laqiya* (see Appendix B).

(2) The imperfect—active and passive—is inflected on the model of *yalqā* (see Appendix B).

(3) The formation of the subjunctive, jussive, active and passive participles should be familiar by now. Formative principles are like those of the Form VIII weak-*lām* (see §60.2).

(4) The verbal noun deserves special attention. The character-isitic C_2 vowel *-u-* of the sound form is lost, and the noun is inflected exactly like the active participle.

70 Intensive Noun Pattern: FA''ĀL-. The noun/adjective pattern FA''ĀL- indicates someone intensely engaged in an activity or something that exhibits the quality intensely. Note that a weak third radical shows up as *hamza*, whereas weak second radicals take their original form, *y* or *w*.

اكل < اكّال *'akala* > *'akkāl-* 'glutton'
امر < امّار *'amara* > *'ammār-* 'imperious'
بكي < بكّاء *bakā* > *bakkā'*- 'weeper'
دلّ < دلّال *dalla* > *dallāl-* 'guide'
سار < سيّار *sāra* > *sayyār-* 'wanderer, planet'
غفر < غفّار *ğafara* > *ğaffār-* 'prone to forgive'
كذب < كذّاب *kaðaba* > *kaððāb-* 'inveterate liar'

This is also the pattern par excellence for trades and crafts.

باب < بوّاب *bāb-* 'gate' > *bawwāb-* 'gatekeeper'
ورق < ورّاق *waraq-* 'leaf, folio' > *warrāq-* 'manuscript copier'
خبز < خبّاز *xabaza* 'bake' > *xabbāz-* 'baker'
طبخ < طبّاخ *ṭabaxa* 'cook' > *ṭabbāx-* 'cook'

71 The Arabic Personal Name.

71.1 In its simplest form the personal name consists of (1) the given name *(ism-)* and (2) the patronymic, i.e., the father's name preceded by *ibn-*. When the patronymic follows the given name, (a) the nunation is removed from triptote given names and (b) the *alif* of *ibn-* is dropped. Since *-bn-* is in apposition to the given name, it is in whatever case the given name is. The father's name is, of course, in construct with *-bn-*.

محمد بن عبد الله	*muḥammadu bnu 'abdi llāhi*	Muhammad son of Abdullah
على بن ابى طالب	*'alīyu bnu 'abī ṭālibin*	Ali son of Abu-Talib

Patronymics carried back to the fourth or fifth generation are not uncommon.

جعفر بن محمد بن على بن حسن بن على	*ja'faru bnu muḥammadi bni 'alīyi bni ḥasani bni 'alīyin*	Ja'far b. Muhammad b. Ali b. Hasan b. Ali

For women the patronymic is introduced by *bint-* or *ibnat-*.

فاطمة بنت (ابنة) محمد	*fāṭimatu bintu (bnatu) muḥammadin*	Fatima daughter of Muhammad

71.2 To the given name and patronymic may be added the "filionymic" *(kunyat-)*, the name of a man's eldest son, with *'abū*. The filionymic usually precedes the given name.

ابو الحسن على بن ابى طالب	*'abu l-ḥasani 'alīyu bnu 'abī ṭālibin*	Abu'l-Hasan Ali b. Abu-Talib

71.3 To the given name, patronymic and filionymic may be added the agnomen *(laqab-)*, an honorific or nickname. It may also be an occupational name.

ابو نصر بشر بن الحارث الحافى	*'abū naṣrin bišru bnu l-ḥāriθi l-ḥāfī*	Abu-Nasr Bishr b. al-Harith "the Barefoot"
ابو بكر الصديق	*'abū bakrin*^{i} *ṣ-ṣiddīqu*	Abu-Bakr "the Righteous"
ابو المغيث الحسين بن منصور الحلاج	*'abu l-muġīθi l-ḥusaynu bnu manṣūrin*^{i} *l-ḥallāju*	Abu'l-Mughith al-Husayn b. Mansur "the Cotton-carder"

Agnomens may also be nicknames with *'abū*.

ابو هريرة	*'abū hurayrata*	Abu-Hurayra ("father of a little cat")
ابو الفرج	*'abu l-faraji*	Abu'l-Faraj ("father of joy")

In later Islamic times *laqab*s in *ad-dīn-* became common as part of the given name.

علاء الدين على	*'alā'u d-dīni 'alīyun*	Ala' al-Din Ali
شمس الدين محمد	*šamsu d-dīni muḥammadun*	Shams al-Din Muhammad

71.4 The final part of the name, the attributive *(nisbat-)* in *-iyy-* may indicate (1) tribal or dynastic affiliation

ابو على الزبير بن بكار القرشى	*'abū 'alīyin^{i} z-zubayru bnu bakkārin^{i} l-qurašiyyu*	Abu Ali al-Zubayr b. Bakkar al-Qurashi ("of Quraysh")

or (2) place of origin.

ابو جعفر محمد بن جرير بن يزيد الطبرى	*'abū ja'farin muḥammadu bnu jarīri bni yazīda ṭ-ṭabariyyu*	Abu-Ja'far Muhammad b. Jarir b. Yazid al-Tabari ("of Tabaristan")

The attributive may properly belong either to the individual, in which case it follows the case of the given name, or to the father or grandfather's name, in which case it is in the genitive.

71.5 An individual may be known by any one or more of his names. For instance,

ابو الفرج محمد بن ابى يعقوب بن اسحق النديم الوراق البغدادى	*'abu l-faraji muḥammadu bnu 'abī ya'qūba bni 'isḥāqa n-nadīmi l-warrāqu l-baġdādiyyu*	Abu'l-Faraj Muhammad b. Abu-Ya'qub b. Ishaq al-Nadim al-Warraq al-Baghdadi

GIVEN NAME: Muḥammad
FATHER'S NAME: Abu-Ya'qūb
GRANDFATHER'S NAME: Isḥāq
AGNOMEN: Abu'l-Faraj

Either his father or grandfather (likely the former) was a *nadīm-*, a "boon companion," probably to a caliph.

He himself was a copier of manuscripts *(warrāq-)* and was a native of Baghdad.

He is known historically (his *šuhrat-*) as Ibn al-Nadim.

Vocabulary

VERBS

بشر II *baššara* announce (*bi-* something) as good news to (acc.)

حرم *ḥaruma (u) ḥarām-* be forbidden; II *ḥarrama* make unlawful, proscribe (*'alā* for)

خبر *xabura (u) xibr-/xibrat-* know thoroughly, be fully acquainted (*bi-/-hu* with)

رزق *razaqa (i) rizq-* provide with sustenance, means of subsistence

قضى *qaḍā (ī) qaḍā'-* decide, foreordain; VII *inqaḍā* be completed, concluded

منو V *tamannā* wish for, desire; make a wish for

وفى II *waffā* give (*-hu* someone) full due; give a full share of; V *tawaffā* take / get one's full share of, receive fully; V passive *tuwuffiya* die, pass on (euphemistic)

NOUNS

ام/امهات *'umm-* pl *'ummahāt-* mother

بشرى *bušrā* (fem.) good news

خبر/اخبار *xabar-* pl *'axbār-* news, piece of information

سوء *sū'-* evil, ill

OTHERS

انى *'annā* how? (Koranic)

كلما *kullamā* whenever (+ conditional type)

نعم *na'am(i)* yes

PROPER NAMES

اسحق *'isḥāqu* Isaac

زكريا(ء) *zakariyyā('u)* Zacharias

مسيح *masīḥ-* Messiah

Exercises

(a) Read and translate:

١ وقال رسول الله ان أدنى مقعد[1] احدكم من الجنة ، إن هيّئ له ، أن يقال له
«تمنّ». فيتمنّى ويتمنّى فيقال له «هل تمنّيت؟» فيقول «نعم» فيقول له الله
«فإنّ لك ما تمنّيت ومثله معه.»

٢ الذى خلق السموات والارض وما بينهما فى ستة ايام ثم استوى على
العرش[2] الرحمن فاسأل به خبيراً.

٣ ما أبرّئ نفسى. ان النفس لأمارة بالسوء إلاّ ما رحم ربى.

٤ ولقد جاءت رسلنا ابرهيم بالبشرى وقالوا «سلاماً». قال «سلام». فجاء بعجل
حنيذ[3] فلما رآهم لا ياكلون خاف. قالوا «لا تخف. إنّا رسل الى قوم لوط»
وامرأته قائمة فضحكت. فبشّرناها باسحق ومن وراء اسحق ، يعقوب.

٥ لا تقتلوا النفس التى حرّم الله إلا بالحق.

٦ لما ولدت مريم قالت امها «ربى انى سمّيتها مريم وانها لك» فتقبلها ربها بقبول
حسن. فكلما دخل عليها زكريا وجد عندها رزقاً. قال «يا مريم أنّى لك
هذا؟» قالت «هو من عند الله. ان الله يرزق من يشاء.»

٧ وقضى ربكم ألاّ تعبدوا الا اياه.

٨ من يتخذ الشيطان ولياً من دون الله فقد خسر خسراناً مبيناً.

٩ كل نفس ذائقة الموت ، ثم الينا ترجعون.

١٠ لو أن قرآناً سُيّرت به الجبالُ او قُطّعت به الارضُ او كُلّم به الموتى بل
لله الامر جميعاً.

١١ تبارك الذى نزّل الفرقان على عبده ليكون للعالمين نذيراً - الذى له ملك
السموات والارض ولم يتخذ ولداً ولم يكن له شريك فى الملك وخلق كل
شىء فقدّره تقديراً - واتخذوا من دونه آلهة لا يخلقون شيئاً وهم يُخلقون
ولا يملكون لأنفسهم ضراً ولا نفعاً ولا يملكون موتاً ولا حياةً.[4]

١٢ ألم تر أن الله يسجد له من فى السموات ومن فى الارض والشمس والقمر
والنجوم والجبال والشجر والدوابّ[5] وكثير من الناس.

---

[1] *'Adnā maq'ad-* "the lowest seat."

[2] *'Arš-* throne.

[3] *'Ijl- ḥanīð-* roasted calf.

[4] *Tabāraka* "blessed be"; *furqān-* the meaning of this word is not fully understood; it is often equated with the Koran and may possibly be borrowed from the Aramaic פרקא 'chapter, division (of a book)'; *naðir-* warner.

[5] *Dābbat-* pl *dawābbu* beast.

١٢ الله يتوفّى الأنفس حين موتها.

(b) Translate into Arabic:

1. It appears to us that you (pl) have aspired to a way that has been made unlawful to you.

2. When the Children of Israel said to Moses, "Make us a god like the gods of Egypt," he said to them, "You are a people who are ignorant."

3. Those who follow their lusts as itinerants follow the stars will not be shown the right way.

4. Umm-'Ali passed away, and her children wept much over her.

5. The Merciful does not accept the sacrifice of him who wishes for other than the truth in his heart.

Reading Selection: *Sūrat Āl-'Imrān (3):45–51.*

The Annunciation

اذ قالت الملائكة «يا مريم إنَ الله يبشّرك بكلمة منه اسمُه المسيح عيسى
ابن مريم وجيهاً فى الدنيا والآخرة ومن المقرّبين (٤٥)[1]
ويكلّم الناسَ فى المهد وكهلاً ومن الصالحين (٤٦)[2]
قالت «ربى أنّى يكون لى ولد ولم يمسسنى بشر؟» قال «كذلك الله يخلق
ما يشاء: اذا قضى امراً فإنما يقول له كن فيكون» (٤٧)
ويعلّمه الكتاب والحكمة والتوراة والانجيل (٤٨)[3]
ورسولاً[4] الى بنى اسرئيل أنى قد جئتكم بآية من ربكم، أنى أخلق
لكم من الطين كهيئة الطير فأنفخ فيه فيكون طيراً بإذن الله
وأبرئ الأكمه والأبرص وأحيى الموتى بإذن الله
وأنبّئكم بما تاكلون وما تدّخرون فى بيوتكم. إنَ فى ذلك لآيةً لكم
إن كنتم مؤمنين (٤٩)[5]
ومصدّقاً[6] لما بين يدىَ من التوراة ولأحلَ لكم بعض الذى حُرّم عليكم.
وجئتكم بآية من ربكم فاتّقوا الله وأطيعونى (٥٠)[7]

---

[1]*Wajīh*- eminent, illustrous.

[2]*Mahd*- cradle; *kahl*- man of mature age.

[3]*Ḥikmat*- wisdom.

[4]Assume an elipsed verb, "and he will make him…"

[5]*'Annī* introduces direct quotation, translate as "saying"; *nafaxa (u)* blow; *'akmahu* born blind; *'abraṣu* leprous; *'uḥyī* "I will bring to life"; *iddaxara* store up.

[6]A subjective complement for *ji'tukum* in verse 49.

[7]*Li-'uḥilla* "in order that I make lawful"; *'aṭī'ū* "obey" (pl. imperative).

ان الله ربی وربکم فاعبدوه. هذا صراط مستقیم (٥١)[1]

[1]*Ṣirāṭ- mustaqīm*- straight path.

Lesson Thirty-One

72 The Construct of Qualification; The Adjectival Relative Phrase.

72.1 The construct of qualification, also known as the "improper construct," consists of an adjective followed in construct by a noun qualifying the adjective, e.g.

رجل حسن الوجه	*rajulun ḥasanu̲ l-wajhi̲*	a man handsome of/in face
امرأة طاهرة القلب	*imra'atu̲n̲ ṭāhiratu̲ l-qalbi̲*	a woman pure of heart

The adjective agrees in case, number and gender with the preceding noun, as any attributive adjective would. The adjective also has the definite article or not according to the state of the modified noun. However, since the adjective is in construct with the following noun (which is usually definite), its inflectional ending is *always definite*. The reason this construction is called "improper" is because what appears to be a first member of a construct state may take the definite article.

الرجل الحسن الوجه	*a̲r̲-rajulu̲ l̲-ḥasanu̲ l-wajhi̲*	the man handsome of face
المرأة الطاهرة القلب	*a̲l̲-mar'atu̲ t̲-ṭāhiratu̲ l-qalbi̲*	the woman pure of heart
الملوك الكثيرو المال	*a̲l̲-mulūku̲ l̲-kaθīrū̲ l-māli̲*	the kings with much wealth

The construction may be summarized by the following scheme:

رجل كريم النفس	*rajulun karīmu n-nafsi*	a man of noble soul

الرجل الكريم النفس *ar-rajulu l-karīmu n-nafsi* the man of noble soul

NOUN	ADJECTIVE Adjective agrees in case, number, gender and article; ending definite	NOUN qualifying noun in construct; usually definite
rajulun	***karīmu***	***n-nafsi***
ar-rajulu	***l-karīmu***	***n-nafsi***

72.2 The Adjectival Relative Clause. In this adjectival/relative type of clause, a noun is followed by an adjective that agrees with the preceding noun in *case only;* in number and gender the adjective agrees with a noun that follows in the *nominative case.*[1]

للمراة المقتول ابوها *lil-mar'ati l-maqtūli 'abūhā* for the woman whose father is / was killed

من النبى المسموعة كلماته *mina n-nabīyi l-masmū'ati kalimātuhu* from the prophet whose words are / were heard

NOUN I	ADJECTIVE < case agreement only with noun I number/gender agreement with noun II >	NOUN II nominative case; resumptive pronoun refers to noun I
l-mar'ati	*l-maqtūli*	*'abū-hā*
n-nabīyi	*l-masmū'ati*	*kalimātu-hu*

73 Uses of *Mâ*.

73.1 The particle *mā* followed by the affirmative perfect gives the equivalent of the English "as / so long as." Followed by *lam* + jussive, *mā* means "so long as...not" or "until."

[1] In this construction the definite article on the adjective is equivalent to the relative pronoun; the two examples are equivalent to the phrases للمراة التى مقتول ابوها and من النبى الذى مسموعة كلماته .

ما عصيتنى أعذبك	*mā 'aṣaytanī 'u'aððibuka*	As long as you disobey me, I will punish you.
لا نخاف ما كنتم معنا	*lā naxāfu mā kuntum ma'anā*	We do not fear so long as you are with us.
لا جناح عليكم إن طلقتم النساء ما لم تمسوهن	*lā junāḥa 'alaykum 'in ṭallaqtumu n-nisā'a mā lam tamassū-hunna*	It is no sin for you if you divorce women so long as you have not touched them.

73.2 The enlitic particle *-mā* combines with the interrogatives to give the indefinite relatives *'ayna-mā* 'wherever,' *'iðā-mā* 'whenever,' *miθla-mā* 'however,' *kulla-mā* 'whenever, as often as.' The indefinite relative 'whatever' is an anomalous form, *mahmā*. These are commonly followed by the perfect or jussive as conditional types.

هو معكم اينما كنتم	*huwa ma'akum 'ayna-mā kuntum*	He is with you wherever you are (may be).
اينما تكونوا يدرككم الموت	*'ayna-mā takūnū yud-rikkumu l-mawtu*	Wherever you may be, death will reach you.
كلما دخلت وجدتهم يتكلمون	*kulla-mā daxaltu, wajadtuhum yatakallamūna*	Whenever I entered, I found them speaking.
مهما تأتنا به من آية فما نحن لك بمؤمنين	*mahmā ta'tinā bihi min 'āyatin fa-mā naḥnu laka bi-mu'minīna*	Whatever sign you may bring us, we will not believe in you.

73.3 A similar *-mā* may be added to any indefinite noun to heighten the sense of indefiniteness or nonspecificity.

يوماً ما خرجنا	*yawman-mā xarajnā*	We went out one day.

74 Auxiliary Verbs. Arabic has very few verbs that can be classed as auxiliary, but the following three are worth noting:

(1) *kāda / yakādu,* followed by the imperfect indicative, gives the sense of 'almost, scarcely' to the following verb.

ان القوم كادوا يقتلوننى	*'inna l-qawma kādū yaqtulūnanī*	The people almost killed me.
وجد قوماً لا يكادون يفقهون قولاً	*wajada qawman lā yakādūna yafqahūna qawlan*	He found a people who could scarcely understand a word.

(2) *mā zāla / lā yazālu* followed by the imperfect indicative means 'to keep on, to be still' doing something.

هم لا يزالون يقولون كذلك	*hum lā yazālūna yaqūlūna ka-ðālika*	They will keep on (are still) saying the same thing.

(3) *ja'ala* (and in post-Koranic *'axaða*) + imperfect indicative means 'to begin to.'

جعلت الارض تميد	*ja'alati l-'arḍu tamīdu*	The earth began to sway.

Vocabulary

تم *tamma (i)* be completed, finished, fulfilled

حسب *ḥasiba (a) ḥisbān-* reckon, consider someone (acc.) as (acc.); *ḥasaba (u) ḥisāb-* figure, make an account

خلف *xalafa (u)* come after, take the place of, lag (*'an* behind); II *xallafa* appoint as successor; VIII *ixtalafa* differ (*'an* from), dispute (*fī* over), frequent (*'ilā* a place)

زال *zāla (zul-) (ū) zawāl-* pass away, come to an end; (negative) continue, abide

ما زال *mā zāla (mā zil-) (lā yazālu, lam yazal)* (occurs in the negative + imperf. ind. or act. part.) keep on, be still (doing something)

سرع *saru'a (u) sur'at-* be quick, fast

كسر *kasara (i) kasr-* break; II *kassara* smash, break to pieces; VII *inkasara* get broken

كاد *kāda (kid-) (ā)* (+ imperf. ind.) almost, scarcely

طهر *ṭahura (u) ṭahārat-* be pure, clean; II *ṭahhara* purify; V *taṭahhara*/ *iṭṭahhara* cleanse oneself, perform ablutions

لام *lāma (ū) lawm-/malāmat-* blame, reproach (*'alā* for)

NOUNS

اجل *'ajl-* sake; *min/li-'ajli* (+ const.) for the sake of

جن ، جنى/جان *jinn-* (collective), *jinniyy-* (unit sing.) pl *jānn-* genie, the djinn, invisible beings who interfere in men's lives

سيئ *sayyi'-* evil

سيّئة *sayyi'at-* pl *-āt-* evil deed

Exercises

(a) Vocalize, read and translate:

١ العقبى العظيمة العذاب ٤ الملوك الشداد القوة ٧ الرجال الصادقو الوعد
٢ عين كثيرة الماء ٥ الرجل المبسوطة يده ٨ مدينة كثيرة الابواب
٣ العدو القليل السلاح ٦ النساء المخفية وجوههن ٩ المرأة الصالح ابنها

(b) Give the Arabic for the following:

1. a woman pure of heart
2. the women pure of heart
3. a man handsome of face
4. two men handsome of face
5. a boy with a broken arm
6. the boys with broken arm(s)
7. a genie with a big head
8. a tree with many leaves
9. a band few in number
10. a woman of much learning

(c) Read and translate:

١ والذين كفروا اعمالهم كسراب بقيعة: يحسبه الظمآن ماء حتى اذا جاءه لم يجده شيئاً ووجد الله عنده فوفّاه حسابه والله سريع الحساب.[1]
٢ ان ربك واسع المغفرة هو أعلم بكم.
٣ يا ابن آدم ما دعوتني أغفر لك.
٤ ولو شاء ربك لجعل الناس امة واحدة ولا يزالون مختلفين الا من رحم ربك، ولذلك خلقهم وتمّت كلمة ربك «لأملأنّ جهنم من الجن والناس اجمعين».

---

[1]*Sarāb-* mirage; *qi'at-* desert; *ẓam'ānu* thirsty

٥ فتولّ عنهم فما انت بملوم.
٦ وانه لما قام عبد الله يدعو ربه كاد القوم يتولّون عنه.
٧ قال الله «انا عند المنكسرة قلوبهم من اجلى».
٨ ان المرأة الطاهرة القلب لامت نفسها على مرض ابنها.
٩ فكدنا نضلّ عن الهنا لولا أن جاء مبشّر يبشّرنا.
١٠ من عمل سيّئة فلا يجزى[1] الا مثلها ومن عمل صالحاً وهو مؤمن فاولئك يدخلون الجنة يرزقون فيها بغير حساب.
١١ انى أمرت ان اكون اول من حكم بمثل هذا فى الدنيا.

(d) Translate into Arabic:

1. It is not possible for you to exculpate yourself, for what you did was made unlawful beforehand.

2. They will keep on visiting the sick until they are free of their illness.

3. Moses struck the stone, and many springs flowed from it.

4. The two girls beautiful of face guided him to their father.

5. When I saw the old man with his face concealed entering the woman's house, I almost laughed.

6. The heavenly bodies—the sun, moon and stars—will all bow down before those who are pious in heart.

[1] *Yujzā* "he is rewarded."

Reading Selection: *Sūrat al-Kahf (18):83–95.*

Dhu'l-Qarnayn[1]

ويسالونك عن ذى القرنين. قل ساتلو عليكم منه ذكراً (٨٣)[2]

إنّا مكنّا له فى الارض وآتيناه من كل شىء سبباً (٨٤)[3]

فاتبع سبباً (٨٥)[4]

حتى اذا بلغ مغرب الشمس وجدها تغرب فى عين حمئة ووجد

عندها قوماً. قلنا «يا ذا القرنين إمّا أن تعذّب واما أن تتخذ

فيهم حسناً» (٨٦)[5]

قال «أمّا من ظلم فسوف نعذّبه ثُم يُردَ الى ربه فيعذّبه

عذاباً نكراً (٨٧)[6]

وأمّا من آمن وعمل صالحاً فله جزاءً الحُسنى وسنقول له من امرنا

يسراً (٨٨)[7]

ثُم أتبع سبباً (٨٩)

حتى اذا بلغ مطلع الشمس وجدها تطلع على قوم لم نجعل

لهم من دونها ستراً (٩٠)[8]

---

[1]Dhū'l-Qarnayn is a Koranic figure usually identified with Alexander the Great.

[2]*Qarn-* horn.

[3]*Makkana* establish, make firm; *'ātā* give to; *sabab-* road, way.

[4]*'Atba'a sababan* take one's way.

[5]*Balağa* reach; *mağrib-* setting place (of the sun); *ğaraba (u)* set (sun); *ḥami'-* muddy; *'immā…'immā* either…or; *ḥusn-* favor, kindness.

[6]*Nukr-* awful.

[7]*'Āmana* believe; *jazā'an* "as a reward"; *yusr-* ease.

[8]*Maṭla'-* rising place (of the sun); *min dūnihā* "beneath it (the sun)"; *sitr-* covering, shelter.

... ثُم أتبع سبباً (٩٢)

حتى اذا بلغ بين السدّين وجد من دونهما قوماً لا يكادون

يفقهون قولاً (٩٣)[1]

قالوا «يا ذا القرنين إنَ ياجوج وماجوج مفسدون فى الارض

فهل نجعل لك خرجاً على أن تجعل بيننا وبينهم سداً؟» (٩٤)[2]

قال «ما مكَنّى فيه ربى خير [من خرجكم]. فأعينونى بقوّة ، أجعلْ

بينكم وبينهم ردماً (٩٥)[3]

---

[1]*Sadd-* mountain; *faqiha (a)* understand.

[2]*Yājūju wa-mājūju* Gog and Magog; *mufsid-* corrupting; *xarj-* tribute; *'alā 'an* on condition that; *sadd-* barrier.

[3]*Makkannī* for *makkananī* see note 3 above; *'a'īnū* help (masc. pl. imperative); *radm-* dam, dike.

Lesson Thirty-Two

75 Causative Verbs: Form IV. Characteristic of the causative Form IV is prefixed *'a-* in the perfect and the vowel *-u-* on the personal prefixes of the imperfect. The base pattern is 'AF'ALA.

75.1 As a causative / factitive verb, Form IV is—with few exceptions—necessarily transitive.

انزل < نزل *nazala* > IV *'anzala* 'cause someone (acc.) to go / come down'

اخرج < خرج *xaraja* > IV *'axraja* 'cause someone (acc.) to go out, expel'

Form IV verbs from transitive G-forms often become doubly transitive.

اسمع < سمع *sami'a* > IV *'asma'a* 'cause someone (acc.) to hear something (acc.)'

اورث < ورث *wariθa* > IV *'awraθa* 'make someone (acc.) heir to something (acc.)'

Stative G-forms tend to be factitive in Form IV.

اكبر < كبر *kabura* > IV *'akbara* 'make important, praise'

Since both Form II and Form IV give factitive connotations, the question arises as to the difference in meaning between the two. In general, the two forms take different connotations of the base idea into the factitive. For example, *ḥasuna* means both 'to be good' and 'to be beautiful': Form II *ḥassana* has the meaning of 'to make beautiful, make better,' while Form IV *'aḥsana* generally means 'to do a good deed, to do (something) well.' G-form *karuma* means both 'to be noble' and 'to be hospitable': Form II *karrama* generally means 'to make noble, exalt,' while Form IV *'akrama* means 'to treat with hospitality, honor.' On the other hand, many verbs that produce both Form II and Form IV show little or no appreciable difference in meaning between the two.

Form II, to a much greater extent than Form IV, makes denominative verbs, so that Form II may make a verb from a noun with a root identical with—but unrelated to—a G-form causative in Form IV, e.g., IV *'aðhaba* 'to make go away' is derived from *ðahaba* 'to go (away),' while II *ðahhaba* is derived from the noun *ðahab-* 'gold' and means 'to gild.'

75.2 Synopsis of Form IV:

	ACTIVE	PASSIVE
PERFECT	افعل *'af'ala*	افعل *'uf'ila*
IMPERFECT	يفعل *yuf'ilu*	يفعل *yuf'alu*
SUBJUNCTIVE	يفعل *yuf'ila*	يفعل *yuf'ala*
JUSSIVE	يفعل *yuf'il*	يفعل *yuf'al*
IMPERATIVE	افعل *'af'il*	— —
PARTICIPLE	مفعل *muf'il-*	مفعل *muf'al-*
VERBAL NOUN	إفعال *'if'āl-*	

Example from √*NZL*:

PERFECT	انزل *'anzala*	انزل *'unzila*
IMPERFECT	ينزل *yunzilu*	ينزل *yunzalu*
SUBJUNCTIVE	ينزل *yunzila*	ينزل *yunzala*
JUSSIVE	ينزل *yunzil*	ينزل *yunzal*
IMPERATIVE	أنزل *'anzil*	— —
PARTICIPLE	منزل *munzil-*	منزل *munzal-*
VERBAL NOUN	إنزال *'inzāl-*	

REMARKS:

(1) The *hamzas* of the perfect, imperative and verbal nouns are true *hamzas* and *not elidible*.

(2) The imperfect passive is identical to the imperfect passive of the G-form.

75.3 Synopsis of Form IV Doubled Verbs. The patterns to which the doubled verb conforms in Form IV should be familiar and predictable by now. Example from √*TMM:*

PERFECT	أَتَمَّ	*'atamma*	أُتِمَّ	*'utimma*
IMPERFECT	يُتِمُّ	*yutimmu*	يُتَمُّ	*yutammu*
SUBJUNCTIVE	يُتِمَّ	*yutimma*	يُتَمَّ	*yutamma*
JUSSIVE	يُتِمَّ	*yutimma/i*	يُتَمَّ	*yutamma/i*
	يُتْمِمْ	*yutmim*	يُتْمَمْ	*yutmam*
IMPERATIVE	أَتِمَّ	*'atimma/i*		
	أَتْمِمْ	*'atmim*	—	—
PARTICIPLE	مُتِمّ	*mutimm-*	مُتَمّ	*mutamm-*
VERBAL NOUN	إتمام	*'itmām-*		

75.4 Synopsis of Form IV C_1' Verbs. Example from √*'MN:*

PERFECT	آمن	*'āmana*	أومن	*'ūmina*
IMPERFECT	يؤمن	*yu'minu*	يؤمن	*yu'manu*
SUBJUNCTIVE	يؤمن	*yu'mina*	يؤمن	*yu'mana*
JUSSIVE	يؤمن	*yu'min*	يؤمن	*yu'man*
IMPERATIVE	آمن	*'āmin*	—	—
PARTICIPLE	مؤمن	*mu'min-*	مؤمن	*mu'man-*
VERBAL NOUN	إيمان	*'īmān-*		

REMARKS: *Hamza*-initial verbs are regular in Form IV *except* where the pattern would result in two adjacent *hamza*s:

(1) In the perfect active and passive, the *hamza* of the radical is lost; compensation is effected by lengthening the preceding vowel.

(2) The imperfect is regular with the notable exception of the first-person singular, **'u'minu* → *'ūminu*. The same compensatory lengthening is seen in the imperative: **'a'min* → *'āmin*.

(3) The verbal noun undergoes the same loss of the radical *hamza* with compensatory lengthening of the preceding vowel: *$*'i'mān- \rightarrow 'īmān-$.*

75.5 Synopsis of Form IV C1*w/y* **verbs.** Both *w* and *y* are *unaffected and remain as sound consonants* when preceded in the pattern by the vowel *-a-*. When preceded by *-u-*, they both assimilate to *w (*$*uw = ū$, *$*uy \rightarrow ū$); when preceded by *-i-*, they both assimilate to *y (*$*iw \rightarrow ī$, *$*iy = ī$) to form long vowels in both cases.

Example from √*WRθ*:

PERFECT	أورث	*'awraθa*	أورث	*'ūriθa*
IMPERFECT	يورث	*yūriθu*	يورث	*yūraθu*
IMPERATIVE	أورث	*'awriθ*	—	—
PARTICIPLE	مورث	*mūriθ-*	مورث	*mūraθ-*
VERBAL NOUN		إيراث	*'īrāθ-*	

Example from √*YQN*:

PERFECT	أيقن	*'ayqana*	أوقن	*'ūqina*
IMPERFECT	يوقن	*yūqinu*	يوقن	*yūqanu*
IMPERATIVE	أيقن	*'ayqin*	—	—
PARTICIPLE	موقن	*mūqin-*	موقن	*mūqan-*
VERBAL NOUN		إيقان	*'īqān-*	

75.6 Here follow Form IV verbs from radicals previously introduced:

أبرأ	heal, make free	أدخل	admit to, allow in
أبعد	banish, exile	أذهب	make go away
أتمّ	finish, fulfill	أرسل	send, dispatch
أجمع	make a consensus	أسكن	settle, make dwell
أحسن	do good, do well	أسمع	make hear
أخرج	expel, turn out	أشرك	ascribe as partner (*bi-* to)
أخلف	go back on one's word	أضرّ	compel, coerce

أضلّ lead astray
أطلع inform, apprise
أطلق set free
أعلم let know, norify
اكبر laud
اكرم treat hospitably
انزل send / bring / take down
أوجد bring into existence
أورث make heir to

Vocabulary

VERBS

امن *'amina (a) 'amn-/'amān-* be / feel safe, trust (*'alā* with); IV *'āmana* believe (*bi-* in)

حب IV *'aḥabba* love, like, want (*ḥubb-* and *maḥabbat-* are used as verbal nouns, not the predictable formation from the pattern)

دبر IV *'adbara* turn one's back (*'an/'alā* on), go back, flee, run away

سلم *salima (a) salāmat-* be safe and sound, intact; II *sallama* keep from harm, hand over intact; IV *'aslama* submit, surrender

عقل *'aqala (i) 'aql-* be reasonable, be endowed with reason; II *'aqqala* make reasonable, bring to reason

قبل IV *'aqbala* come / go forward, advance (*'alā* on / to)

NOUNS

دبر/ادبار *dub(u)r-* pl *'adbār-* the back / rear side of anything

سلطان/سلاطين *sulṭān-* pl *salāṭīnu* power, authority

عقل/عقول *'aql-* pl *'uqūl-* reason, rationality; intellect, mind

قبل/اقبال *qub(u)l-* pl *'aqbāl-* the fore / front side of anything

OTHER

و *wa-* (+ gen.) by (used in oaths, as *wa-llāhi* "by God")

IDIOM

ولّى دبره *wallā dub(u)rahu* "he turned and ran away"

Exercises

(a) Read and translate:

١ اجماع	٥ نورثهم اياها	٩ أخرجناهم	١٣ لم يُسمَعوا
٢ أسكنّاهم	٦ كتب منزلة	١٠ يخرجون	١٤ نبى مرسل
٣ المشركون به	٧ لم تتممه	١١ إطلاق عبد	١٥ لم أضللك
٤ أحبّك	٨ محسن	١٢ ليعلمنا	١٦ يحَبّ المحِبّون

(b) Read and translate:

١ وقال الشيطان لما قُضى الامر «ان الله وعدكم وعد الحق ووعدتكم فاستجبتم لى فلا تلومونى ولوموا انفسكم. ما انا بمصرخكم وما انتم بمصرخىّ. إنى كفرت بما أشركتمونى من قبل. إن الظالمين لهم عذاب اليم».[1]

٢ وكيف أخاف ما أشركتم ولا تخافون انكم أشركتم بالله ما لم ينزّل به عليكم سلطاناً؟

٣ ثم أورثنا الكتاب الذين اصطفينا[2] من عبادنا.

٤ اانتم اضللتم عبادى هؤلاء ام هم ضلوا السبيل؟

٥ وانزلنا من السماء ماء فاسكنّاه فى الارض وإنّا على ذهاب به لقادرون.

٦ وبالحق انزلناه وبالحق نزل وما أرسلناك الا شاهداً مبشّراً.

٧ يقولون «ربنا أتمم لنا نورنا واغفر لنا. إنك على كل شىء قدير».

٨ هو الذى أنزل السكينة فى قلوب المؤمنين ليزدادوا إيماناً مع إيمانهم لِيدخل المؤمنين والمؤمنات جنات تجرى من تحتها الانهار خالدين فيها.[3]

٩ ومن يشرك بالله فقد ضل ضلالاً بعيداً.

١٠ أتهدون من أضل الله؟ ومن يضلل الله فلن تجد له سبيلاً. ودّوا لو تكفرون كما كفروا فتكونون سواء. فلا تتخذوا منهم اولياء حتى يهاجروا[4] فى سبيل الله فإن تولّوا فخذوهم واقتلوهم حيث وجدتموهم ولا تتخذوا منهم ولياً.

١١ فيه رجال يحبّون أن يتطهروا والله يحب المطّهّرين.

١٢ كان الناس أمة واحدة فبعث الله النبيين مبشرين وأنزل معهم الكتاب

---

[1] *Istajabtum* "you responded"; *'aṣraxa* help; *'alīm-* painful.

[2] *Iṣṭafā* chose.

[3] *Sakīnat-* tranquility; *izdāda* increase (int.).

[4] *Hājara/yuhājiru* migrate.

بالحق ليحكم بين الناس.

(c) Translate into Arabic:

1. I have been commanded to be the first to submit ("the first who submitted") to the Lord of the Universe.

2. We told them to advance on the enemy and to be quick, but they lagged behind the others and so were killed.

3. And he smashed the stones on which had been written the king's orders.

4. We shall never believe in the prophet so long as he does not bring us evidence.

5. Those who love the truth are kept safe from the evil of the devil.

6. If they turned and ran away, they should not be blamed for that.

Reading Selection: *Sūrat al-A'rāf (7):73–79.*

The Prophet Salih and the Tribe of Thamud

والى ثمود [ارسلنا] اخاهم صالحاً قال «يا قوم اعبدوا الله! ما لكم

من اله غيرُه؟ قد جاءتكم بينة من ربكم: هذا ناقة الله لكم آيةً

فذروها تاكل فى ارض الله ولا تمسّوها بسوء فياخذكم

عذاب اليم» ... (٧٣)[1]

قال الملأ الذين استكبروا من قومه للذين استضعفوا لِمن آمن منهم

«أتعلمون أن صالحاً مرسل من ربه؟» قالوا «إنّا بما أرسِل به

مؤمنون» (٧٥)[2]

قال الذين استكبروا «إنّا بالذى آمنتم به كافرون» (٧٦)

[1]*θamūd*- Thamud, a north Arabian tribe; *Ṣāliḥ*- Salih, prophet to Thamud; *nāqat*- she-camel; *ðarūhā* (+ imperf. ind.) "let her."

[2]*Istakbara* be scornful; *ustuḍ'ifū* "they were despised."

فعقروا الناقة وعتوا عن امر ربهم وقالوا «يا صالح ائتنا بما تعدنا

إن كنت من المرسلين» (٧٧)[1]

فأخذهم الرجفة فأصبحوا فى دارهم جاثمين (٧٨)[2]

فتولى عنهم وقال «يا قوم لقد أبلغتكم رسالة ربى ونصحت لكم

ولكن لا تحبّون الناصحين» (٧٩)[3]

---

[1] *'Aqara (i)* hamstring; *'atā (ū)* be insolent (*'an* toward)

[2] *Rajfat-* tremor; *'aṣbaḥa* be/become in the morning; *dār-* abode; *jaθama (u/i)* lie prone.

[3] *'Ablağa* deliver; *risālat-* message.

Lesson Thirty-Three

76 Form IV: Weak Verbs.

76.1 Synopsis of Form IV weak-*lām* verbs. Example from √*LQY:*

PERFECT	القى *'alqā*	القى *'ulqiya*
IMPERFECT	يلقى *yulqī*	يلقى *yulqā*
SUBJUNCTIVE	يلقى *yulqiya*	يلقى *yulqā*
JUSSIVE	يلق *yulqi*	يلق *yulqa*
IMPERATIVE	الق *'alqi*	— —
PARTICIPLE	ملقٍ *mulqin*	ملقًى *mulqan*
VERBAL NOUN	إلقاء *'ilqā'*-	

REMARKS: The forms of these verbs should be perfectly familiar by now.

(1) Note that in the verbal noun C3 appears as *hamza* after the -*ā*-, as in Forms VII and VIII.

(2) The vowel of the *hamza*-prefix in the imperative is -*a*-.

76.2 Synopsis of Form IV hollow verbs. Example from √*MWT:*

PERFECT	اماتَ *'amāta*	اميت *'umīta*
IMPERFECT	يميت *yumītu*	يمات *yumātu*
SUBJUNCTIVE	يميت *yumīta*	يمات *yumāta*
JUSSIVE	يمت *yumit*	يمت *yumat*
IMPERATIVE	امت *'amit*	— —

PARTICIPLE	مميت	*mumīt-*	ممات	*mumāt-*
VERBAL NOUN	إماتة	*'imātat-*		

REMARKS:

(1) Here, throughout, the vowel that would have been on C_2 in the sound pattern is thrown back to C_1 and lengthened in compensation.

(2) In the verbal noun the vowel on C_2 is long and cannot be further lengthened for compensation; hence, the pattern receives a *ta' marbūṭa* in compensation for the loss of C_2.

76.3 Here follows a list of Form IV verbs from radicals already introduced:

آتى	give ("make come to")	ادرى	make know
ابدى	make apparent	اذاق	make taste
ابكى	make cry	ارضى	make satisfied
ابان	make clear	ازال	make pass away
اجرى	make flow	اقام	perform
اخاف	make fear	القى	cast, throw
اخفى	hide, conceal	امات	make die

76.4 Form IV of *ra'ā, 'arā* 'to cause to see, to show.' As in the G-form imperfect, *ra'ā* loses its middle radical glottal stop. As the synopsis below shows, it becomes basically a weak-*lām* verb with a few characteristics of the hollow verb too.

PERFECT	أرى	*'arā*	أرى	*'uriya*
IMPERFECT	يرى	*yurī*	يرى	*yurā*
SUBJUNCTIVE	يرى	*yuriya*	يرى	*yurā*
JUSSIVE	ير	*yuri*	ير	*yura*
IMPERATIVE	أر	*'ari*	—	—
PARTICIPLE	مرٍ	*murin*	مرًى	*muran*
VERBAL NOUN	إراءة	*'irā'at-*		

Vocabulary

بدل II *baddala* substitute something (acc.) (*bi-* for something else); V *tabaddala* change, exchange (*bi-* something) for something else (acc.)

بلغ *balağa (u) bulūğ-* reach, attain, amount to; IV *'ablağa* make someone / thing (acc.) reach; announce, inform

حيّ/يحيا ، يحيّ *ḥayya / yaḥyā* and *yaḥayyu* live, be alive; IV أحيا/يحيي *'aḥyā / yuḥyī* (note spelling) bring to life, revivify

خطئ/يخطأ *xaṭi'a (a) xaṭa'-* be mistaken, make a mistake, sin; IV *'axṭa'a* err, miss, be off target

رود IV *'arāda* want

صوب IV *'aṣāba* hit the mark, afflict; (passive *'uṣība*) be stricken, afflicted

طوع IV *'aṭā'a* obey

عطو IV *'a'ṭā* give someone (acc.) something (acc.)

وحي IV *'awḥā* inspire (*'ilā* someone) (*bi-* or acc., with something) *or* (*'an* that)

NOUNS

حيّ/احياء *ḥayy-* pl *'aḥyā'-* alive

ظلمة/ظلمات *ẓulmat-* pl *ẓulumāt-* darkness

OTHERS

ابداً *'abadan* ever; (+ negative) never

على أن *'alā 'an* (+ subjunctive) on condition that

IDIOM

بلغ اشدّه *balağa 'ašuddahu* "he reached maturity"

Exercises

(a) Read and translate orally:

١ امر مطاع ٥ سجدوا له اطاعة ٩ ملق مصيب ١٣ مقيمو الصلاة

٢ رام مخطئ ٦ احجار ملقاة ١٠ محيي الدين ١٤ مميت الاحياء

٣ إحياء الموتى ٧ مريد مطيع ١١ موحًى اليه ١٥ لمخيفى الناس

٤ المصاب مرضاً ٨ مطيعو الاوامر ١٢ إخفاء الوجه ١٦ ملقيات

١٧ إزالة الحياة ١٨ يذيقهم عذاباً ١٩ أصبت ٢٠ المراد

(b) Read and translate:

١ ان الله خلق خلقه فى ظلمة فالقى عليهم من نوره، فمن أصابه من ذلك النور اهتدى ومن أخطاه ضل.

٢ أرنى الدنيا كما تريها صالحى عبادك.

٣ قل اى شىء اكبر شهادة؟ قل الله شهيد بينى وبينكم وأوحى الىّ هذا القرآن لأنذركم[1] به ومن بلغ. أئنكم لتشهدون أن مع الله آلهة اخرى؟ قل لا أشهد. قل انما هو اله واحد واننى برىء مما تشركون.

٤ وقال موسى «يا فرعون انى رسولٌ من رب العالمين حقيقٌ[2] على أن لا أقول على الله الا الحق. قد جئتكم ببينة من ربكم فارسل معى بنى اسرئيل». قال «إن كنت جئت بآية فأت بها إن كنت من الصادقين». فالقى عصاه فاذا هى ثعبان[4] مبين. فقال الملأ من قوم فرعون «إن هذا لساحر[3] عليم يريد ان يخرجكم من ارضكم. فماذا تأمرون؟» قالوا «ارجه[5] واخاه وارسل فى المدائن حاشرين[6] يأتوك بكل ساحر عليم». وجاء السحرة فرعون أن «لنا لأجراً[8] إن كنا نحن الغالبين[7]؟» قال «نعم وإنكم لمن المقربين». قالوا «يا موسى إما أن تلقى وإما أن نكون نحن الملقين؟» قال «ألقوا». فلما ألقوا سحروا اعين الناس وجاءوا بسحر عظيم.

٥ يوم تُقلب وجوههم فى النار يقولون «يا ليتنا أطعنا الله وأطعنا الرسول».

٦ ألم تعلم ان الله له ملك السموات والارض وما لكم من دون الله من ولى؟ ام تريدون ان تسالوا رسولكم كما سئل موسى من قبل؟ ومن يتبدل الكفر بالايمان فقد ضل سواء السبيل.

٧ كيف تكفرون بالله وكنتم امواتاً فاحياكم ثم يميتكم ثم يحييكم؟

٨ ولما جاء موسى الجبل وكلّمه ربه قال «رب أرنى أنظر اليك». قال «لن

---

[1] *'Anðara* warn.
[2] *Ḥaqīq-* worthy.
[3] *Sāḥir-* sorcerer.
[4] *θa'bān-* serpent.
[5] *'Arjā* put off.
[6] *Ḥāšir-* announcer, herald.
[7] *Ğalaba* win.
[8] *'Ajr-* reward.

ترانى».

٩ ويقول الانسان أئذا ما متّ لسوف أخرَج حياً؟

١٠ إن اول ما خلق الله العقل فقال له «أقبل» فاقبل وقال له «أدبر» فادبر فقال «ما خلقت شيئاً احسن الىّ منك او أحبّ الىّ منك. بك آخذ وبك أعطى».

١١ لو اراد الله أن لا يغفر للعباد لما خلق ابليس.

(c) Translate into Arabic:

1. When you have reached (the end of) your stipulated term, perhaps you will want to be reasonable and submit yourself.

2. When we advanced upon the band of the enemy, they drew back, then laid down their arms and turned and ran away, retracing their steps.

3. God inspires the prophets with his commands for the people, and the people believe and obey.

4. God said, "Whoever loves me, I keep on drawing near him until I am his eye, his ear and his hand."

5. I wanted to depart for the prayer, but I was unmindful of what had happened.

6. If you (m pl) had not mistaken the way, you would not have gotten lost in the darkness.

Reading Selection: *Sūrat al-Mā'ida (5):20–25*

Moses and the Israelites at the Holy Land

وإذ قال موسى لقومه «اذكروا نعمة الله عليكم إذ جعل فيكم

انبياء وجعلكم ملوكاً وآتاكم ما لم يؤت احداً من العالمين (٢٠)[1]

يا قومى ادخلوا الارض المقدّسة التى كتب الله لكم ولا ترتدّوا على

ادباركم فتنقلبوا خاسرين» (٢١)[2]

قالوا «يا موسى ان فيها قوماً جبّارين وانا لن ندخلها

[1]*Ni'mat*- favor.

[2]*Muqaddas*- sacred; *irtadda* turn back.

حتى يخرجوا منها. فإن يخرجوا منها فإنا داخلون» (٢٢)[1]

قال رجلان من الذين يخافون أنعم الله عليهما «ادخلوا عليهم الباب

فإذا دخلتموه فإنكم غالبون، وعلى الله فتوكلوا إن كنتم

مؤمنين» (٢٣)[2]

قالوا «يا موسى انا لن ندخلها ابداً ما داموا فيها فاذهب انت وربك

فقاتلا. انا ههنا قاعدون» (٢٤)[3]

قال «ربى انى لا أملك الا نفسى واخى فافرق بيننا وبين القوم

الفاسقين» قال «فإنها محرّمة عليهم اربعين سنة يتيهون فى الارض.

فلا تأس على القوم الفاسقين» (٢٥)[4]

---

[1]*Jabbār-* giant.

[2]*'An'ama 'alā* show favor to; *ğalaba (i)* vanquish; *tawakkala 'alā* rely on.

[3]*Dāma (ū)* remain; *qātala/yuqātilu* fight; *hāhunā* right here; *qa'ada (u)* sit.

[4]*Faraqa (u)* distinguish; *fasaqa (u/i)* be dissolute; *'arba'īna sanatan* "for forty years"; *tāha (ī)* wander; *'asiya (ā)* grieve.

Lesson Thirty-Four

77 Reflexive/Medio-Passive Verbs: Form X. Characteristic of Form X is prefixed *st-*. The base pattern is ISTAF'ALA. This form is assumed to be the reflexive of an unused *SAF'ALA causative form, a few examples of which are to be met with in the Hebrew and Aramaeo-Syriac *shaph'el* (שפעל) pattern, as שעבד *(ša'bed)* 'to enslave' and its reflexive/medio-passive אשתעבד *(išta'bad).* Causatives in *ša-* are quite regular in Akkadian.

77.1 Form X in Arabic has three major connotations:

(1) Reflexive/medio-passive of factitive Form IV, as IV *'aslama* 'to turn over, submit' > X *istaslama* 'to turn oneself over, give up,' and IV *'axraja* 'to make (someone / something) go / come out' > X *istaxraja* 'to get (something) out for oneself, extract.'

(2) From stative G-forms, Form X denotes thinking that a thing has the quality of the G-form, sometimes with reference to oneself, as *ḥasuna* 'to be good' > X *istaḥsana* 'to think / consider (something) good, to approve,' and *kabura* 'to be big, great' > X *istakbara* 'to consider (someone / something or oneself) great, important.'

(3) Form X quite commonly denotes seeking or asking for what is meant by the G-form, as *'alima* 'to know' > X *ista'lama* 'to seek to know, inquire,' and *ṭa'ām-* 'food' > X *istaṭ'ama* 'to ask for food.'

77.2 Synopsis of Form X:

PERFECT	استفعل	*istaf'ala*	استفعل	*ustuf'ila*
IMPERFECT	يستفعل	*yastaf'ilu*	يستفعل	*yustaf'alu*
SUBJUNCTIVE	يستفعل	*yastaf'ila*	يستفعل	*yustaf'ala*

JUSSIVE	يستفعل	*yastafʻil*	يستفعل	*yustafʻal*
IMPERATIVE	استفعل	*istafʻil*	—	—
PARTICIPLE	مستفعل	*mustafʻil-*	مستفعل	*mustafʻal-*
VERBAL NOUN	استفعال	*istifʻāl-*		

77.3 Form X of the doubled verb. Example from √*DLL:*

PERFECT	استدل	*istadalla*	استدل	*ustudilla*
IMPERFECT	يستدل	*yastadillu*	يستدل	*yustadallu*
SUBJUNCTIVE	يستدل	*yastadilla*	يستدل	*yustadalla*
JUSSIVE	يستدل	*yastadilla/i*	يستدل	*yustadalla/i*
	يستدلل	*yastadlil*	يستدلل	*yustadlal*
IMPERATIVE	استدل	*istadilla/i*	—	—
	استدلل	*istadlil*		
PARTICIPLE	مستدل	*mustadill-*	مستدل	*mustadall-*
VERBAL NOUN	استدلال	*istidlāl-*		

77.4 Form X of C_1*w/y* verbs. The only patterns affected are the verbal noun, which becomes ISTĪʻĀL-, and the perfect passive, which is USTŪʻILA. All other forms retain the *w* or *y* as a sound consonant. Example from √*YQN:*

PERFECT	استيقن	*istayqana*	استوقن	*ustūqina*
IMPERFECT	يستيقن	*yastayqinu*	يستيقن	*yustayqanu*
VERBAL NOUN	استيقان	*istīqān-*		

Example from √*WQF:*

PERFECT	استوقف	*istawqafa*	استوقف	*ustūqifa*
IMPERFECT	يستوقف	*yastawqifu*	يستوقف	*yustawqafu*
VERBAL NOUN	استيقاف	*istīqāf-*		

77.5 Form X of weak-*lām* verbs. Example from √*SQY:*

PERFECT	استسقى	*istasqā*	استسقى	*ustusqiya*
IMPERFECT	يستسقى	*yastasqī*	يستسقى	*yustasqā*
SUBJUNCTIVE	يستسقى	*yastasqiya*	يستسقى	*yustasqā*

JUSSIVE	يستسق	*yastasqi*	يستسق	*yustasqa*
IMPERATIVE	استسق	*istasqi*	—	—
PARTICIPLE	مستسق	*mustasqin*	مستسقى	*mustasqan*
VERBAL NOUN	استسقاء	*istisqā'-*		

All patterns conform to the principles given for weak-*lām* verbs in Forms VII and VIII (see §60.2).

77.6 Form X of hollow verbs. Example from √*QWM*:

PERFECT	استقام	*istaqāma*	استقيم	*ustuqīma*
IMPERFECT	يستقيم	*yastaqīmu*	يستقام	*yustaqāmu*
SUBJUNCTIVE	يستقيم	*yastaqīma*	يستقام	*yustaqāma*
JUSSIVE	يستقم	*yastaqim*	يستقم	*yustaqam*
IMPERATIVE	استقم	*istaqim*	—	—
PARTICIPLE	مستقيم	*mustaqīm-*	مستقام	*mustaqām-*
VERBAL NOUN	استقامة	*istiqāmat-*		

See remarks on the synopsis of Form IV hollow verbs (§76.2).

77.7 A selective list of familiar roots in Form X:

استأذن	ask permission
استحسن	consider good, prefer (*'alā* over)
استدلّ	ask to be shown (*'alā*) something
استشهد	call upon as witness
استعمل	put to work, use, employ
استقام	stand erect, be straight, true, go straight to (*'ilā*)
استحبّ	prefer, consider good / better
استخرج	extract, take out for oneself
استسلم	turn oneself over, submit
استعلم	seek to learn / know, request information
استكبر	be haughty, proud, consider something (acc.) great

Vocabulary

سقى *saqā (ī) saqy-* give water to, give to drink; IV *'asqā* = G; X *istasqā* ask for water

صدق V *taṣaddaqa* give alms

طوع X *istaṭā'a* have the endurance / capability for, be able / capable of

طعم IV *'aṭ'ama* feed; X *istaṭ'ama* ask for food

عجل *'ajila (a) 'ajal(at)-* hurry, hasten (intr.); II *'ajjala* hasten (trs.); V *ta'ajjala* = G, be ahead of, precede; X *ista'jala* be in a hurry, rush

متع II *matta'a* enable someone (acc.) to enjoy *(bi-)* something; equip; V *tamatta'a* enjoy *(bi-)* something; X *istamta'a* enjoy, relish *(bi-)* something

نصر *naṣara (u) naṣr-* help, assist (*'alā* againt); VIII *intaṣara* be victorious, triumph (*'alā* over), take revenge (*min* on); X *istanṣara* ask for assistance

NOUNS

حديد *ḥadīd-* iron

ريح/رياح ، ارياح *rīḥ-* pl *riyāḥ-/'aryāḥ-* wind

طعام/اطعمة *ṭa'ām-* pl *'aṭ'imat-* food, victuals

يتيم/ايتام ، يتامى *yatīm-* pl *'aytām-/yatāmā* orphan

OTHERS

متى *matā* when?

بعدما *ba'da-mā* after (conj.)

Exercises

(a) Read and translate:

١ استدلّه على السبيل

٢ لم يُستحب الاول على الآخر

٣ اقبل مسقياً

٤ يستخرجنها لأنفسهن

٥ متّعونى فاستمتعت به

٦ استطعمانا فأطعمناهما

٧ لم يُستعمل

٨ استحسنوا اعماله

٩ هل استعلمتموه؟

١٠ استقمنا اليهم

١١ استأذنتنى فى الخروج

١٢ لا تستكبروا فى الارض

١٣ أستشهدهم عليك

١٤ لن نستسلم للعدو

١٥ استنصر ننصرك

(b) Read and translate:

١ «يا ابن آدم استطعمتك فلم تطعمنى» قال «يا رب وكيف اطعمك وانت رب العالمين؟» قال «اما علمت انه استطعمك عبدى فلان فلم تطعمه؟ اما علمت انك لو اطعمته لوجدت ذلك عندى؟ يا ابن آدم استسقيتك فلم تسقنى» قال «يا رب كيف اسقيك وانت رب العالمين؟» قال «استسقاك عبدى فلان فلم تسقه. اما علمت انك لو سقيته لوجدت ذلك عندى؟»

٢ لا تتخذوا آباءكم واخوانكم اولياء إن استحبوا الكفر.

٣ اراد ربك ان يبلغ اليتيمان اشدهما ويستخرجا كنزهما.

٤ انظر كيف ضربوا لك الامثال فضلوا فلا يستطيعون سبيلاً.

٥ انما الهكم اله واحد فاستقيموا اليه واستغفروه.

٦ اذا استأذنوك للخروج فقل لن تخرجوا معى ابداً.

٧ لا تحسبنّ الذين قتلوا فى سبيل الله امواتاً بل احياء عند ربهم يرزقون.

٨ الله ولى الذين آمنوا - يخرجهم من الظلمات الى النور. والذين كفروا اولياؤهم الطاغوت[1] - يخرجونهم من النور الى الظلمات. اولئك اصحاب النار هم فيها خالدون.

٩ خلق الانسان من عجل. سأريكم آياتى فلا تستعجلونى ويقولون «متى هذا الوعد إن كنتم صادقين؟»

١٠ الذين من قبلكم كانوا اشد منكم قوةً واكثر اموالاً واولاداً فاستمتعوا بخلاقهم[2] فاستمتعتم بخلاقكم كما استمتع الذين من قبلكم.

١١ ألم تر أنهم يقولون ما لا يفعلون الا الذين آمنوا وعملوا الصالحات وذكروا الله.

١٢ ربنا اعف عنا واغفر لنا وارحمنا انت مولانا فانصرنا على القوم الكافرين.

١٣ لما خلق الله الارض جعلت تميد فخلق الجبال وألقاها عليها فاستقامت. فعجبت الملائكة من شدة الجبال فقالت «يا رب هل من خلقك شىء اشد من الجبال؟» قال «نعم، الحديد». فقالت «يا رب هل من خلقك شىء اشد من

[1]*Ṭāğūt*- false gods.
[2]*Xalāq*- lot.

الحديد ؟» قال «نعم ، النار». فقالت «يا رب هل من خلقك شيء اشد من النار؟» قال «نعم ، الماء». فقالت «يا رب هل من خلقك شيء اشد من الماء ؟» قال «نعم ، الريح». فقالت «يا رب هل من خلقك شيء اشد من الريح ؟» قال «نعم ، الانسان . يتصدق بيمينه فيخفيها عن شماله» (من احاديث انس بن مالك)[1]

(c) Translate into Arabic:

1. Ask (fem. sing.) forgiveness, for you have sinned greatly.
2. Not everyone who casts hits the mark.
3. When Adam's two sons made a sacrifice in obedience to God, it was accepted from one of them and not from the other.
4. If they follow that which avails them not, their hearts will be filled with the darkness of unbelief.
5. God inspired the prophet with the word of truth.
6. Are the women able to go on foot?

[1]*Māda (ī)* sway; *'ajiba (a)* wonder, be astonished; *šiddat-* might.

Lesson Thirty-Five

78 Effective Verbs: Form III. Characteristic of the effective Form III is a lengthening of the vowel of C_1. The base pattern is FĀʻALA.

78.1 Since the basic notion of Form III is the qualitative or active effect one person has upon another, the form is necessarily transitive. There are three common connotations of Form III:

(1) From stative and qualitative G-forms, Form III indicates that the subject employs that quality towards the object, as *ḥasuna* 'to be good' > III *ḥāsana* 'to treat (someone) kindly, well.'

(2) When the G-form denotes an act, the receiver of which is indicated through a preposition, Form III takes the receiver of the action as a direct object, sometimes with reciprocal overtones, as *qāma 'ilā* 'to rise up against' > III *qāwama* 'to resist, oppose'; *šarika* 'to participate' > III *šāraka* 'to enter into partnership with'; *xalafa* 'to lag behind, stay away' > III *xālafa* 'to be at variance with, differ from.'

(3) When the G-form immediately affects an object, Form III denotes an attempt to perform that act upon the object, often with the idea of competition, as *qatala* 'to kill' > III *qātala* 'to attempt to kill, fight with'; *ṣaraʻa* 'to throw down' > III *ṣāraʻa* 'to wrestle with.'

78.2 Synopsis of Form III.

	ACTIVE	PASSIVE
PERFECT	فاعل *fāʻala*	فوعل *fūʻila*
IMPERFECT	يفاعل *yufāʻilu*	يفاعل *yufāʻalu*
SUBJUNCTIVE	يفاعل *yufāʻila*	يفاعل *yufāʻala*

JUSSIVE	يفاعل	*yufā'il*	يفاعل	*yufā'al*
IMPERATIVE	فاعل	*fā'il*	—	—
PARTICIPLE	مفاعل	*mufā'il-*	مفاعل	*mufā'al-*
VERBAL NOUN	مفاعلة	*(1) mufā'alat-*		
	فعال	*(2) fi'āl-*		

Example from √*ŠHD:*

PERFECT	شاهد	*šāhada*	شوهد	*šūhida*
IMPERFECT	يشاهد	*yušāhidu*	يشاهد	*yušāhadu*
SUBJUNCTIVE	يشاهد	*yušāhida*	يشاهد	*yušāhada*
JUSSIVE	يشاهد	*yušāhid*	يشاهد	*yušāhad*
IMPERATIVE	شاهد	*šāhid*	—	—
PARTICIPLE	مشاهد	*mušāhid-*	مشاهد	*mušāhad-*
VERBAL NOUN	مشاهدة	*(1) mušāhadat-*		
	شهاد	*(2) šihād-*		

REMARKS:

(1) The basic lengthening of the C_1 vowel characteristic of this form applies to the perfect passive as well as the active.

(2) The pronominal prefix vowel of the imperfect is *-u-*. Form III completes the set of forms that take this characteristic vowel in the imperfect: Forms II, III & IV.

(3) Form III alone of all increased forms regularly produces two verbal nouns. With some roots usage is the sole criterion as to which of the two is produced. Where both are in use, it can be said generally that MUFĀ'ALAT- retains more of the verbal sense, while FI'ĀL- tends to be slightly more nominalized, as from √*QTL, muqātalat-* 'fighting, doing battle' and *qitāl-* 'battle, combat.'

78.3 Synopsis of Form III doubled verbs. Example from √*ḌRR:*

PERFECT	ضارّ	*ḍārra*	ضورر	*ḍūrira*
IMPERFECT	يضارّ	*yuḍārru*	يضارّ	*yuḍārru*
SUBJUNCTIVE	يضارّ	*yuḍārra*	يضارّ	*yuḍārra*

JUSSIVE	يضارّ	*yuḍārra/i*	يضارّ	*yuḍārra/i*
	يضارر	*yuḍārir*	يضارر	*yuḍārar*
PARTICIPLE	مضارّ	*muḍārr-*	مضارّ	*muḍārr-*
VERBAL NOUN	مضارّة	(1) *muḍārrat-*		
	ضرار	(2) *ḍirār-*		

REMARKS:

(1) This is the only verbal form in Arabic to produce regularly a long vowel followed by a doubled consonant, but only long *-ā-* followed by a doubled consonant is tolerated phonetically.

(2) The vocalic structure of the perfect passive overrides the tendency of the two like consonants to coalesce, hence *ḍūrira*. In all other forms, except the second jussive, the distinction between the active and passive is obscured.

78.4 Synopsis of Form III weak-*lām* verbs. Example from √NDW:

PERFECT	نادى	*nādā*	نودى	*nūdiya*
IMPERFECT	ينادى	*yunādī*	ينادى	*yunādā*
SUBJUNCTIVE	ينادى	*yunādiya*	ينادى	*yunādā*
JUSSIVE	يناد	*yunādi*	يناد	*yunāda*
IMPERATIVE	ناد	*nādi*	—	—
PARTICIPLE	مناد	*munādin*	منادًى	*munādan*
VERBAL NOUN	مناداة	(1) *munādāt-*		
	نداء	(2) *nidā'-*		

By this time these forms should not need explanation. Note especially that C3*w/y* → glottal stop after *-ā-* in the second noun.

79 Reciprocal Verbs: Form VI. Characteristic of the reflexive pattern of the reciprocal Form VI is the prefixed *ta-* of Form V. Form VI thus stands in relation to Form III exactly as Form V does to Form II. The basic pattern for Form VI is TAFĀʻALA.

79.1 Form VI does not give a reflexive connotation so much as the sense of mutuality and reciprocity with regards to the signification of

Form III. Being mutual, or reciprocal, Form VI of necessity involves more than one person, and there is commonly no passive. Examples: *raḍiya* 'to be satisfied' > III *rāḍā* 'to try to please, conciliate' > VI *tarāḍā* 'to come to mutually satisfactory terms'; III *xālafa* 'to differ with' > VI *taxālafa* 'to be at odds one with another.'

A second—and fairly common—connotation of Form VI is the pretence of a quality, as *jahila* 'not to know' > VI *tajāhala* 'to feign ignorance'; *mariḍa* 'to be ill' > VI *tamāraḍa* 'to feign illness'; *nasiya* 'to forget' > VI *tanāsā* 'to pretend to forget.'

	ACTIVE		PASSIVE (rare)	
PERFECT	تفاعل	*tafā'ala*	تفوعل	*tufū'ila*
IMPERFECT	يتفاعل	*yatafā'alu*	يتفاعل	*yutafā'alu*
SUBJUNCTIVE	يتفاعل	*yatafā'ala*	يتفاعل	*yutafā'ala*
JUSSIVE	يتفاعل	*yatafā'al*	يتفاعل	*yutafā'al*
IMPERATIVE	تفاعل	*tafā'al*	—	—
PARTICIPLE	متفاعل	*mutafā'il-*	متفاعل	*mutafā'al-*
VERBAL NOUN	تفاعل	*tafā'ul-*		

See remarks (1) and (4) for Form V (§67.1).

79.3 Synopsis of Form VI for weak-*lām* verbs. Example from √*NSY*:

PERFECT	تناسى	*tanāsā*
IMPERFECT	يتناسى	*yatanāsā*
SUBJUNCTIVE	يتناسى	*yatanāsā*
JUSSIVE	يتناس	*yatanāsa*
IMPERATIVE	تناس	*tanāsa*
PARTICIPLE	متناسٍ	*mutanāsin*
VERBAL NOUN	تناسٍ	*tanāsin*

See remarks on Form V weak-*lām* verbs (§69.1).

79.4 A selective list of familiar roots in Forms III and VI:

FORM III		FORM VI	
آخذ	take to task (*bi-* for)		
راود	entice		
سالم	make peace	تسالم	be reconciled
شاهد	witness		
عامل	trade, do business with	تعامل	trade, do business with each other
قابل	confront, stand opposite	تقابل	be face to face, get together
قاتل	fight with		
قاوم	oppose, resist	تقاوم	resist each other
كاتب	write to	تكاتب	correspond with each other
كاثر	outnumber	تكاثر	band together
كالم	speak with		
		تلاوم	blame each other
ماثل	resemble	تماثل	resemble each other, be alike
		تمارض	pretend to be sick
مانع	put up resistance to		
		تناسى	pretend to forget
ناظر	argue, debate	تناظر	dispute with one another
		تحابّ	love one another

Vocabulary

انس *'anisa (a) / 'anusa (u) 'uns-* be friendly, on intimate terms (*bi-/'ilā* with); perceive; II *'annasa* put at ease, tame; III *'ānasa* be friendly, cordial to; IV *'ānasa* keep company, observe, espy; X *ista'nasa* be sociable, on familiar terms with

اوى *'awā (ī)* seek shelter, refuge; IV *'āwā* take refuge (*'ilā* at), give shelter to

برك III *bāraka* bless *(fī)* someone/thing; VI *tabāraka* be blessed

جهد III *jāhada* endeavor, strive; VIII *ijtahada* work hard, be industrious

جاع *jā'a (ū) jaw'-* be hungry

علو *'alā (ū) 'ulūw-* be high, tall, rise (*'an* above); VI *ta'ālā* be exalted (*'an* over), be sublime; (VI imperative) *ta'āla* come on!; X *ista'lā* rise, tower (*'alā* over), be master (*'alā* of)

ندو III *nādā* call / cry out to, proclaim

نفق III *nāfaqa* be hypocritical, dissimulate; IV *'anfaqa* spend, expend

هجر *hajara (i) hajr-/hijrān-* part company with, be separated from; III *hājara* migrate; VI *tahājara* desert each other, break up

NOUNS

إنس *'ins-* humanity (as opposed to beasts, djinn, &c.)

بركة/بركات *barakat-* pl *-āt-* blessing

ذنب/ذنوب *ðamb-* pl *ðunūb-* sin

قبر/قبور *qabr-* pl *qubūr-* grave

OTHER

سبحان *subḥāna* (+ construct) "glory be to"

Exercises

(a) Read and translate:

١ إنهما يتحابّان
٢ الباب المقابل
٣ تعال
٤ تبارك الله
٥ اوخذنا بما عملنا
٦ لم يؤانسونا
٧ الجهاد الاكبر
٨ تكاثُر المجاهدين
٩ بارك الله فيك
١٠ النساء لم يكالمنه
١١ قاتلوا فى سبيل الله
١٢ ان الاخوين يتماثلان
١٣ مقاومتهم الاعداء
١٤ مهاجرون ومهاجرات
١٥ ليسالموا عدوّهم
١٦ تقابلت الطائفتان

(b) Read and translate:

١ يجاهدون فى سبيل الله ولا يخافون لومة لائم.
٢ ألم تر الى الذى حاجّ ابرهيم فى ربه أن آتاه الله الملك إذ قال ابرهيم «ربى الذى يحيى ويميت» قال «انا أحيى وأميت» قال ابرهيم «فإن الله ياتى

بالشمس من المشرق فأت بها من المغرب» فبُهت الذى كفر والله لا يهدى
القوم الظالمين.[1]

٣ إن الذين آمنوا وهاجروا وجاهدوا باموالهم وانفسهم فى سبيل الله والذين
آووا ونصروا اولئك بعضهم اولياء بعض. والذين آمنوا ولم يهاجروا ما لكم من
ولايتهم من شىء حتى يهاجروا. وإن استنصروكم فى الدين فعليكم النصر الا
على قوم بينكم وبينهم ميثاق. والله بما تعملون بصير.[2]

٤ تبارك الذى بيده الملك وهو على كل شىء قدير.

٥ إذ قال موسى لاهله «إنى آنست ناراً سآتيكم منها بخبر او آتيكم بشهاب
قبس» فلما جاءها نودى أن «بورك من فى النار ومَن حولها، وسبحان الله
رب العالمين. انه انا الله العزيز الحكيم»[3]

٦ وهذا كتاب أنزلناه مبارك فاتبعوه واتّقوا لعلكم تُرحمون.

٧ وما أصابكم فبإذن الله وليَعلم المؤمنين وليَعلم الذين نافقوا وقيل لهم
«تعالوا قاتلوا فى سبيل الله او ادفعوا» قالوا «لو[4] نعلم قتالاً لاتّبعناكم»، هم
للكفر يومئذٍ أقرب منهم للايمان. يقولون بأفواههم ما ليس فى قلوبهم والله
أعلم بما يكتمون.[5]

٨ فاقبل بعضهم على بعض يتلاومون.

٩ قال الله تبارك وتعالى «يا عبادى انى حرّمت الظلم على نفسى وجعلته بينكم
محرّماً فلا تظالموا. يا عبادى كلكم ضالّ الا من هديته فاستهدونى أهدكم. يا
عبادى كلكم جائع الا من اطعمته فاستطعمونى أطعمكم. يا عبادى كلكم عارٍ
الا من كسوته فاستكسونى اكسكم. يا عبادى انكم تخطئون بالليل والنهار
وانا أغفر الذنوب جميعاً فاستغفرونى أغفر لكم.[6]

١٠ لا تمارضوا[8] فتمرضوا ولا تحفروا قبوركم فتموتوا.[7]

(c) Translate into Arabic:

---

[1]*Ḥājja* dispute with; *mašriq-* east; *maǧrib-* west; *buhita* be flabbergasted.

[2]*Walāyat-* friendship; *mīθāq-* pact.

[3]*Šihāb- qabas-* borrowed flame; *ḥawla* around.

[4]*Law* followed by the imperf. ind. gives the sense of "if only."

[5]*Dafa'a (a)* repel; *yawma'iðin* "on that day"; *fam-* pl *'afwāh-* mouth; *katama (u)* conceal.

[6]*'Ariya* be naked; *kasā (ū)* clothe.

[7]*Ḥafara (i)* dig.

[8]See §67.4.

1. It is not seemly for you to rush to the spring. Ask me for water and I will give you to drink of what I have.

2. Let them enjoy their triumph over those who have oppressed the orphans of their people.

3. A proclaimer called out to the people of the city, saying, "Let the women and children take refuge at the mountain, and let the men strive until the fighting is concluded."

4. The hypocrites say that they have spent much to feed the poor, but they have spent nothing and the poor have not been provided with sustenance.

5. The messenger was sent but was killed on his way, and so he was not able to give them the good news.

Lesson Thirty-Six

80 The Adjectival Pattern of Colors and Characteristics: 'AF'ALU. Adjectives of colors and characteristics (generally physical defects) have special patterns that differ from the regular adjectival patterns encountered so far.

MASC. SING.	FEM. SING.	COMMON PL.
افعل *'af'alu*	فعلاء *fa'lā'u*	فعل *fu'l-*

The plural of this pattern is used with *all plurals,* including inanimate things. Examples are:

'green'	اخضر *'axḍaru*	خضراء *xaḍrā'u*	خضر *xuḍr-*
'yellow'	اصفر *'aṣfaru*	صفراء *ṣafrā'u*	صفر *ṣufr-*
'mute'	ابكم *'abkamu*	بكماء *bakmā'u*	بكم *bukm-*

80.2 C_2w roots are perfectly regular in formation.

'black'	اسود *'aswadu*	سوداء *sawdā'u*	سود *sūd-*
'one-eyed'	اعور *'a'waru*	عوراء *'awrā'u*	عور *'ūr-*

80.3 The only exception in the formation of C_2y roots is the harmonization of the vowel of the plural to the *y* radical *(*uy → ī).*

'white'	ابيض *'abyaḍu*	بيضاء *bayḍā'u*	بيض *bīḍ-*

80.4 The weakness of C_2w/y roots appears as *alif maqṣūra* in the masculine singular and *-y-* in the feminine and plural.

'blind'	اعمى *'a'mā*	عمياء *'amyā'u*	عمى *'umy-*

80.5 In the masculine singular of doubled roots, the vowel that would have separated C_2 and C_3 is thrown back onto the first consonant. The feminine and plural patterns are unaffected.

'deaf'	اصمّ *'aṣammu*	صمّاء *ṣammā'u*	صمّ *ṣumm-*

81 Verbs of Colors and Characteristics: Form IX and Form XI. Characteristic of the verb of colors and (physical) characteristics, Form IX, is the doubling of C_3. The base pattern is IF'ALLA. There is no passive of this form.

81.1 Synopsis of Form IX. Example from √SWD:

PERFECT	افعلّ *if'alla*	اسودّ *iswadda*
IMPERFECT	يفعلّ *yaf'allu*	يسودّ *yaswaddu*
SUBJUNCTIVE	يفعلّ *yaf'alla*	يسودّ *yaswadda*
JUSSIVE	يفعلّ *yaf'alla/i*	يسودّ *yaswadda/i*
	يفعلل *yaf'alil*	يسودد *yaswadid*
PARTICIPLE	مفعلّ *muf'all-*	مسودّ *muswadd-*
VERBAL NOUN	افعلال *if'ilāl-*	اسوداد *iswidād-*

81.2 The verbs of this form are vitually limited to roots of color and physical characteristics, as *'aswadu* 'black' > IX *iswadda* 'to become black, be blackened'; *'aṣfaru* 'yellow' > IX *iṣfarra* 'to turn yellow, become jaundiced'; *'a'waju* 'crooked' > IX *i'wajja* 'to be bent, crooked.'

81.3 Form XI (IF'ĀLLA) is characterized by lengthening the vowel before the doubled C_3 of Form IX. Form XI is quite rare and is indistinguishable from Form IX in meaning.

82 Other Verbal Forms: XII–XV. The remaining increased forms of the verb are too rare to deserve more than a passing listing. Almost all known examples of these are stative or qualitative and hence have no passive.

افعوعل XII IF'AW'ALA

افعوّل XIII IF'AWWALA

افعنلل XIV IF'ANLALA

افعنلى XV IF'ANLĀ

Vocabulary

بصر *baṣura (u) / baṣira (a) baṣar- + bi-* look, see, understand; II *baṣṣara* make see, enlighten; IV *'abṣara* see, behold; V *tabaṣṣara* reflect (*bi-/fī* on); X *istabṣara* be able to see

صبح IV *'aṣbaḥa* become (in the morning); get / wake up in the morning

فتو IV *'aftā* give / issue a (legal) opinion / counsel; X *istaftā* seek opinion / counsel from someone (acc.) (*fī* concerning)

فرق *faraqa (u) farq-* separate, part (int.), distinguish (*bayna* between / among); II *farraqa* part, separate (trs.); III *fāraqa* disengage oneself from, part with, quit; V *tafarraqa* be separated, divided, scattered; VIII *iftaraqa* = V

NOUNS AND ADJECTIVES

أبكم *'abkamu* mute, dumb

أبيض *'abyaḍu* white

أحمر *'aḥmaru* red

أخضر *'axḍaru* green

أزرق *'azraqu* blue

أسود *'aswadu* black

أصفر *'aṣfaru* yellow

أصمّ *'aṣammu* deaf

أعمى *'a'mā* blind

بصر/ابصار *baṣar-* pl *'abṣār-* vision, sight, insight

دابّة/دوابّ *dābbat-* (usually masc.) pl *dawābbu* beast, (riding) animal

فتوى/فتاوٍ ، فتاوى *fatwā* pl *fatāwin/fatāwā* (legal) opinion, counsel

صبح ، صباح *ṣubḥ- / ṣabāḥ-* morning, dawn, daybreak

OTHERS

اما *'ammā* as for (topicalizer, with main clause introduced by *fa-*)

بلى *balā* yes (affirmative response to a negative question, like *si* in French)

وان *wa-'in* even if

Exercises

(a) Give the Arabic:

1. red stones
2. black kings
3. a green tree
4. a blind hypocrite
5. a black book
6. yellow houses
7. a one-eyed devil
8. white queens
9. green trees
10. deaf mutes
11. a black calf
12. blue birds

(b) Read and translate:

١ استفت قلبك وان أفتاك المفتون.

٢ لا تسمع الصمّ الدعاء اذا ولّوا مدبرين.

٣ يوم تبيضّ وجوه وتسودّ وجوه فاما الذين اسودّت وجوههم اكفرتم بعد ايمانكم؟ فذوقوا العذاب بما كنتم تكفرون. واما الذين ابيضّت وجوههم ففى رحمة الله هم فيها خالدون.

٤ الم تر ان الله انزل من السماء ماء فتصبح الارض مخضرّة؟

٥ قل «من رب السموات والارض؟» قل «الله» أفاتخذتم من دونه اولياء لا يملكون لانفسهم نفعاً ولا ضراً؟ قل «هل يستوى الاعمى والبصير ام هل تستوى الظلمات والنور ام جعلوا لله شركاء خلقوا كخلقه؟» قل «الله خالق كل شيء وهو الواحد»

٦ فلا تطع الكافرين وجاهدهم جهاداً كبيراً.

٧ يا ايها الذين آمنوا لا تدخلوا بيوتاً غير بيوتكم حتى تستأذنوا وتسلّموا على اهلها. ذلك خير لكم لعلكم تذكّرون.

٨ اذا جاءك المنافقون قالوا «نشهد انك لَرسول الله» والله يعلم انك لرسوله والله يشهد ان المنافقين لكاذبون.

٩ قل لئن اجتمعت الانس والجن على ان ياتوا بمثل هذا القرآن لا ياتون بمثله.

١٠ واذ اخذ ربك من بنى آدم من ظهورهم ذريتهم وأشهدهم على انفسهم «ألست بربكم؟» قالوا «بلى شهدنا» أن تقولوا يوم القيامة «إنا كنا عن هذا غافلين» او تقولوا «إنما أشرك آباؤنا من قبل وكنا ذرية من بعدهم أفتهلكنا

بما فعل المبطلون؟»[1]

١١ ان شر الدواب عند الله الصم البكم.

(c) Translate into Arabic:

1. He almost appointed the worst of men as his successor, but a voice cried out from heaven, saying, "Your deeds will be reckoned."

2. As for those who disobey God's commands, the judge issued an opinion that they be killed.

3. At the end of this world God's promise will be fulfilled, and everything—the sun, the moon and the stars, the stones and rivers of the earth, and the birds and beasts, and humankind and the djinn—will pass away; but God will abide.

4. Solomon was blessed by God as a prophet and king, and the djinn were tamed for him in order to break the stones for God's house.

5. When they arose in the morning they beheld a green genie entering the city on a white beast.

6. The man pure of heart disengaged himself from his people in order to strive to draw near to God.

7. The hypocrites said, "Give us refuge from our enemy." But when they entered among us they laid a plot to strike the black stone so that it would be broken.

---

[1] *Ẓuhūr-* loins; *ðurriyyat-* progeny; *'an* here, "lest"; *'ahlaka* destroy; *'abṭala* talk idly.

Lesson Thirty-Seven

83 The Pattern of the Noun of Place: MAF‘AL-. The pattern for the place where an activity takes place is MAF‘AL-.

83.1 G-form verbs that have *-a-* or *-u-* as the characteristic vowel of C_2 in the imperfect usually form the noun of place of the pattern MAF‘AL(AT)-, the presence or absence of the feminine sign not being predictable. Verbs with *-i-* as the imperfect vowel form the noun of place on the pattern MAF‘IL(AT)-. The plural of both MAF‘AL(AT)- and MAF‘IL(AT)- is MAFĀ‘ILU.

Here follows a list of nouns of place derived from familiar roots:

مامن	safe place	معمل	workshop
ماوى	shelter	مفرق	junction, intersection
مجرى	river-/watercourse	مقتل	mortal spot
محجر	quarry	مقام	place, position
محكمة	court	مكتب	school
مخرج	exit	مكان	place
مدخل	entrance	مملكة	kingdom
مذهب	way, route	منار	lighthouse
مسجد	mosque	منزل	halting-place, stage
مسكن	dwelling	منظر	watchtower
مسيَر	itinerary	مهجر	place of emigration
مطلَع	point of ascent (sun, star)	موضِع	position, place

Note in this list that the third radical of C3*w/y* roots is replaced by *alif maqṣūra*. Since the *alif maqṣūra* takes the place of a radical consonant, the indefinite triptote ending is retained, i.e., they end in *-an* in the indefinite and *-ā* in the definite.

83.2 The noun of place for the increased forms is identical to the masculine-singular passive participle. Plurals are in *-āt-*. Examples of such relatively rare nouns of place are:

مجتمع/مجتمعات	meeting-place, communal gathering
متّكا/متّكآت	cushion, couch (< *ittaka'a* to lean, recline)
مصلًّى/مصلّيات	place of prayer, oratory
ملتقًى/ملتقيات	meeting place, rendezvous, battlefield

84 The Pattern of the Noun of Instrumentality: MIF'AL-. The pattern of nouns indicating implements and instruments is MIF'AL-. The vowel between C2 and C3 may be long, giving MIF'ĀL-. The plural of MIF'AL- is MAFĀ'ILU; the plural of MIF'ĀL- is MAFĀ'ĪLU. Examples of these patterns are:

مئكال/مآكيلُ	implement for eating (< *'akala* to eat)
مبرد/مباردُ	file (< *barada* to file)
مثقال/مثاقيلُ	mithcal, a unit of weight (< *θaqula* to be heavy)
مجمر/مجامرُ	brazier (< *jamr-* embers)
مرآة/مرايا	mirror (< *ra'ā* to see)
مصباح/مصابيحُ	lantern, light (< *ṣabuḥa* to be radiant)
مضراب/مضاريبُ	plectrum (< *ḍaraba* to strike)
مفتاح/مفاتيحُ	opener, key (< *fataḥa* to open)

85 The Patterns of Nouns of Instance (FA'LAT-) and Manner (FI'LAT-).

85.1 The noun of instance, i.e., the noun that indicates the action or state of the verb done once, is on the pattern FA'LAT-. These nouns are used almost exclusively as cognate accusatives (see §29). Whereas the normal cognate accusative with the verbal noun may either strengthen or intensify the connotation of the verb or serve as a "dummy" carrier for an adjective used adverbially, the noun of instance as cognate accusative means "once," "one time." For instance, in the construction

ضربنى ضرباً شديداً	*ḍarabanī ḍarban šadīdan*	He struck me sharply.

the cognate verbal noun may be replaced by the noun of instance:

ضربنى ضربةً	*ḍarabanī ḍarbatan*	He struck me once.
ضربنى ضربتين	*ḍarabanī ḍarbatayni*	He struck me twice.

The noun of instance may also be modified like any cognate accusative.

ضربنى ضربةً شديدةً	*ḍarabanī ḍarbatan šadīdatan*	He gave me a sharp blow.
ضربنى ضربتين شديدتين	*ḍarabanī ḍarbatayni šadīdatayni*	He gave me two sharp blows.

85.2 The noun of manner, which indicates the manner in which something is done, is on the pattern FI'LAT-, e.g.:

ضحك > ضحكة	*ḍaḥika > ḍiḥkat-*	manner of laughing
خلق > خلقة	*xalaqa > xilqat-*	disposition
مشى > مشية	*mašā > mišyat-*	manner of walking, gait

Theoretically all G-form verbs are susceptible to these two patterns; however, only a limited number of the potentially available ones are in actual use.

86 Optative and Assertory Uses of the Perfect. The verb in the perfect (negative with *lā*) is used to assert what is assumed or hoped to be a fact. This occurs in wishes, prayers, curses, &c. Such phrases commonly follow proper names.

النبى محمد صلى الله عليه وسلم	*an-nabīyu muḥam-madun ṣallā llāhu 'alayhi wa-sallama*	The Prophet Muham-mad—may God pray for him and grant him peace!
ابو بكر الصديق رضى الله عنه	*abū-bakrin^{i} ṣ-ṣiddīqu raḍiya llāhu 'anhu*	Abu-Bakr the Right-eous—may God be pleased with him.

فلان بن فلان رحمه الله	*fulānu bnu fulānin raḥimahu llāhu*	So-and-So son of So-and-So—may God have mercy upon him.
الشيخ فلان كرّم الله وجهه	*aš-šayxu fulānun karrama llāhu wajhahu*	Shaykh So-and-So—may God ennoble his countenance.
ابليس لعنه الله	*'iblīsu la'anahu llāhu*	Iblis—may God curse him!
السلطان فلان دام ملكه	*as-sulṭānu fulānun dāma mulkuhu*	Sultan So-and-So—may his kingdom endure forever!

The standard phrases *tabāraka* and *ta'ālā*, which follow the name of God, may be translated as optatives, although it should be realized that they are clearly assertory in nature.

الله تبارك وتعالى	*allāhu tabāraka wa-ta'ālā*	God—blessed and exalted is (be) He!

Vocabulary

VERBS

جزى *jazā (ī) jazā'* - requite, reward, punish (*bi-*/*'alā* for); III *jāzā* = G

حفظ *ḥafiẓa (a) ḥifẓ-* preserve, protect, memorize; III *ḥāfaẓa* watch out (*'alā* for), be mindful (*'alā* of); VIII *iḥtafaẓa* + *bi-* guard, maintain; X *istaḥfaẓa* commit something (acc.) to the charge of (acc.)

حوط IV *'aḥāṭa* surround *(bi-/-hu)* someone (*bi-/-hu* with); VIII *iḥtāṭa* be careful, on one's guard

سرق *saraqa (i) sariqat-* steal, rob; VII *insaraqa* be / get stolen; VIII *istaraqa* filch, pilfer

فسد *fasada (u) fasād-* rot, decay, be wicked, vain; IV *'afsada* spoil, corrupt, act wickedly

نكر *nakira (a)* not to know / recognize, deny, disown; IV *'ankara* refuse to acknowledge, disavow, disclaim

وكل *wakala (i) wakl-/wukūl-* entrust (*'ilā* to); II *wakkala* authorize, put in charge (*bi-* of); V *tawakkala 'alā* rely on, depend upon, put one's confidence in; VIII *ittakala* = V

NOUNS

بضاعة/بضائع *biḍāʻat-* pl *baḍāʼiʻu* wares, merchandise
شهاب/شهب *šihāb-* pl *šuhub-* flame, shooting star
مثقال/مثاقيل *miθqāl-* pl *maθāqīlu* small weight
معروف *maʻrūf-* act of favor / kindness, good deed (opposite of *munkar-*)
مرجع/مراجع *marjiʻ-* pl *marājiʻu* refuge, recourse, retreat
منكر *munkar-* abomination, objectionable act

IDIOM

استرق السمع *istaraqa s-samʻa* "he eavesdropped"

Exercises

(a) Read and translate:

١ يا ابن آدم أقم الصلاة وأمر بالمعروف وآنه عن المنكر واصبر على ما أصابك.
٢ إن المتقين فى مقام امين فى جنات وعيون لا يذوقون فيها الموت الا الموتة الأولى - وقاهم عذاب الجحيم[1].
٣ يا بُنى إنها إن تك[2] مثقال حبة من خردل فتكن فى صخرة او فى السموات او فى الارض يات بها الله. إن الله خبير.[3]
٤ ولتكن منكم امة يدعون الى الخير ويامرون بالمعروف وينهون عن المنكر واولئك هم المفلحون[4] ولا تكونوا كالذين تفرقوا واختلفوا من بعد ما جاءهم البينات واولئك لهم عذاب عظيم.
٥ وقالوا «اذا ضللنا فى الارض أئنّا لفى خلق جديد؟» بل هم بلقاء ربهم كافرون. قل «يتوفاكم ملك الموت الذى وُكّل بكم ثم الى ربكم تُرجَعون».
٦ ولقد جعلنا فى السماء بروجاً وزيّنّاها للناظرين وحفظناها من كل شيطان الا من استرق السمع فأتبعه شهاب مبين.[5]
٧ قالت [ملكة سبأ] «يا ايها الملأ إنى ألقى الىّ كتابٌ كريم - انه من سليمان وانه

---

[1]*Jaḥīm-* hell.
[2]*Taku*, apocopated form of *takun*.
[3]*Ḥabbat-* seed; *xardal-* mustard; *ṣaxrat-* rock.
[4]*ʼAflaḥa* be successful.
[5]*Burj-* pl *burūj-* constellation; *zayyana* decorate, embellish.

باسم الله الرحمن الرحيم الاّ تعلوا علىّ واتونى مسلمين» قالت «يا ايها الملأ أفتونى فى امرى ، وما كنت قاطعةً امراً حتى تشهدونى» قالوا «نحن اولو قوة والامر اليك فانظرى ماذا تامرين» قالت «إن الملوك اذا دخلوا قرية أفسدوها وجعلوا اعزّة اهلها اذلّة ، وكذلك يفعلون. وانى مرسلة اليهم بهديّة فناظرة بما يرجع المرسلون»[1]

٨ من اجل ذلك كتبنا على بنى اسرئيل انه من قتل نفساً بغير نفس او فساد فى الارض فكأنما قتل الناس جميعاً ، ومن أحياها فكأنما أحيا الناس جميعاً. ولقد جاءتهم رسلنا بالبينات ثم ان كثيراً منهم بعد ذلك فى الارض لمسرفون[2].

٩ الهكم اله واحد فالذين لا يؤمنون بالآخرة قلوبهم مُنكِرة وهم مستكبرون.

(b) Translate into Arabic:

1. He put his brothers, whom he loved, in charge of all the kingdom.

2. When the evil-doers subjugated the village, some of the people submitted, others turned and fled, and others fought until they were slain.

3. The meaning of the prophet's words is to command the good and forbid the abomination.

4. The beasts can see and touch and taste; but man, to the exclusion of all beasts, has reason.

5. The friends of God who recite the beautiful verses of the Koran are rewarded with paradise, beneath which flow rivers eternally.

6. Go to the village of your fathers and hand over this legal opinion. If the inhabitants of the village refuge to acknowledge my rule over them, punish them severely for their disobedience.

7. I and my partners sought a legal opinion from the learned men of the religion.

8. Only the purified may touch this book.

---

[1] *Qaṭaʿa ʾamran* make a final decision; *ʿazīz-* pl *ʾaʿizzat-* powerful; *ðalīl-* pl *ʾaðillat-* base; *hadīyat-* pl *hadāyā* gift.

[2] *ʾAsrafa* squander.

Lesson Thirty-Eight

87 Quadriliteral and Reduplicative Verbs. There are many roots that are composed of four consonants instead of the normal three. These fall into two categories: they are either (1) of four different radicals, FA'LALA, or (2) of two radical consonants reduplicated, FALFALA.

The majority of quadriliterals appear to be extensions in some fashion of existing triliteral roots, as *daḥraja* 'to roll (trs.)' from *daraja* 'to roll up.' Others are clearly denominative, as *tarjama* 'to translate' from *tarjumat-* 'translation.'

Reduplicative verbs are almost all onomatopoeic in nature, as *waswasa* 'to whisper,' *xašxaša* 'to rustle,' and *qa'qa'a* 'to clank, clatter.'

The base form of the quadriliterals and reduplicatives conforms to Form II of the triliteral in vocalic patterning and participial formation. An example is *tarjama* 'to translate.'

	ACTIVE		PASSIVE	
PERFECT	ترجم	*tarjama*	ترجم	*turjima*
IMPERFECT	يترجم	*yutarjimu*	يترجم	*yutarjamu*
IMPERATIVE	ترجم	*tarjim*	—	—
PARTICIPLE	مترجم	*mutarjim-*	مترجم	*mutarjam-*

The verbal noun of G-form quadriliterals, though not predictable, tends to one of the patterns FA'LALAT- (as here, *tarjamat-*) or FI'LĀL-.

87.1 Form II of the quadriliteral, TAFAʻLALA, corresponds in both form and meaning to Form V of the triliteral, as *tadaḥraja* 'to roll along (int.)' and *tašayṭana* 'to act like a devil' (< *šayṭān-* 'devil').

PERFECT	تدحرج	*tadaḥraja*	تشيطن	*tašayṭana*
IMPERFECT	يتدحرج	*yatadaḥraju*	يتشيطن	*yatašayṭanu*
PARTICIPLE	متدحرج	*mutadaḥrij-*	متشيطن	*mutašayṭin-*
VERBAL NOUN	تدحرج	*tadaḥruj-*	تشيطن	*tašayṭun-*

87.2 Form III of the quadriliteral—quite rare—corresponds formally to Form VII of the triliteral. The -*n*- is infixed between C_2 and C_3, however, rather than prefixed to the radical, IFʻANLALA. An example is √SLṬḤ *islanṭaḥa* 'to be broad, to be laid down flat.'

87.3 Form IV of the quadriliteral corresponds formally to Form IX of the triliteral. The pattern is IFʻALALLA. Examples are *iṭmaʼanna* 'to be calm, assured,' *iqšaʻarra* 'to be horrified,' and *išmaʼazza* 'to be disgusted.'

PERFECT	اطمأنّ	*iṭmaʼanna*	اقشعرّ	*iqšaʻarra*
IMPERFECT	يطمئنّ	*yaṭmaʼinnu*	يقشعرّ	*yaqšaʻirru*
PARTICIPLE	مطمئنّ	*muṭmaʼinn-*	مقشعرّ	*muqšaʻirr-*
VERBAL NOUN	اطمئنان	*iṭmiʼnān-*	اقشعرار	*iqšiʻrār-*

88 Impersonal Passives. Verbs such as *ğaḍiba ʻalā* 'to be angry with' and *rağiba fī* 'to be desirous of'—or almost any intransitive verb that takes a semantic object through a preposition—may form an impersonal passive construction. In the passive, the verb (or participle) is impersonal in the third-person masculine singular, and the semantic object of the active voice remains the prepositional complement in the passive.

غضبت عليهم	*ğaḍibtu ʻalayhim* (act.)	I got angry with them.
غُضب عليهم	*ğuḍiba ʻalayhim* (pass.)	They suffered wrath.
المغضوب عليهم	*al-mağḍūbu ʻalayhim* (pass. part.)	those who are the object of (someone's) wrath

سجدوا للاصنام	*sajadū lil-'aṣnāmi* (act.)	They bowed down to the idols.
سُجد للاصنام	*sujida lil-'aṣnāmi* (pass.)	The idols were bowed down to.
الاصنام المسجود لها	*al-'aṣnāmu l-masjūdu lahā* (pass. part.)	the idols that were bowed down to
رغبوا فيها	*rağibū fīhā* (act.)	They desired her.
رُغب فيها	*ruğiba fīhā* (pass.)	She was desired.
المرغوب فيها	*al-marğūbu fīhā* (pass. part.)	the one (fem.) who is desired
أشار الى المرأة	*'ašāra 'ilā l-mar'ati* (act.)	He pointed to the woman.
أشير الى المرأة	*'ušīra 'ilā l-mar'ati* (pass.)	The woman was pointed to.
المرأة المشار اليها	*al-mar'atu l-mušāru 'ilayhā* (pass. part.)	the woman who is / was pointed to

Whereas verbs that are wholly intransitive (like *ğaḍiba* 'to get angry') or complete transitives in and of themselves (like *'ašāra* 'to make an indication') form impersonal passives only, transitive verbs like *ba'aθa* and quasi-transitives like *'atā bi-* form both personal and impersonal passives. In the personal passive the direct object (or, in the case of quasi-transitives like *'atā* that take an accusative of motion, the accusative) of the active becomes the subject of the passive, and the prepositional complement remains as in the active.

بعثوك اليّ	*ba'aθūka 'ilayya*	They sent you to me.
بعثت اليّ	*bu'iθta 'ilayya*	You were sent to me.
أتيتني بالكتاب	*'ataytanī bil-kitābi*	You brought me the book.
أتيت بالكتاب	*'utītu bil-kitābi*	I was brought the book.

In the impersonal passive the verb is 3rd-person masculine singular, and the complement of the preposition remains as in the active.

بعث اليّ	*bu'iθa 'ilayya*	I was sent to (for).

اتى بالكتاب	*'utiya bil-kitābi*	The book was brought.

89 The *Mâ...Min* Clause. The use of the indefinite relative pronoun *mā* 'that which' followed by the partitive-*min* construction will be frequently encountered. Although the construction is not difficult, it differs enough from the English mode of expression sometimes to cause problems in translation. Example:

ما تنفقوا من خير فلانفسكم	*wa-mā tunfiqū min xayrin fa-li-'anfusikum*	Whatever good you spend, it is for yourselves.

The example would be literally translated, "what you spend of good...." By and large, the most successful method of dealing with the *mā...min* construction is to translate what follows *min* first and then what follows *mā* as an English relative clause.[1]

ما يفتح الله للناس من رحمة فلا ممسك لها	*mā yaftaḥi llāhu lin-nāsi min raḥmatin fa-lā mumsika lahā*	No one can withhold the mercy God opens to people.
غفر له ما تقدم من ذنبه وما تأخر	*ğafara lahu mā taqaddama min ðambihi wa-mā ta'axxara*	He forgave him his sins past and future.

Vocabulary

VERBS

رد *radda (u) radd-* send / bring / take back, ward off, return; reply (*'alā* to); V *taraddada* be reflected, recur; waver, be uncertain, hesitate; VIII *irtadda* go back, revert, apostasize (*'an* from); X *istaradda* reclaim, get back

حزن *ḥazina (a) ḥuzn-* be sad, grieved

طمان IV *iṭma'anna/yaṭma'innu* be tranquil, at peace, assured

[1]For a *mā...min* clause with *mahmā*, see p. 190, §73.2, last example.

عوذ *'āδa (ū) ma'āδ-* seek protection (*bi-* with) (*min* from); II *'awwaδa* place someone (acc.) under the protection (*bi-* of) (*min* against); X *ista'āδa* = G

غاب *ğāba (ī) ğayb-/ğiyāb-* be absent, vanish

قر *qarra (a/i) qarr-* be cool; *qarrat 'aynuhu* he was glad, delighted (*bi-/fī* in)

هلك *halaka (i) halāk-* perish, die; IV *'ahlaka* destroy, cause to perish; X *istahlaka* exhaust oneself

وذر √WδR (no perfect) *yaδaru* leave; (+ jussive) let, allow

يئس/يياس *ya'isa (a) ya's-* despair, give up hope (*min* of); IV *'ay'asa* deprive of hope; X *istay'asa* = G

NOUNS

حزن/احزان *ḥuzn-* pl *'aḥzān-* sorrow, grief

صدقة/صدقات *ṣadaqat-* pl *-āt-* alms, charity

غيب/غيوب *ğayb-* pl *ğuyūb-* that which is invisible, the transcendental / supernatural (realm)

قرة العين *qurratu l-'ayni* joy, delight

OTHER

لا...ولا *lā...wa-lā* neither...nor (in such constructions *lā* functions as an ordinary negative, affecting no case)

Exercises

(a) Read and translate:

١ يا ايتها النفس المطمئنة ارجعى الى ربك راضيةً مرضيةً فادخلى فى عبادى وادخلى جنتى.

٢ الا ان اولياء الله لا خوفٌ عليهم ولا هم يحزنون؟ الذين آمنوا وكانوا يتقون لهم البشرى فى الحياة الدنيا وفى الآخرة.

٣ ولا يزالون يقاتلونكم حتى يردّوكم عن دينكم إن استطاعوا ، ومن يرتدد منكم عن دينه فيمت وهو كافر.

٤ أنفقوا من ما رزقناكم من قبل أن ياتى أحدكم الموت فيقول "رب لولا

اخّرتنى[1] الى اجل قريب فاصّدّق واكن من الصالحين» ولن يؤخّر الله نفساً اذا
جاء اجلها والله خبير بما تعملون.

٥ قل ان الموت الذى تفرّون منه فانه ملاقيكم ثم تُردّون الى عالم الغيب
والشهادة فينبّئكم بما كنتم تعملون.

٦ تلك آيات الكتاب وقرآن مبين ربما يودّ الذين كفروا لو كانوا مسلمين. ذرهم
ياكلوا ويتمتعوا فسوف يعلمون وما أهلكنا من قرية الا ولها كتاب معلوم.

٧ فاذا قرأت القرآن فاستعذ بالله من الشيطان الرجيم[2]. انه ليس له سلطان
على الذين آمنوا وعلى ربهم يتوكلون.

٨ عذابى أصيب به من أشاء ورحمتى وسعت كل شىء فساكتبها للذين يتّقون
ويؤتون الزكاة والذين هم بآياتنا يؤمنون.

٩ اوحينا الى ام موسى أن «ارضعيه فاذا خفت عليه فالقيه فى اليمّ ولا تخافى ولا
تحزنى. إنا رادّوه اليك وجاعلوه من المرسلين». فرددناه الى امّه كى تقرّ عينها
ولا تحزن ولتعلم أن وعد الله حق ولكن اكثر الناس لا يعلمون. ولما بلغ
اشدّه واستوى آتيناه حكماً وعلماً وكذلك نجزى المحسنين.[3]

١٠ إنا أنزلنا التوراة فيها هدى ونور يحكم بها النبيون الذين أسلموا للذين
هادوا والربّانيّون والأحبار بما استُحفظوا من كتاب الله وكانوا عليه شهداء
ومن لم يحكم بما أنزل الله فاولئك الكافرون.

(b) Translate into Arabic:

1. When a man's appointed time has come, he gives up hope of life and is made to perish; but they sorrow not over him, for he will be sent forth at the day of resurrection.

2. Iblis disobeyed God's command to bow down to Adam, and so God punished him, and he was cast from heaven into the darkness.

3. We have been surrounded and are not able to go back, so let us seek refuge with those who will watch out for us.

4. All Muslims memorize verses from the Koran and recite them while they pray.

---

[1] *Law-lā* here introduces a question of rebuke, "Why did you not…?" In a conditional-type sentence with a following jussive, as here, it is best translated as an affirmative modal, "If you would only…"; *'axxara* reprieve, postpone.

[2] *Rajīm-* stoned, accursed.

[3] *'Arḍa'a* suckle; *yamm-* sea.

5. O you (m s) who pray, turn your face toward Mecca.

6. You (m pl) who have been put in charge of these orphans, when they have reached maturity give them their due.

7. The poor woman had despaired of life when a pious man passed by her dwelling and gave her alms.

Lesson Thirty-Nine

90 Higher Numbers. The tens of numbers above 19 are formed as masculine plurals of the units—except for 20, which is formed from the root of 10.

20	عشرون	*'išrūna*	60	ستون	*sittūna*
30	ثلاثون	*θalāθūna*	70	سبعون	*sab'ūna*
40	اربعون	*'arba'ūna*	80	ثمانون	*θamānūna*
50	خمسون	*xamsūna*	90	تسعون	*tis'ūna*

As sound masuline plurals, these numbers take genitive and accusative endings in *-īna*.

Compound numbers are formed from the declined units followed by *wa-* and the tens:

احد وعشرون	*'aḥadun wa-'išrūna*	twenty-one (masc. nom.)
اثنان وعشرون	*iθnāni wa-'išrūna*	twenty-two (masc. nom.)
ثلاثة وعشرون	*θalāθatun wa-'išrūna*	twenty-three, &c.

Note that the 'one' in 'twenty-one' &c. is *'aḥad-* (fem. *'iḥdā*), as in 'eleven' (see §63).

90.1 From 11 through 99, things counted are normally in the *accusative singular* following the number.

ثلاثون يوماً	*θalāθūna yawman*	thirty days

بلغ اربعين سنةً	*balağa 'arba'īna sanatan*	he attainted (the age of) forty years
تسعة وتسعون اسماً	*tis'atun wa-tis'ūna sman*	ninety-nine names

Occasionally other cases and the plural number will be found after the numbers from 11 through 99.

90.2 'Hundred' is *mi'at-* (note irregular spelling). The hundreds are quite regularly formed as follows:

100	مائة	*mi'at-*	500	خمسمائة	*xamsu-mi'atin*
200	مائتان	*mi'atāni* (nom.)	600	ستمائة	*sittu-mi'atin*
	مائتين	*mi'atayni* (obl.)	700	سبعمائة	*sab'u-mi'atin*
300	ثلثمائة	*θalātu-mi'atin*	800	ثمانمائة	*θamāni-mi'atin*
400	اربعمائة	*'arba'u-mi'atin*	900	تسعمائة	*tis'u-mi'atin*

The hundreds are normally followed in construct by the *genitive singular* of the thing counted.

مائة سنة	*mi'ata sanatin*	for a hundred years
قبل مائتى سنة	*qabla mi'atay sanatin*	two hundred years ago

The hundreds are also occasionally followed by the *accusative plural* as an accusative of respect.

90.3 'Thousand' is *'alf-* (pl. *'ālāf-* and *'ulūf-*). It is counted like any regular masculine noun and is followed by the thing counted in the *genitive singular* in construct or with the partitive-*min* construction.

الف سنة	*'alfu sanatin*	a thousand years
ثلاثة آلاف من الملائكة	*θalāθatu 'ālāfin mina l-malā'ikati*	three thousand (of the) angels

90.4 Synopsis of the case and number governance of numbers.

NUMBER	COUNTED NOUN	CONCORD
1	*wāḥid(at)-* follows the singular as a regular attributive adjective	

2	*iθn(at)āni/-ayni* follows the dual as a regular attributive adjective	
3–10	genitive plural	chiastic concord applies
11–99	accusative singular	chiastic concord applies to units 3–9; 'ten' in teens takes normal concord; tens from 20 on unaffected
100–999	gen. sing. in construct; occasionally acc. pl.	chiastic concord applied to units 3–9 only
1000+	gen. sing. in construct; or *min* + plural	chiastic concord applies to units 3–9 only

90.5 Mixed numbers are generally read in the following order: thousands, hundreds, units, tens. *The last element read determines the number and case of the thing counted.*

اربعة آلاف وخمسمائة وستة فراسخ	*'arba'atu 'ālāfin wa-xamsu-mi'atin wa-sittatu farāsixa*	4506 leagues
الفان وسبعة عشر فرسخاً	*'alfāni wa-sab'ata-'ašara farsaxan*	2017 leagues
الف ومائتا فرسخ	*'alfun wa-mi'atā farsaxin*	1200 leagues

91 Numerals and the *Abjad* System. The numerals in common use in Arabic for the last millennium or so, the immediate source of our own "Arabic" numerals, were borrowed by Islamic civilization from the Indian subcontinent.

١	1	٣	3	٥	5	٧	7	٩	9
٢	2	٤	4	٦	6	٨	8	١٠	10

Compound numbers are written from left to right, exactly as our own numbers.

Except for mathematical calculation, the "Indian" numerals were not commonly used for numbering; instead, the *abjad* system, common to

Semitic languages, was used. In this system each letter of the alphabet stands for a number, the order of which preserves the ancient Semitic alphabetical order that was discarded by the Arabic philologians in favor of the order by shape common today.

ا	1	ك	20	ش	300
ب	2	ل	30	ت	400
ج	3	م	40	ث	500
د	4	ن	50	خ	600
ه	5	س	60	ذ	700
و	6	ع	70	ض	800
ز	7	ف	80	غ	900
ح	8	ص	90	ظ	1000
ط	9	ق	100		
ى	10	ر	200		

These numbers are indicated in the manuscript tradition by a *madda* or line placed over the numerical letters, e.g. شسه = 365.

Vocabulary

VERBS

توب *tāba (ū) tawbat-* turn away (*'an* from), renounce, relent, repent (*'ilā* towards)

شور IV *'ašāra* + *'ilā* make a sign, indicate

صوم *ṣāma (ū) ṣiyām-/ṣawm-* fast

عد *'adda (u) 'add-* count, number

غلب *ğalaba (i) ğalabat-* subdue, vanquish

نكح *nakaḥa (i) nikāḥ-* marry

وضع VI *tawāḍa'a* be humble

NOUNS AND ADJECTIVES

الف/آلاف ، الوف *'alf-* pl *'ālāf-/'ulūf-* thousand

سنة/سنون ، سنوات *sanat-* pl *sinūna / sanawāt-* year

شهر/شهور ، اشهر *šahr-* pl *šuhūr-/'ašhur-* month

عام/اعوام *ʿām-* pl *ʾaʿwām-* year

عدة *ʿiddat-* number

مائة/مئات *miʾat-* pl *miʾāt-* hundred

متتابع *mutatābiʿ-* consecutive

مرة/مرات ، مرار *marrat-* pl *-āt-/mirār-* time, instance

مسكين/مساكين *miskīn-* pl *masākīnu* poor, unfortunate

Exercises

(a) Read and translate

١ افترقت اليهود على احدى وسبعين فرقة وتفرقت النصارى على اثنتين وسبعين فرقة وستفترق امتى على ثلاث وسبعين ملة كلها فى النار الا واحدة. (حديث نبوى)

٢ يا ايها النبى حرّض[1] المؤمنين على القتال - إن يكن منكم عشرون صابرون يغلبوا مائتين. وإن يكن منكم مائة يغلبوا الفاً. وإن يكن منكم الف يغلبوا الفين باذن الله والله مع الصابرين.

٣ استغفر لهم او لا تستغفر لهم - إن تستغفر لهم سبعين مرة فلن يغفر الله لهم. ذلك بأنهم كفروا بالله ورسوله والله لا يهدى القوم الفاسقين.

٤ فمن لم يستطع ذلك فصيام شهرين متتابعين فمن لم يستطع فإطعام ستين مسكيناً.

٥ الزانية والزانى فاجلدوا كل واحد منهما مائة جلدة ولا تأخذكم بهما رأفة فى دين الله إن كنتم تؤمنون بالله واليوم الآخر وليشهد عذابهما طائفة من المؤمنين. الزانى لا ينكح الا زانية او مشركة والزانية لا ينكحها الا زانٍ او مشرك وحُرّم ذلك على المؤمنين. والذين يرمون المحصنات ثم لم يأتوا باربعة شهداء فاجلدوهم ثمانين جلدة ولا تقبلوا لهم شهادة ابداً واولئك هم الفاسقون الا الذين تابوا من بعد ذلك وأصلحوا فإن الله غفور رحيم.[2]

٦ ان الله خلق الارواح قبل الاجسام[3] بالفى سنة.

٧ ان الله ينظر فى كل يوم وليلة ثلثمائة وستين نظرة الى قلب المؤمن.

---

[1] *Ḥarraḍa* encourage.

[2] *Jalada (i)* flog; *jaldat-* lash; *raʾfat-* pity; *ramā* here means "cast aspersions, accuse"; *muḥṣanat-* chaste woman; *ʾaṣlaḥa* reform.

[3] *Jism-* pl *ʾajsām-* body.

٨ خُيِّرتُ بين أن اكون نبياً مَلِكاً او اكون نبياً عبداً فاشار الىّ جبريل (عليه السلام) أن «تواضعْ» فقلت «بل اكون نبياً عبداً - اشبع يوماً واجوع يوماً».[1]

٩ ان عدّة الشهور عند الله اثنا عشر شهراً فى كتاب الله يوم خلق السموات والارض.

١٠ وما كان لمؤمن أن يقتل مؤمناً الا خطأً ومن قتل مؤمناً خطأً فتحرير رقبة مؤمنة ودية مسلّمة الى اهله الا أن يصّدّقوا فإن كان من قوم عدو لكم وهو مؤمن فتحرير رقبة مؤمنة وإن كان من قوم بينكم وبينهم ميثاق فدية مسلّمة الى اهله وتحرير رقبة مؤمنة فمن لم يجد فصيام شهرين متتابعين توبةً من الله وكان الله عليماً حكيماً.[2]

---

[1] *Xayyara* give a choice; *šabiʻa* be satiated, full.

[2] *Ḥarrara* manumit, set free; *raqabat-* slave; *diyat-* bloodmoney; *tatābaʻa* be consecutive.

Lesson Forty

92 Ordinal Numbers. The ordinal numbers are formed from the radicals of the cardinal numbers on the active-participial pattern FĀ'IL-, which is in every respect a regular adjectival pattern. The chiastic concord of the cardinals does not apply to the ordinals. The only irregularly formed ordinals are *'awwal-* 'first' (fem. *'ūlā*), a suppletion form that does not derive from the number 'one,' and *sādis-* 'sixth,' which reflects the original radicals of 'six,' which have fallen together as *-tt-* in the cardinal number.

1st	الاول	*al-'awwalu* (m)	5th	الخامس	*al-xāmisu*
	الاولى	*al-'ūlā* (f)	6th	السادس	*as-sādisu*
2nd	الثانى	*aθ-θānī* (m)	7th	السابع	*as-sābi'u*
	الثانية	*aθ-θāniyatu* (f)	8th	الثامن	*aθ-θāminu*
3rd	الثالث	*aθ-θāliθu*	9th	التاسع	*at-tāsi'u*
4th	الرابع	*ar-rābi'u*	10th	العاشر	*al-'āširu*

92.1 From '11th' through '19th,' the ordinals are indeclinable in *-a*. Both parts of the number agree in gender with the noun described.

MODIFYING MASCULINE NOUNS		MODIFYING FEMININE NOUNS	
الحادى عشر	*al-ḥādiya 'ašara*	الحادية عشرة	*al-ḥādiyata 'ašrata*
الثانى عشر	*aθ-θāniya 'ašara*	الثانية عشرة	*aθ-θāniyata 'ašrata*
الثالث عشر	*aθ-θāliθa 'ašara*	الثالثة عشرة	*aθ-θāliθata 'ašrata*
الرابع عشر	*ar-rābi'a 'ašara*	الرابعة عشرة	*ar-rābi'ata 'ašrata*

and so on.

92.2 The ordinals from '1st' through '10th' may be (1) the first member of a construct phrase followed by a plural, as

| هو رابع الرجال | *huwa rābi'u r-rijāli* | He is the fourth of the men. |
| هى خامستهن | *hiya xāmisatuhunna* | She is the fifth of them. |

or (2) a regular attributive adjective following the modified noun.

| الجزء السابع | *al-juz'u s-sābi'u* | the seventh section |
| فى جزءين الرابع والخامس | *fi l-juz'ayni r-rābi'i wal-xāmisi* | in the fourth and fifth sections |

92.3 From '11th' on, the ordinals must follow the nouns they modify as attributive adjectives. From '11th' through '19th,' the ordinals are indeclinable. From '20th' on, the units are fully declinable and the tens are identical to the cardinal tens.

الجزء الرابع عشر	*al-juz'u r-rābi'a̱ 'ašara̱*	the 14th section
فى الليلة التاسعة عشرة	*fi l-laylati t-tāsi'ata̱ 'ašrata̱*	on the 19th night
الجزء الحادى والعشرون	*al-juz'u l-ḥādī wal-'išrūna*	the 21st section
فى الجزء التاسع والعشرين	*fi l-juz'i t-tāsi'i̱ wal-'išrī̱na*	in the 29th section

93 Fractions. From 'a third' through 'a tenth,' the fractions are formed on the pattern FUʿUL- (exclusively in Koranic Arabic) or FUʿL- (more common in post-Koranic). The plural of both is on the pattern ʾAFʿĀL-. As in most languages, 'half' is a suppletion form and has nothing to do with the number 'two.'

1/2	نصف	*niṣf-*	3/4	ثلاثة ارباع	*θalāθatu 'arbā'in*
1/3	ثلث	*θul(u)θ-*	5/6	خمسة اسداس	*xamsatu 'asdāsin*
2/3	ثلثان	*θul(u)θāni*	7/10	سبعة اعشار	*sab'atu 'a'šarin*

| ربع الارض المسكون | *rub'u l-'arḍi l-maskūnu* | the inhabited quarter of the earth |

فى ثلثى الجزء	*fī θul(u)θayi l-juz'i*	in two thirds of the section

Above 'a tenth,' fractions must be expressed periphrastically.

وزعموا ان جرم القمر جزء من تسعة وثلاثين جزءاً وربع جزء من جرم الارض	*wa-za amū 'anna jirma l-qamari juz'un min tis'atin wa-θalāθīna juz'an wa-rub'i juz'in min jirmi l-'arḍi*	And they have asserted that the mass of the moon is one part of $39^1/_4$ parts of the earth's mass (i.e., $^1/_{39.25}$ of the earth's mass).

94 Distributives. The distributive numbers from 'three by three' up to 'ten by ten' are formed on the diptote pattern FU'ĀLU. 'Two by two' is an exceptional form, *maθnā*.

فدخلوا مثنى وثلاث ورباع	*fa-daxalū maθnā wa-θulāθa wa-rubā'a*	And they entered two by two, three by three, and four by four.

95 The Islamic Calendar. The Hegira Era begins with the migration *(hijrat-)* of the Prophet Muhammad from Mecca to Medina in A.D. 622. The Islamic year is based on the old Arabian succession of twelve lunar months, which are:

محرم	*muḥarram-*	رجب	*rajab-*
صفر	*ṣafar-*	شعبان	*ša'bānu*
ربيع الاول	*rabī'u l-'awwalu*	رمضان	*ramaḍānu*
ربيع الثانى	*rabī'u θ-θānī*	شوال	*šawwālu*
جمادى الاولى	*jumāda l-'ūlā*	ذو القعدة	*ðu l-qa'dati*
جمادى الآخرة	*jumāda l-'āxiratu*	ذو الحجة	*ðu l-ḥijjati*

Since the year is lunar, it bears no readily discernable relation to the solar year and falls $11^1/_4$ days short of the solar year annually. The formulae for conversion are:

$$\text{A.D.} = (\text{A.H.} \times 0.970225) + 621.54$$

$$\text{A.H.} = (\text{A.D.} - 621.54) \div 0.970225$$

For the Syro-Mesopotamian months and the days of the week, see Appendix H.

Vocabulary

VERBS

حج *ḥajja (u) ḥajj-* make the pilgrimage to Mecca

دفع *dafaʻa (a) dafʻ-* push away, repel

زيد *zāda (ī) ziyādat-* be more (*ʻalā* than), increase (int.); II *zayyada* increase (trs.); VIII *izdāda* grow, multiply

طاب *ṭāba (ī) ṭībat-* be good, pleasant

وصى II *waṣṣā* & IV *'awṣā* charge (*bi-* with), recommend; bequeath *(bi-)* something (*li-* to)

وقع *waqaʻa (a) wuqūʻ-* befall, occur, fall down

NOUNS

انثى *'unθā* female

جزء/اجزاء *juz'-* pl *'ajzā'-* part, section

ذكر *ðakar-* male

طيب *ṭayyib-* good, pleasant, agreeable; *ṭīb-* perfume, pleasant aroma

نصف *niṣf-* half

وصية/وصايا *waṣīyat-* pl *waṣāyā* bequest, legacy; directive, commandment

Exercises

(a) Read and translate:

١ لقد كفر الذين قالوا ان الله ثالث ثلاثة.

٢ قال النبى «حُبِّبَ الىّ من دنياكم ثلاث - الطيب والنساء وجُعلت قرة عينى فى الصلاة».

٣ وان خفتم ألا تقسطوا فى اليتامى فانكحوا ما طاب لكم من النساء مثنى وثلاث ورباع.[1]

٤ يستعجلونك بالعذاب ولن يخلف الله وعده وان يوماً عند ربكم كألف

---

[1] *'Aqsaṭa fī* be equitable to.

سنة مما تعدّون.

٥ سأل سائل بعذاب واقع للكافرين - ليس له دافع من الله ذى المعارج - تعرج الملائكة والروح اليه فى يوم كان مقداره خمسين الف سنة فاصبر صبراً جميلاً إنهم يرونه بعيداً ونراه قريباً- يوم تكون السماء كالمهل وتكون الجبال كالعهن.[1]

٦ يوصيكم الله فى اولادكم - للذكر مثل حظ الانثيين. فإن كنّ نساء فوق اثنتين فلهم ثلثا ما ترك. وإن كانت واحدة فلها النصف. ولأبويه لكل واحد منهما السدس مما ترك إن كان له ولد. فإن لم يكن له ولد وورثه ابواه فلأمه الثلث. فإن كان له اخوة فلأمه السدس من بعد وصية يوصى بها ودين.[2]

٧ ولكم نصف ما ترك ازواجكم إن لم يكن لهن ولد. فإن كان لهن ولد فلكم الربع مما تركن من بعد وصية يوصين بها او دين. ولهن الربع مما تركتم إن لم يكن لكم ولد. فإن كان لكم ولد فلهن الثمن مما تركتم من بعد وصية توصون بها او دين. وإن كان رجل يورث كلالة او امرأة وله اخ او اخت فلكل واحد منهما السدس. فإن كانوا اكثر من ذلك فهم شركاء فى الثلث من بعد وصية يوصى بها ودين غير مضارّ - وصيةً من الله والله عليم حكيم.[3]

---

[1]*Ma'raj-/ma'āriju* height; *'araja (u)* ascend; *muhl-* molten metal; *'ihn-* tufts of wool.

[2]*Ḥaẓẓ-* portion; *dayn-* debt.

[3]*Kalālat-* distant heir.

Supplementary Readings from the *Hadith* Literature

(Glossed words marked with asterisks)

I. The First Three Sent to Hell

عن* ابى هريرة (رضى الله عنه) عن النبى (صلى الله عليه وسلم) قال ان الله تبارك وتعالى اذا كان يوم القيامة ينزل الى العباد ليقضى بينهم وكل امة جاثية* فأول من يدعونه رجل جمع* القرآن ورجل قُتل فى سبيل الله ورجل كثير المال. فيقول الله للقارئ «ألم أعلّمك ما أنزلتُ على رسولى؟» قال «بلى يا رب» قال «فماذا عملت فيما* علمت؟» قال «كنت أقوم به آناء* الليل وآناء النهار» فيقول الله له «كذبت» وتقول له الملائكة «كذبت» ويقول الله «بل أردت أن يقال إن فلاناً قارئ فقد قيل ذاك*»

فيؤتى بصاحب المال فيقول الله له «ألم أوسّع عليك حتى لم أدعْك تحتاج* الى احد؟» قال «بلى يا رب» قال «فما عملت فيما آتيتك؟» قال «كنت أصل الرحم* وأتصدق» فيقول الله له «كذبت» وتقول له الملائكة «كذبت» ويقول الله تعالى «بل اردت ان يقال فلان جواد*، فقد قيل ذاك»

'an in a *hadith* indicates a transmitter
jaθā (ū) bend the knee
jama'a (a) l-qur'āna memorize the Koran
fīmā = fī mā with regards to that which
'ānā'a throughout
ðāka variant of *ðālika*
wada'a (a) let (+ imperf. ind.)
iḥtāja 'ilā be in need of
waṣala (i) r-raḥima maintain family ties
jawād- generous

ويؤتى بالذى قُتل فى سبيل الله فيقول الله له «فيماذا قُتلت؟» فيقول «أُمرتُ بالجهاد* فى سبيلك فقاتلت حتى قتلت» فيقول الله تعالى له «كذبت» وتقول له الملائكة «كذبت» ويقول الله «بل اردت ان يقال فلان جرىء* فقد قيل ذاك»

ثم ضرب رسول الله صلى الله عليه وسلم على ركبتى* فقال «يا ابا هريرة اولئك الثلاثة اول خلق الله تسعّر* بهم النار يوم القيامة.»

jihād- holy war
jarī' - bold, courageous
rukbat- knee
tasa''ara (issa''ara, see §67.3) *bi*- be kindled with

II. Intercession on Judgment Day

عن آنس (رضى الله عنه) عن النبى (صلى الله عليه وسلم) قال: يجتمع* المؤمنون يوم القيامة فيقولون «لو* استشفعنا* الى ربنا» فيأتون آدم فيقولون «انت ابو الناس. خلقك الله بيده واسجد لك ملائكته وعلّمك اسماء كل شىء فاشفع* لنا عند ربك حتى يريحنا* من مكاننا هذا» فيقول «لست هناكم*» ويذكر ذنبه فيستحيى* فيقول «اؤتوا نوحاً فانه اول رسول بعثه الله الى اهل الارض» فيأتونه فيقول «لست هناكم. اؤتوا موسى عبدالله كلّمه الله واعطاه التوراة» فيأتونه فيقول «لست هناكم» ويذكر قتل النفس بغير نفس* فيستحيى من ربه فيقول «اؤتوا عيسى عبد الله ورسوله وكلمة الله وروحه» فيأتونه فيقول «لست هناكم. اؤتوا محمداً صلى الله عليه وسلم

ijtama'a be gathered
law (optative) "if only we could"
istašfa'a 'ilā seek intercession with
šafa'a (a) intercede
'arāḥa relieve
lastu hunākum "I'm not in a position to help you" (for the *-kum* ending on *hunāka* "there," see p. 110, note 3)
istaḥyā be ashamed
xalīl- friend (*Xalīlu llāhi* is Abraham's epithet)
qatlu n-nafsi bi-ğayri nafsin "to take a life other than in compensation for another" (for the circumstances of Moses' murder of an Egyptian, see Kor. 28:15–19)

عبداً غفر الله له ما تقدم من ذنبه وما تاخر*» فيأتوننى* فانطلق حتى أستأذن على ربى فيؤذن. فاذا رايت ربى وقعت* ساجداً فيدعنى* ما شاء الله. ثم يقال «ارفع* رأسك وسل* ، تُعطَه. وقل ، يُسمعْ. واشفع، تُشفَعْ.» فأرفع راسى فاحمَده* بتحميد يعلّمنيه ثم أشفع فيحدّ* لى حداً فادخلهم الجنة. ثم أعود اليه فاذا رأيت ربى مثله ثم أشفع فيحدّ لى حداً فأدخلهم الجنة. ثم أعود الثالثة ثم أعود الرابعة فأقول «ما بقى* فى النار إلا من حبسه* القرآن ووجب* عليه الخلود.»

mā taqaddama min ðambihi wa-mā ta'axxara "his sins past and future" (see §89)
ya'tūnanī the Prophet is speaking here
waqa'a (a) fall down
wada'a (a) allow
rafa'a (a) raise
sal (alternative imperative of *sa'ala*).
The three constructions that follow are conditionals in which the protasis is imperative.
ḥamida (a) praise; *ḥammada* extol
ḥadda (u) ḥadd- limit
baqiya (ā) remain
ḥabasa (i) confine, keep back
wajaba (i) 'alā be incumbent upon

III. The Prophet's Ascension to Heaven

حدثنا شَيبان بن فَرُّوخ. حدثنا حمّاد بن سَلَمة. حدثنا ثابت البُنانى عن أنَس بن مالك ان رسول الله صلى الله عليه وسلم قال: أتيت بالبراق* وهو دابة ابيض طويل* فوق الحمار* ودون البغل* يضع حافره عند منتهى طرفه*. قال فركبته* حتى أتيت

burāq- Buraq, the mythical animal on which the Prophet ascended into heaven; it is often depicted as a winged horse with with head of a human female
ṭawīl- tall
ḥimār- donkey
baġl- mule
ḥāfir- hoof
yaḍa'u ḥāfirahu 'inda muntahā ṭarfihi "which in one step could go as far as it could see"
rakiba (a) ride, mount

بيت المقدس*. قال فربطته* بالحلقة* التى يربط بها الانبياء. قال ثم دخلت المسجد فصلّيت فيه ركعتين*. ثم خرجت فجاءنى جبريل عليه السلام بإناء* من خمر* واناء من لبن* فاخترت اللبن فقال جبريل «اخترت الفطرة*»

ثم عرج* بنا الى السماء الاولى فاستفتح* جبريل فقيل له «من انت؟» قال «جبريل» قيل «ومن معك؟» قال «محمد» قيل «وقد بُعث اليه؟» قال «قد بعث اليه» ففُتح* لنا فاذا انا بآدم فرحّب* بى ودعا لى بخير.

ثم عرج بنا الى السماء الثانية فاستفتح جبريل عليه السلام فقيل «من انت؟» قال «جبريل» قيل «ومن معك؟» قال «محمد» قيل «وقد بعث اليه؟» قال «قد بعث اليه» ففتح لنا فاذا انا بابنى الخالة* عيسى ابن مريم ويحيى* بن زكرياء صلوات الله عليهما فرحّبا ودعوا لى بخير.

ثم عرج بى الى السماء الثالثة فاستفتح جبريل عليه السلام فقيل «من انت؟» قال «جبريل» قيل «ومن معك؟» قال «محمد» قيل «وقد بعث اليه؟» قال «قد بعث اليه» ففتح لنا فاذا انا بيوسف اذا هو قد أُعطى شطر الحسن* فرحّب ودعا لى بخير.

ثم عرج بنا الى السماء الرابعة فاستفتح جبريل عليه السلام فقيل «من هذا؟» قال «جبريل» قيل «ومن معك؟» قال «محمد» قيل «وقد بعث اليه؟» قال «قد بعث اليه» ففتح لنا فاذا انا بادريس فرحب

baytu l-maqdisi Jerusalem
rabaṭa (i) tie
ḥalqat- (hitching) ring
rak'at- kneeling
'inā'- vessel
xamr- wine
laban- milk
fiṭrat- innate disposition (to Islam)
'araja (u) ascend
istaftaḥa ask for something to be opened, request admittance
fataḥa (a) open
raḥḥaba bi- welcome
xālat- maternal aunt (according to legend, John's mother Elizabeth was Mary's aunt; John and Jesus were thus maternal cousins)
Yaḥyā John
šaṭru l-ḥusn half of (all) beauty

ودعا لى بخير. قال الله عزّ وجلّ• وَرَفَعْناهُ مَكاناً عَلِيًّا (سورة مريم آية ٥٧).

ثم عرج بى الى السماء الخامسة فاستفتح جبريل. قيل «من انت؟» قال «جبريل» قيل «ومن معك؟» قال «محمد» قيل «وقد بعث اليه؟» قال «قد بعث اليه» ففتح لنا فاذا انا بهرون فرحب ودعا لى بخير.

ثم عرج بى الى السماء السادسة فاستفتح جبريل عليه السلام قيل «من هذا؟» قال «جبريل» قيل «ومن معك؟» قال «محمد» قيل «وقد بعث اليه؟» قال «قد بعث اليه» ففتح لنا فاذا انا بموسى فرحب ودعا لى بخير.

ثم عرج بى الى السماء السابعة فاستفتح جبريل فقيل «من هذا؟» قال «جبريل» قيل «ومن معك؟» قال «محمد» قيل «وقد بعث اليه؟» قال «قد بعث اليه» ففتح لنا فاذا انا بابرهيم مسنداً ظهره• الى البيت المعمور• واذا هو يدخله كل يوم سبعون الف ملك لا يعودون اليه.

ثم ذهب بى الى السدرة المنتهى• واذا ورقها كآذان الفيلة• واذا ثمرها• كالقلال•. قال فلما غشيها• من امر الله ما غشى تغيّرت• فما احد من خلق الله يستطيع أن ينعتها• من حسنها. فأوحى الله الىّ ما أوحى. ففرض• علىّ خمسين صلاة فى كل يوم وليلة.

فنزلت الى موسى فقال «ما فرض ربك على امتك؟» قلت «خمسين صلاة» قال «ارجع الى ربك فاسأله التخفيف• فإن امتك لا يطيقون•

'azza wa-jalla mighty and glorious is he
'asnada lean
ẓahr- back
al-baytu l-ma'mūru the prototype of the Ka'ba in heaven
as-sidratu l-muntahā the heavenly lote-tree
fīlat- elephant
θamar- fruit
qullat- pl *qilāl-* jug
ğašiya (ā) cover
tağayyara change (int.)
na'ata (a) describe
faraḍa (i) ordain, assign
xaffafa lighten, reduce
'aṭāqa bear, endure

ذلك فإني قد بلوت* بني اسرئيل وخبرتهم» قال فرجعت الى ربي فقلت «يا رب خفّف على امتي» فحط* عني خمساً فرجعت الى موسى فقلت «حط عني خمساً» قال «ان امتك لا يطيقون ذلك فارجع الى ربك فاسأله التخفيف»

قال فلم أزل أرجع بين ربي تبارك وتعالى وبين موسى عليه السلام حتى قال «يا محمد إنهن خمس صلوات كل يوم وليلة. لكل صلاة عشر فذلك خمسون صلاة. ومن همّ* بحسنة فلم يعملها كُتبت له حسنةً، فإن عملها كتبت له عشراً. ومن هم* بسيئة فلم يعملها لم يُكتب شيئاً فإن عملها كتبت سيئةً واحدة»

قال فنزلت حتى انتهيت* الى موسى فأخبرته فقال «ارجع الى ربك فاسأله التخفيف» فقال رسول الله «فقلت قد رجعت الى ربي حتى استحييت* منه»

balā (ū) put to the test
ḥaṭṭa (u) decrease, reduce
hamma (u) bi- intend
intahā 'ilā reach
istaḥyā be ashamed

Appendix A

BROKEN PLURAL TYPES

Classed by Singular (See Locator Index, p. 263)

1. Singular FA‘L-

1a. plural ’AF‘ĀL-

انف/آناف   رب/ارباب   قول/اقوال   نهر/انهار

حي/احياء   زوج/ازواج   قوم/اقوام   يوم/ايّام

خير/اخيار   شيء/اشياءُ   موت/اموات

1b. plural FU‘ŪL-

امر/امور   شمس/شموس   عين/عيون   نجم/نجوم

انف/انوف   شهر/شهور   غيب/غيوب   نفس/نفوس

بيت/بيوت   شيخ/شيوخ   قلب/قلوب   وجه/وجوه

حق/حقوق   عقل/عقول   كنز/كنوز

1c. plural FI‘ĀL-   عبد/عباد   مرة/مرار

1d. plural ’AF‘UL-   شهر/اشهر   نجم/انجم   نهر/انهر

عين/اعين   نفس/انفس   يد/ايدٍ

1e. plural FAWĀ‘ILU   امر/اوامر

2. **Singular FA‘AL- (FA‘IL-/FA‘UL-/FU‘UL-; FĀL- for C_2w)**

2a. plural ’AF‘ĀL- (’Ā‘ĀL- for C_1’)   اجل/آجال   اذن/آذان

احد/آحاد   باب/ابواب

بصر/ابصار　صنم/اصنام　قمر/اقمار　نبأ/انباء

حجر/احجار　عام/اعوام　مال/اموال　هوى/اهواء

خبر/اخبار　عدد/اعداد　مثل/امثال　ورق/اوراق

ذكر/اذكار　عقب/اعقاب　مرض/امراض　ولد/اولاد

شجر/اشجار　عمل/اعمال　مطر/امطار

2b. plural FI'ĀL-　جبل/جبال　رجل/رجال　ماء/مياه

2c. plural FU'ŪL-　ملك/ملوك

3. Singular FU'L-/FI'L-/FA'L-

3a. plural FU'AL-/FI'AL-　امة/امم　قصة/قصص

فرقة/فرق　قرية/قرى　قوة/قوى　ملة/ملل

3b. plural 'AF'ĀL-

جسم/اجسام　حكم/احكام　دين/اديان　قبل/اقبال

جزء/اجزاء　حين/احيان　روح/ارواح　مثل/امثال

حزن/احزان　دبر/ادبار　سن/اسنان　نور/انوار

3b. plural FU'ŪL-　برج/بروج　علم/علوم

4. Singular FĀ'IL- (FĀ'AL-)

4a. plural FU''ĀL-　حاكم/حكام　كافر/كفار

4b. plural FAWĀ'ILU　آخرة/اواخر　طائفة/طوائف

دابة/دواب　عالم/عوالم　فاكهة/فواكه　آدم/اوادم

4c. plural 'AF'ĀL-　صاحب/اصحاب

4d. plural FU'ĀT-　داعٍ/دعاة　قاضٍ/قضاة

5. Singular FA'ĪL-

5a. plural FI'ĀL-　صغير/صغار　قليل/قلال　كثير/كثار

عظيم/عظام　كبير/كبار　كريم/كرام

5b. plural FU'ALĀ'U

بريء/برآء   شهيد/شهداء   غريب/غرباء   كريم/كرماء
شريك/شركاء   عليم/علماء   فقير/فقراء   وكيل/وكلاء

5c. plural FU‘UL-   جديد/جدد   سبيل/سبل   مدينة/مدن

5d. plural ’AF‘ILĀ’U (’AFILLĀ’U for doubled roots)

بريء/ابرياء   عزيز/اعزاء   قوى/اقوياء
تقى/اتقياء   غنى/اغنياء   نبى/انبياء
شديد/اشداء   قليل/اقلاء   ولى/اولياء

5e. plural FA‘Ā’ILU (for singular FA‘ĪLAT-)   حديقة/حدائق
خليقة/خلائق   صغيرة/صغائر   عظيمة/عظائم   مدينة/مدائن

5f. plural FA‘LĀ   قتيل/قتلى   مريض/مرضى   ميّت/موتى

5g. plural FA‘ĀLĀ   خطيئة/خطايا   وصية/وصايا   يتيم/يتامى

5h. plural ’AF‘ĀL-   يتيم/ايتام   يمين/ايمان

5i. plural ’AFĀ‘ĪLU-   حديث/احاديث

5j. plural ’AFILLAT-   ذليل/اذلة   عزيز/اعزة

6. Singular FI‘ĀL-/FA‘ĀL-/FU‘ĀL-

6a. plural ’AF‘ILAT-   اله/آلهة   سؤال/اسئلة
دعاء/ادعية   طعام/اطعمة   عذاب/اعذبة
سلاح/اسلحة   مكان/امكنة   متاع/امتعة

6b. plural FA‘Ā’ILU   بضاعة/بضائع

6c. plural FU‘UL-   كتاب/كتب

6d. plural ’AFĀ‘ILU   مكان/اماكن

7. Singular FA‘ŪL-

7a. plural ’AF‘ĀL-   عدو/اعداء

7b. plural FU‘UL-   رسول/رسل

8. Singular 'AF'ALU (m), FA'LĀ'U (f), pl FU'L- for colors/defects

ابكم/بكم   احمر/حمر   اسود/سود   اعمى/عمى
ابيض/بيض   اخضر/خضر   اصم/صم

9. Singular 'AF'ALU (m), FU'LĀ (f) for all elatives

9a. masc. plural 'AFĀ'ILU and/or 'AF'ALŪNA   آخَر/آخرون
اكبر/اكابر اكبرون

9b. fem. plural FU'AL- and/or FU'LAYĀT-   اخرى/اخريات
كبرى/كبر كبريات

10. Anomalous noun types

10a. apparently biliteral in singular, C_3 obscured in plural 'AF'Ā'-

اسم/اسماء   اب/آباء   ابن/ابناء

10b. apparently biliteral in singular, FI'LAT- in plural اخ/اخوة

10c. plural FI'LĀN-   اخ/اخوان   نار/نيران

10d. anomalous feminine plurals in -ĀT-
اخت/اخوات   ام/امهات   بنت/بنات

10e. anomalous plurals in 'AFĀ'IN / FA'ĀLIN

ارض/اراضٍ   اهل/اهالٍ   يد/اياد
اسم/اسامٍ   ليلة/ليالٍ

10f. C_3 obscured in singular, plural FA'AWĀT-   زكاة/زكوات
صلاة/صلوات   سنة/سنوات

Quadriliteral Types

11. Plural FA'ĀLILU / MAFĀ'ILU, for all quadriliteral singulars with *short* vowel between C_3 and C_4.

اصبع/اصابع   كوكب/كواكب   فتوى/فتاوٍ   مولى/موالٍ

ملك (ملأك) / ملائك ، ملائكة

12. Plural FA'ĀLĪLU / MAFĀ'ĪLU, for all quadriliteral singulars with *long* vowel between C_3 and C_4.

سلطان / سلاطين　　　مسكين / مساكين قربان / قرابين
شيطان / شياطين

Locator Index for Broken-Plural Types

I. Triptote Types

أفعال 'AF'ĀL- 1a, 2a, 3b, 4c, 5h, 7a, 10e
أفعل 'AF'UL- 1d
أفعلة 'AF'ILAT- 6a
أفلّة 'AFILLAT- 5j
فعال FI'ĀL- 1c, 2b, 5a
فعّال FU''ĀL- 4a
فعل FI'AL-/FU'AL- 3a, 9b
فعل FU'L- 8
فعل FU'UL- 5c, 6c, 7b
فعلان FI'LĀN- 10c
فعلة FI'LAT- 10b
فعول FU'ŪL- 1b, 2c, 3c

II. Diptote Types

أفاعٍ 'AFĀ'IN 10e
أفاعل 'AFĀ'ILU 6d, 9a
أفاعيل 'AFĀ'ĪLU 5i
أفعلاء 'AF'ILĀ'U 5d
فعالٍ FA'ĀLIN 10e
فعالل FA'ĀLILU 11
فعاليل FA'ĀLĪLU 12
فعائل FA'Ā'ILU 5e, 6b
فعلاء FU'ALĀ'U 5b
فواعل FAWĀ'ILU 1e, 4b
مفاعل MAFĀ'ILU 11
مفاعيل MAFĀ'ĪLU 12

III. Indeclinable Types

فعالى FA'ĀLĀ 5g
فعلى FA'LĀ 5f

Appendix B

The Inflection of Weak-*lam*, Hollow and Geminate Verbs

		Weak-*lām* I	Weak-*lām* II	Weak-*lām* III	Hollow	Geminate
Perfect						
Singular	3 m	رَمَى	لَقِيَ	دَعَا	قَالَ	دَلَّ
	f	رَمَتْ	لَقِيَتْ	دَعَتْ	قَالَتْ	دَلَّتْ
	2 m	رَمَيْتَ	لَقِيتَ	دَعَوْتَ	قُلْتَ	دَلَلْتَ
	f	رَمَيْتِ	لَقِيتِ	دَعَوْتِ	قُلْتِ	دَلَلْتِ
	1 c	رَمَيْتُ	لَقِيتُ	دَعَوْتُ	قُلْتُ	دَلَلْتُ
Dual	3 m	رَمَيَا	لَقِيَا	دَعَوَا	قَالَا	دَلَّا
	f	رَمَتَا	لَقِيَتَا	دَعَتَا	قَالَتَا	دَلَّتَا
	2 c	رَمَيْتُمَا	لَقِيتُمَا	دَعَوْتُمَا	قُلْتُمَا	دَلَلْتُمَا
Plural	3 m	رَمَوْا	لَقُوا	دَعَوْا	قَالُوا	دَلُّوا
	f	رَمَيْنَ	لَقِينَ	دَعَوْنَ	قُلْنَ	دَلَلْنَ
	2 m	رَمَيْتُمْ	لَقِيتُمْ	دَعَوْتُمْ	قُلْتُمْ	دَلَلْتُمْ
	f	رَمَيْتُنَّ	لَقِيتُنَّ	دَعَوْتُنَّ	قُلْتُنَّ	دَلَلْتُنَّ
	1 c	رَمَيْنَا	لَقِينَا	دَعَوْنَا	قُلْنَا	دَلَلْنَا
Imperfect Indicative						
Singular	3 m	يَرْمِي	يَلْقَى	يَدْعُو	يَقُولُ	يَدُلُّ
	f	تَرْمِي	تَلْقَى	تَدْعُو	تَقُولُ	تَدُلُّ
	2 m	تَرْمِي	تَلْقَى	تَدْعُو	تَقُولُ	تَدُلُّ
	f	تَرْمِينَ	تَلْقَيْنَ	تَدْعِينَ	تَقُولِينَ	تَدُلِّينَ
	1 c	أَرْمِي	أَلْقَى	أَدْعُو	أَقُولُ	أَدُلُّ
Dual	3 m	يَرْمِيَانِ	يَلْقَيَانِ	يَدْعُوَانِ	يَقُولَانِ	يَدُلَّانِ
	f	تَرْمِيَانِ	تَلْقَيَانِ	تَدْعُوَانِ	تَقُولَانِ	تَدُلَّانِ

	2 c	تَرْمِيَانِ	تَلْقَيَانِ	تَدْعُوَانِ	تَقُولَانِ	تَدُلَّانِ
Plural	3 m	يَرْمُونَ	يَلْقَوْنَ	يَدْعُونَ	يَقُولُونَ	يَدُلُّونَ
	f	يَرْمِينَ	يَلْقَيْنَ	يَدْعُونَ	يَقُلْنَ	يَدْلُلْنَ
	2 m	تَرْمُونَ	تَلْقَوْنَ	تَدْعُونَ	تَقُولُونَ	تَدُلُّونَ
	f	تَرْمِينَ	تَلْقَيْنَ	تَدْعُونَ	تَقُلْنَ	تَدْلُلْنَ
	1 c	نَرْمِي	نَلْقَى	نَدْعُو	نَقُولُ	نَدُلُّ

Subjunctive

Singular	3 m	يَرْمِيَ	يَلْقَى	يَدْعُوَ	يَقُولَ	يَدُلَّ
	f	تَرْمِيَ	تَلْقَى	تَدْعُوَ	تَقُولَ	تَدُلَّ
	2 m	تَرْمِيَ	تَلْقَى	تَدْعُوَ	تَقُولَ	تَدُلَّ
	f	تَرْمِي	تَلْقَيْ	تَدْعِي	تَقُولِي	تَدُلِّي
	1 c	اَرْمِيَ	اَلْقَى	اَدْعُوَ	اَقُولَ	اَدُلَّ
Dual	3 m	يَرْمِيَا	يَلْقَيَا	يَدْعُوَا	يَقُولَا	يَدُلَّا
	f	تَرْمِيَا	تَلْقَيَا	تَدْعُوَا	تَقُولَا	تَدُلَّا
	2 c	تَرْمِيَا	تَلْقَيَا	تَدْعُوَا	تَقُولَا	تَدُلَّا
Plural	3 m	يَرْمُوا	يَلْقَوْا :	يَدْعُوا	يَقُولُوا	يَدُلُّوا
	f	يَرْمِينَ	يَلْقَيْنَ	يَدْعُونَ	يَقُلْنَ	يَدْلُلْنَ
	2 m	تَرْمُوا	تَلْقَوْا	تَدْعُوا	تَقُولُوا	تَدُلُّوا
	f	تَرْمِينَ	تَلْقَيْنَ	تَدْعُونَ	تَقُلْنَ	تَدْلُلْنَ
	1 c	نَرْمِيَ	نَلْقَى	نَدْعُوَ	نَقُولَ	نَدُلَّ

Jussive

Singular	3 m	يَرْمِ	يَلْقَ	يَدْعُ	يَقُلْ	يَدُلَّ/يَدْلُلْ
	f	تَرْمِ	تَلْقَ	تَدْعُ	تَقُلْ	تَدُلَّ/تَدْلُلْ
	2 m	تَرْمِ	تَلْقَ	تَدْعُ	تَقُلْ	تَدُلَّ/تَدْلُلْ
	f	تَرْمِي	تَلْقَيْ	تَدْعِي	تَقُولِي	تَدُلِّي
	1 c	اَرْمِ	اَلْقَ	اَدْعُ	اَقُلْ	اَدُلَّ/اَدْلُلْ
Dual	3 m	يَرْمِيَا	يَلْقَيَا	يَدْعُوَا	يَقُولَا	يَدُلَّا
	f	تَرْمِيَا	تَلْقَيَا	تَدْعُوَا	تَقُولَا	تَدُلَّا

	2 c	تَرْمِيَا	تَلْقَيَا	تَدْعُوَا	تَقُولاَ	تَدُلاَّ
Plural	3 m	يَرْمُوا	يَلْقَوْا	يَدْعُوا	يَقُولُوا	يَدُلُّوا
	f	يَرْمِينَ	يَلْقَيْنَ	يَدْعُونَ	يَقُلْنَ	يَدْلُلْنَ
	2 m	تَرْمُوا	تَلْقَوْا	تَدْعُوا	تَقُولُوا	تَدُلُّوا
	f	تَرْمِينَ	تَلْقَيْنَ	تَدْعُونَ	تَقُلْنَ	تَدْلُلْنَ
	1 c	نَرْمِ	نَلْقَ	نَدْعُ	نَقُلْ	نَدُلَّ/نَدْلُلْ

Imperative

Singular	m	اِرْمِ	اِلْقَ	اُدْعُ	قُلْ	دُلَّ/اُدْلُلْ
	f	اِرْمِي	اِلْقَيْ	اُدْعِي	قُولِي	دُلِّي
Dual		اِرْمِيَا	اِلْقَيَا	اُدْعُوَا	قُولاَ	دُلاَّ
Plural	m	اِرْمُوا	اِلْقَوْا	اُدْعُوا	قُولُوا	دُلُّوا
	f	اِرْمِينَ	اِلْقَيْنَ	اُدْعُونَ	قُلْنَ	اُدْلُلْنَ

Passive

Perfect	رُمِيَ	لُقِيَ	دُعِيَ	قِيلَ	دُلَّ (دُلِلْتَ)
Imperfect	يُرْمَى	يُلْقَى	يُدْعَى	يُقَالُ	يُدَلُّ

Active Participles

Singular masc.	رَامٍ	لاَقٍ	دَاعٍ	قَائِلٌ	دَالٌّ
Singular fem.	رَامِيَةٌ	لاَقِيَةٌ	دَاعِيَةٌ	قَائِلَةٌ	دَالَّةٌ
Dual masc.	رَامِيَانِ	لاَقِيَانِ	دَاعِيَانِ	قَائِلاَنِ	دَالاَّنِ
Dual fem.	رَامِيَتَانِ	لاَقِيَتَانِ	دَاعِيَتَانِ	قَائِلَتَانِ	دَالَّتَانِ
Plural masc.	رَامُونَ	لاَقُونَ	دَاعُونَ	قَائِلُونَ	دَالُّونَ
Plural fem.	رَامِيَاتٌ	لاَقِيَاتٌ	دَاعِيَاتٌ	قَائِلاَتٌ	دَالاَّتٌ

Passive Participles

masc. sing.	مَرْمِيٌّ	مَلْقِيٌّ	مَدْعُوٌّ	مَقُولٌ	مَدْلُولٌ
fem. sing.	مَرْمِيَّةٌ	مَلْقِيَّةٌ	مَدْعُوَّةٌ	مَقُولَةٌ	مَدْلُولَةٌ

masc. dual	مَرْمِيَّانِ	مُلْقِيَانِ	مَدْعُوَّانِ	مَقُولَانِ	مَدْلُولَانِ
fem. dual	مَرْمِيَّتَانِ	مُلْقِيَتَانِ	مَدْعُوَّتَانِ	مَقُولَتَانِ	مَدْلُولَتَانِ
masc. pl.	مَرْمِيُّونَ	مُلْقِيُونَ	مَدْعُوُّونَ	مَقُولُونَ	مَدْلُولُونَ
fem. pl.	مَرْمِيَّاتٌ	مُلْقِيَاتٌ	مَدْعُوَّاتٌ	مَقُولَاتٌ	مَدْلُولَاتٌ

Appendix C: Synopses of the Increased Forms

ROOT TYPE	FORM II	FORM III	FORM IV	FORM V	FORM VI	FORM VII	FORM VIII	FORM IX	FORM X
1. Sound Triliteral									
perf. act.	قَتَّلَ	قَاتَلَ	أَقْتَلَ	تَقَتَّلَ	تَقَاتَلَ	اِنْقَتَلَ	اِقْتَتَلَ	اِقْتَلَّ	اِسْتَقْتَلَ
perf. pass.	قُتِّلَ	قُوتِلَ	أُقْتِلَ	تُقُتِّلَ	تُقُوتِلَ	—	اُقْتُتِلَ	—	اُسْتُقْتِلَ
impf. act.	يُقَتِّلُ	يُقَاتِلُ	يُقْتِلُ	يَتَقَتَّلُ	يَتَقَاتَلُ	يَنْقَتِلُ	يَقْتَتِلُ	يَقْتَلُّ	يَسْتَقْتِلُ
impf. pass.	يُقَتَّلُ	يُقَاتَلُ	يُقْتَلُ	يُتَقَتَّلُ	يُتَقَاتَلُ	—	يُقْتَتَلُ	—	يُسْتَقْتَلُ
subj. act.	يُقَتِّلَ	يُقَاتِلَ	يُقْتِلَ	يَتَقَتَّلَ	يَتَقَاتَلَ	يَنْقَتِلَ	يَقْتَتِلَ	يَقْتَلَّ	يَسْتَقْتِلَ
juss. act.	يُقَتِّلْ	يُقَاتِلْ	يُقْتِلْ	يَتَقَتَّلْ	يَتَقَاتَلْ	يَنْقَتِلْ	يَقْتَتِلْ	يَقْتَلَّ يَقْتَلِلْ	يَسْتَقْتِلْ
impt.	قَتِّلْ	قَاتِلْ	أَقْتِلْ	تَقَتَّلْ	تَقَاتَلْ	اِنْقَتِلْ	اِقْتَتِلْ	اِقْتَلَّ	اِسْتَقْتِلْ
act. part.	مُقَتِّلٌ	مُقَاتِلٌ	مُقْتِلٌ	مُتَقَتِّلٌ	مُتَقَاتِلٌ	مُنْقَتِلٌ	مُقْتَتِلٌ	مُقْتَلٌّ	مُسْتَقْتِلٌ

pass. part.	مُقَتَّلٌ	مُقاتَلٌ	مُقْتَلٌ	مُتَقَتَّلٌ	مُتَقاتَلٌ	—	مُقْتَتَلٌ	—	مُسْتَقْتَلٌ
noun	تَقْتِيلٌ	مُقاتَلَةٌ قِتالٌ	إِقْتالٌ	تَقَتُّلٌ	تَقاتُلٌ	اِنْقِتالٌ	اِقْتِتالٌ	اِقْتِلالٌ	اِسْتِقْتالٌ

2. Initial *hamza*

perf. act.	أَنَّسَ	آنَسَ	آنَسَ	تَأَنَّسَ	تَآنَسَ	—	اِئْتَنَسَ	—	اِسْتَأْنَسَ
impf. act.	يُؤَنِّسُ	يُؤانِسُ	يُؤْنِسُ	يَتَأَنَّسُ	يَتَآنَسُ	—	يَأْتَنِسُ	—	يَسْتَأْنِسُ
impt.	أَنِّسْ	آنِسْ	آنِس	تَأَنَّسْ	تَآنَسْ	—	اِئْتَنِسْ	—	اِسْتَأْنِسْ
act. part.	مُؤَنِّسٌ	مُؤانِسٌ	مُؤْنِسٌ	مُتَأَنِّسٌ	مُتَآنِسٌ	—	مُؤْتَنِسٌ	—	مُسْتَأْنِسٌ
noun	تَأْنِيسٌ	مُؤانَسَةٌ إِناسٌ	إِيناسٌ	تَأَنُّسٌ	تَآنُسٌ	—	اِئْتِناسٌ	—	اِسْتِئْناسٌ

3. Initial *wâw* (C_1w)

perf. act.	وَفَّقَ	وافَقَ	أَوْفَقَ	تَوَفَّقَ	تَوافَقَ	—	اِتَّفَقَ	—	اِسْتَوْفَقَ
impf. act.	يُوَفِّقُ	يُوافِقُ	يُوفِقُ	يَتَوَفَّقُ	يَتَوافَقُ	—	يَتَّفِقُ	—	يَسْتَوْفِقُ

impt.	وَفِّقْ	وافِقْ	أَوْفِقْ	تَوَفَّقْ	تَوافَقْ	—	اِتَّفِقْ	—	اِسْتَوْفِقْ
act. part.	مُوَفِّقٌ	مُوافِقٌ	مُوفِقٌ	مُتَوَفِّقٌ	مُتَوافِقٌ	—	مُتَّفِقٌ	—	مُسْتَوْفِقٌ
noun	تَوْفِيقٌ	مُوافَقَةٌ وِفاقٌ	إِيفاقٌ	تَوَفُّقٌ	تَوافُقٌ	—	اِتِّفاقٌ	—	اِسْتِيفاقٌ

4. Medial *wâw* (C_2w)

perf. act.	قَوَّمَ	قاوَمَ	أَقامَ	تَقَوَّمَ	تَقاوَمَ	اِنْقامَ	اِقْتامَ	اِقْوَمَّ	اِسْتَقامَ
impf. act.	يُقَوِّمُ	يُقاوِمُ	يُقِيمُ	يَتَقَوَّمُ	يَتَقاوَمُ	يَنْقامُ	يَقْتامُ	يَقْوَمُّ	يَسْتَقِيمُ
juss. act.	يُقَوِّمْ	يُقاوِمْ	يُقِمْ	يَتَقَوَّمْ	يَتَقاوَمْ	يَنْقَمْ	يَقْتَمْ	يَقْوَمَّ يَقْوَمِمْ	يَسْتَقِمْ
impt.	قَوِّمْ	قاوِمْ	أَقِمْ	تَقَوَّمْ	تَقاوَمْ	اِنْقَمْ	اِقْتَمْ	—	اِسْتَقِمْ
act. part.	مُقَوِّمٌ	مُقاوِمٌ	مُقِيمٌ	مُتَقَوِّمٌ	مُتَقاوِمٌ	مُنْقامٌ	مُقْتامٌ	مُقْوَمٌّ	مُسْتَقِيمٌ
pass. part.	مُقَوَّمٌ	مُقاوَمٌ	مُقامٌ	مُتَقَوَّمٌ	مُتَقاوَمٌ	—	مُقْتامٌ	—	مُسْتَقامٌ
noun	تَقْوِيمٌ	مُقاوَمَةٌ	إِقامَةٌ	تَقَوُّمٌ	تَقاوُمٌ	اِنْقِيامٌ	اِقْتِيامٌ	اِقْوِمامٌ	اِسْتِقامَةٌ

قِوامٌ

5. Medial *yâ'* (C_2y)

perf. act.	بَيَّعَ	بايَعَ	أَباعَ	تَبَيَّعَ	تَبايَعَ	اِنْباعَ	اِبْتاعَ	اِبْيَعَّ	اِسْتَباعَ
perf. pass.	بُيِّعَ	بُويِعَ	أُبِيعَ	تُبُيِّعَ	تُبُويِعَ	—	أُبْتِيعَ	—	أُسْتُبِيعَ
impf. act.	يُبَيِّعُ	يُبايِعُ	يُبِيعُ	يَتَبَيَّعُ	يَتَبايَعُ	يَنْباعُ	يَبْتاعُ	يَبْيَعُّ	يَسْتَبِيعُ
impf. pass.	يُبَيَّعُ	يُبايَعُ	يُباعُ	يُتَبَيَّعُ	يُتَبايَعُ	—	يُبْتاعُ	—	يُسْتَباعُ
juss. act.	يُبَيِّعْ	يُبايِعْ	يُبِعْ	يَتَبَيَّعْ	يَتَبايَعْ	يَنْبَعْ	يَبْتَعْ	يَبْيَعَّ	يَسْتَبِعْ
act. part.	مُبَيِّعٌ	مُبايِعٌ	مُبِيعٌ	مُتَبَيِّعٌ	مُتَبايِعٌ	مُنْباعٌ	مُبْتاعٌ	مُبْيَعٌّ	مُسْتَبِيعٌ
pass. part.	مُبَيَّعٌ	مُبايَعٌ	مُباعٌ	مُتَبَيَّعٌ	مُتَبايَعٌ	—	مُبْتاعٌ	—	مُسْتَباعٌ
noun	تَبْيِيعٌ	مُبايَعَةٌ بِياعٌ	إِباعَةٌ	تَبَيُّعٌ	تَبايُعٌ	اِنْبِياعٌ	اِبْتِياعٌ	اِبْيِعاعٌ	اِسْتِباعَةٌ

6. Final Weakness (C_3w/y)

perf. act.	لَقَّى،	لاقَى،	أَلْقَى،	تَلَقَّى،	تَلاقَى،	اِنْلَقَى،	اِلْتَقَى،	—	اِسْتَلْقَى،

impf. act.	يُلَقِّي	يُلاقِي	يُلْقِي	يَتَلَقَّى	يَتَلاقَى	يَنْلَقِي	يَلْتَقِي	—	يَسْتَلْقِي
subj. act.	يُلَقِّيَ	يُلاقِيَ	يُلْقِيَ	يَتَلَقَّى	يَتَلاقَى	يَنْلَقِيَ	يَلْتَقِيَ	—	يَسْتَلْقِيَ
juss. act.	يُلَقِّ	يُلاقِ	يُلْقِ	يَتَلَقَّ	يَتَلاقَ	يَنْلَقِ	يَلْتَقِ	—	يَسْتَلْقِ
impt.	لَقِّ	لاقِ	أَلْقِ	تَلَقَّ	تَلاقَ	اِنْلَقِ	اِلْتَقِ	—	اِسْتَلْقِ
act. part.	مُلَقٍّ	مُلاقٍ	مُلْقٍ	مُتَلَقٍّ	مُتَلاقٍ	مُنْلَقٍ	مُلْتَقٍ	—	مُسْتَلْقٍ
pass. part.	مُلَقًّى	مُلاقًى	مُلْقًى	مُتَلَقًّى	مُتَلاقًى	مُنْلَقًى	مُلْتَقًى	—	مُسْتَلْقًى
noun	تَلْقِيَةٌ	مُلاقاةٌ لِقاةٌ	إِلْقاءٌ	تَلَقٍّ	تَلاقٍ	اِنْلِقاءٌ	اِلْتِقاءٌ	—	اِسْتِلْقاةٌ

7. Geminate roots

perf. act.	سَبَّبَ	سابَّ	أَسَبَّ	تَسَبَّبَ	تَسابَّ	اِنْسَبَّ	اِسْتَبَّ	اِسْبَبَّ	اِسْتَسَبَّ
impf. act.	يُسَبِّبُ	يُسابُّ	يُسِبُّ	يَتَسَبَّبُ	يَتَسابُّ	يَنْسَبُّ	يَسْتَبُّ	يَسْبَبُّ	يَسْتَسِبُّ
juss act.	يُسَبِّبْ	يُسابَّ	يُسِبَّ	يَتَسَبَّبْ	يَتَسابَّ	يَنْسَبَّ	يَسْتَبَّ	يَسْبَبَّ	يَسْتَسِبَّ

		يُسابِبْ	يُسْبِبْ		يَتَسابَبْ	يَنْسَبِبْ	يَسْتَبِبْ		يَسْتَسْبِبْ
impt.	سَبِّبْ	سابَّ	أَسِبَّ	تَسَبَّبْ	تَسابَّ	اِنْسَبَّ	اِسْتَبَّ	اِسْبَبَّ	اِسْتَسِبَّ
		سابِبْ	أَسْبِبْ		تَسابَبْ	اِنْسَبِبْ	اِسْتَبِبْ		اِسْتَسْبِبْ
act. part.	مُسَبِّبٌ	مُسابٌّ	مُسِبٌّ	مُتَسَبِّبٌ	مُتَسابٌّ	مُنْسَبٌّ	مُسْتَبٌّ	مُسْبَبٌّ	مُسْتَسِبٌّ
pass. part.	مُسَبَّبٌ	مُسابٌّ	مُسَبٌّ	مُتَسَبَّبٌ	مُتَسابٌّ	مُنْسَبٌّ	مُسْتَبٌّ	—	مُسْتَسَبٌّ
noun	تَسْبِيبٌ	مُسابَّةٌ سِبابٌ	إِسْبابٌ	تَسَبُّبٌ	تَسابٌّ	اِنْسِبابٌ	اِسْتِبابٌ	اِسْبِيبابٌ	اِسْتِسْبابٌ

8. Quadriliteral roots	Quad. I	Quad. II	Quad. III	Quad. IV
perf. act.	سَلْطَنَ	تَسَلْطَنَ	اِسْلَنْطَنَ	اِسْلَطَنَّ
impf. act.	يُسَلْطِنُ	يَتَسَلْطَنُ	يَسْلَنْطِنُ	يَسْلَطِنُّ
act. part.	مُسَلْطِنٌ	مُتَسَلْطِنٌ	مُسْلَنْطِنٌ	مُسْلَطِنٌّ
noun	(unpredictable)	تَسَلْطُنٌ	اِسْلِنْطانٌ	اِسْلِطْنانٌ

Appendix D

KORANIC ORTHOGRAPHY

The orthography of Arabic presented in this book is normalized Arabic orthography as established over a millennium ago. The standard orthography of the Koran, however, differs slightly from normalized writing since it antedates the philological normalization. Basically the differences lie in the spelling of internal *-ā-* and the perennially troublesome *hamza.*

The Koran was originally written down in old Arabic letters, which had neither the vowel markings nor the dots for distinguishing the various letters that share a given shape. First developed were signs for the vowels, initially a system of dots above and below the consonants, rather like the Eastern Aramaic system of vocalic points common in Nestorian Syriac. Later, when the dots were invented to distinguish the various consonants, the vowel signs that are current today took the place of the vocalic dots.

In consonance with Aramaic usage, whereas *ī* and *ū* are consistently indicated by the *y* and *w* and final *ā* is indicated by *alif,* internal *ā* is not normally indicated at all. Thus, for *kitāb-* (normalized as كتاب) early Koranic orthography has كتب, reflecting the Aramaeo-Syriac prototype כתבא *(kətābā).*

By the time of vocalization and dotting, the text of the Koran as it stood had obviously already developed a quasi-sacrosanctity that prevented the philologians from inserting into the text any such additional letter as a lengthening *alif,* so the dagger-*alif* was placed over the letter in order not to interfere with the word as it stood, much as the Masoretic pointing was inserted into and around the Hebrew text of the Old Testament without changing or adding to the consonantal skeleton.

Koranic orthography reflects the dialect of Mecca, which differs in small detail from the pronunciation that was later regarded as standard. Notably, the dialect of Mecca had lost internal and final glottal stops. Since the glottal stop was not pronounced, there was no reason to provide it with a consonantal letter. For example, *sa'ala* was pronounced something like *saala* (with an intervocalic glide) and spelled with *alif; yas'alu* was pronounced *yasalu* and so written without *alif,* then standardized as يسـٔل and finally normalized as يسأل. *Su'āl-* and *barī'-* would have been pronounced *suʷāl-* and *barī-* and so spelled. The philologians, based on their analysis of other dialects, "restored" the glottal stop where they determined it should have been, thus the Koranic standardized and normalized سؤال and بريء. This "restoration" accounts for the seemingly random seats of the *hamza* (see Appendix G), a sign invented from an initial *'ayn* because of the close proximity of the two sounds in the throat.

The *alif bi-ṣūrat al-yā'* is another remnant of Meccan dialect and indicates what must have been a vowel something like *-ē-* (as *ma'nē* for *ma'nā* and *waffē* for *waffā).* In Koranic orthography the *alif bi-ṣūrat al-yā'* is maintained as a *yā'* (without dots) even when enclitics are added, as سويك ("he made you"), reflecting a Meccan pronunciation of *sawwēka.* This dialectal variant is preserved in one phrase, لبيك *labbayka* (reflecting Meccan *labbēka* for normalized *labbāka* [*'abduka*] ("[your servant] has responded to you"), a phrase used in the pilgrimage rites.

Other aspects of Koranic orthography that differ from normalized Arabic orthography are:

(1) Otiose letters are indicated by a small circle. This should not be confused with the *sukūn,* which is written as a small initial *j* (without dot) and stands for *jazm*, another word for *sukūn.*

(2) *Madda* indicates abnormal lengthening of a vowel, not *-'ā-* as in normalized orthography. The glottal stop is indicated by *hamza* everywhere, as وفى ءاذانهم for normalized وفى آذانهم.

(3) Final *-ī*, especially the first-person singular objective enclitic *-nī*, is often written defectively, e.g. رَبِّ for normalized رَبِّى, and فَأَرْسِلُونِ for normalized فَأَرْسِلُونِى.

It should be noted that Koranic orthography is maintained only in the Koranic text itself. When quotations were taken from the Koran in the post-normalization period, they were often written in standard orthography.

Cross-Word Assimilations

Assimilations across word boundaries are indicated in Koranic orthography as follows:

WRITTEN	READ AS	EXAMPLE	
-t d-	*-d d-*	أُجِيبَت دَّعْوَتُكُمَا	*'ujībad da'watukumā*
-n b-	*-m b-*	مِنۢ بَعْدِ	*mim ba'di*
		عَدُوٌّۢ بِئْس	*'adūwum bi'sa*
		زَكِيَّةًۢ بِغَيْرِ	*zakīyatam bi-ğayri*
		ءَايَتٍۭ بَيِّنَاتٍ	*'āyātim bayyinātin*
-n l-	*-l l-*	شِفَاءٌ لِّلنَّاسِ	*šifā'ul lin-nāsi*
-n m-	*-m m-*	صِرَاطٍ مُّسْتَقِيمٍ	*ṣirāṭim mustaqīmin*
-n r-	*-r r-*	غَفُورًا رَّحِيمًا	*ğafūrar raḥīman*
-n w-	*-w w-*	أَبَدًا وَلَنْ	*'abadaw wa-lan*
		مَن وَّعَدَنِى	*maw wa'adanī*
-n y-	*-y y-*	أَن يُّعَذِّبَهُمْ	*'ay yu'aððibahum*

The internal assimilation of *-d-* to *-t-* is similarly indicated:

-dt- *-tt-* وَعَدْتُمْ *wa'attum*

The 3rd-person masculine singular enclitic pronoun, *-hu/-hi,* is read with short *ŭ* and *ĭ* when the preceding syllable contains a long vowel or diphthong. When *-hu/-hi* follows a syllable containing a short vowel, however, it is read as *-hū/-hī,* with long vowels, indicated in the Koran by a small *wāw* or *yā'* under the *h* of the enclitic. This variation in length is of no consequence in the normal reading of prose, since it always falls in an unstressable position, but the long-short variation is of importance in the scansion of poetry (i.e., *fīhi* is scanned *fī-hĭ,* but *bihi* is scanned *bĭ-hī.*

Appendix E

KORANIC MARKS OF PERIODIZATION

Arabic only recently—and in imitation of European languages—developed punctuation marks. The late development can be partially explained by the abundance of particles that serve as interrogatives, coordinators and sequentializers, thereby making an elaborate system of periodic marks unnecessary. In the Koran, however, there are numerous passages where incorrect periodization can have disastrous effects on the meaning. In order to prevent such misreadings, a system of markings for pause *(waqf)* is commonly included in Koranic texts.

The marks used in the standard Egyptian Koran are as follows:

(1) م necessary pause: no syntactic connection between what precedes the mark and what follows, e.g.

انما يستجيب الذين يسمعون م والموتى يبعثهم الله	Only those who hear respond—and the dead, God will resurrect them.

This prevents the non-sensical reading

انما يستجيب الذين يسمعون والموتى - يبعثهم الله	Only those who hear and the dead respond—God will resurrect them.

(2) لا no pause: what follows the mark belongs syntactically to what precedes, e.g.

الذين تتوفيهم الملئكة طيّبين لا يقولون سلم عليكم ادخلوا الجنة بما كنتم تعملون	To those whom the angels cause to die [when they are] good, they say, "Peace be unto you. Enter the garden because of what you used to do."

(3) ج indifferent as to pause: preceding word may be taken syntactically as belonging to preceding or following phrase, e.g.

نحن نقصّ عليك نباهم بالحق ج إنهم فتية آمنوا بربهم	We recite to you their news in truth—they are youths who believed in their Lord **or** We recite to you their news—in truth they are youths who believed in their Lord.

(4) صلى pause permissible but no pause preferable.

(5) قلى pause permissible and preferable; no pause also permissible.

(6) ⸪ pause at either place but not both, e.g.

ذلك الكتاب لا ريب ⸪ فيه ⸪ هدى للمتقين	That is the book, no doubt—in it is guidance for the pious **or** That book, in which there is no doubt, is guidance for the pious.

Appendix F

PAUSAL FORMS

The following rules for pronunciation should be observed for pausal forms, i.e., words that fall before a natural pausal point or at the end of a phrase or sentence. Isolated words are also generally pronounced in pausal form.

(1) final short vowels are quiesced (even when written):

إنّك إذاً لمن الظالمينَ read as: *'innaka 'iðan la-mina ẓ-ẓālimīn:*

فقد ظلم نفسَهُ read as: *fa-qad ẓalama nafsah:*

(2) the indefinite endings *-un* and *-in* are quiesced:

وابونا شيخٌ كبيرٌ read as: *wa-'abūnā šayxun kabīr:*

فما له من نورٍ read as: *fa-mā lahu min nūr:*

(3) the indefinite ending *-an* is read as *-ā:*

وامطرنا عليهم مطراً read as: *wa-'amṭarnā 'alayhim maṭarā:*

(4) the inflectional ending and the *-t-* of the *tā' marbūṭa* are quiesced, giving an ending in *-a:*

وآيةٌ لهم الأرضُ الميتةُ read as: *wa-'āyatun lahumu l-'arḍu l-mayta:*

Appendix G

SEATS OF THE *HAMZA*

I. Initial *Hamza*. The seat for all initial *hamza*s is *alif.*

When the vowel of the *hamza* is *-a-* or *-u-*, the *hamza* is commonly written above the *alif,* as in أمر *'amr-* and أنس *'uns-*

When the vowel of the *hamza* is *-i-*, the *hamza* is commonly written beneath the *alif,* as in إنس *'ins-* and إيمان *'īmān-*.

When the vowel of the *hamza* is *-ā-*, the *alif* carries *madda,* as in آية *'āyat-* and آمن *'āmana.*

II. Internal *Hamza*.

(1) If internal *hamza* is (a) preceded by a short vowel and followed by *sukūn,* or (b) preceded by *sukūn,* or (c) both preceded and followed by the same vowel, the seats are:

- *Alif* for *-a'-*, *-'a-* and *-a'a-*, as in رأس *ra's-*, مسألة *mas'alat-* and سأل *sa'ala;*

- *Madda* for *-'ā-*, as in قرآن *qur'ān-* and تآمر *ta'āmara;*

- Dotless *yā'* for *-i'-*, *-'i-* and *-i'i-*, as in ذئب *ði'b-*, أسئلة *'as'ilat-* and قارئه *qāri'ihi;*

- *Wāw* for *-u'-*, *-'u-* and *-u'u-*, as in سؤل *su'l-*, مسؤول *mas'ūl-* and تكافؤه *takāfu'uhu.*

(2) If preceded by a short vowel and followed by a different vowel (long or short), the seats are, in order of preference: (a) *i*—dotless *yā'*, (b) *u*—*wāw,* (c) *a*—*alif.*

سئل *su'ila (i* takes precedence over *u*), قارئه *qāri'uhu (i* takes precedence over *u)*, ذئاب *ði'āb- (i* takes precedence over *a)*, رئيس *ra'īs- (i* takes precedence over *a)*

بؤس *ba'usa (u* takes precedence over *a)*, رؤوف *ra'ūf-*[1] *(u* takes precedence over *a)*, سؤال *su'āl- (u* takes precedence over *a)*, مؤرخ *mu'arrix (u* takes precedence over *a)*

(3) If preceded by a long vowel or diphthong and

(a) followed by *-a-*, the seat is nothing, i.e., the *hamza* "sits" on the line, as in ابناءه *'abnā'ahu*, شيئا *šay'an*,[2] خطيئة *xaṭī'at-*,[3] ضوءه *ḍaw'ahu*, and مروءة *murū'at-*.

(b) followed by *-i-*, the seat is *yā'*, as in ابنائه *'abnā'ihi*, بريئه *barī'ihi*, and سوئل *sū'ila*.

(c) followed by *-u-*, the seat is *wāw*, as in ابناؤه *'abnā'uhu* and بريؤه *barī'uhu*.

III. Final *Hamza*. Final *hamza* (exclusive of inflectional vowels) takes the following seats:

(1) If preceded by a short vowel, the seats are:

(a) *alif* for *-a'*, as in نبأ *naba'-*[4]

(b) dotless *yā'* for *-i'*, as in قارئ *qāri'-*

(c) *wāw* for *-u'-*, as in تكافؤ *takāfu'-*

---

[1]The combination *-a'ū-* is also written with the *hamza* on the line (رءوف).

[2]With the addition of the *alif* for the *-an* termination, *hamza* is no longer reckoned final. This combination is also commonly written with the dotless *yā'* (شيئا), especially in type.

[3]The combination *-ī'a-* is also normalized with the *hamza* on a dotless *yā'* (خطيئة), especially in type.

[4]The indefinite accusative *alif* is not added to words ending in *-a'-* or *-ā'-*, such as نبأ *naba'an* and ابناءً *'abnā'an*.

(2) If preceded by a long vowel, diphthong or *sukūn*, the *hamza* is on the line (no seat), as in ابناء *'abnā'-*, جرىء *jarī'-*, مقروء *maqrū'-*, ضوء *ḍaw'-*, شىء *šay'-*, and جزء *juz'-*.

Appendix H

The Syro-Mesopotamian Months and Days of the Week

The following months were used in Syria and Mesopotamia for fiscal administration throughout the Islamic period. The names are derived from older Semitic usage, and the months are solar (Julian).

نيسان	*nīsānu* April	تشرين الاول	*tišrīnu l-'awwalu* October
ايار	*'ayyāru* May	تشرين الثانى	*tišrīnu θ-θānī* November
حزيران	*ḥazīrānu* June	كانون الاول	*kānūnu l-'awwalu* December
تموز	*tammūzu* July	كانون الثانى	*kānūnu θ-θānī* January
آب	*'ābu* August	شباط	*šubāṭu* February
ايلول	*'aylūlu* September	آذار	*'āδāru* March

Days of the week:

يوم الاحد	*yawmu l-'aḥadi* Sunday
يوم الاثنين	*yawmu l-iθnayni* Monday
يوم الثلاثاء	*yawmu θ-θulāθā'i* Tuesday
يوم الاربعاء	*yawmu l-'arba'ā'i* Wednesday
يوم الخميس	*yawmu l-xamīsi* Thursday
يوم الجمعة	*yawmu l-jum'ati* Friday
يوم السبت	*yawmu s-sabti* Saturday

Appendix I

SUMMARY OF VERBAL SYNTAX

The Perfect

1. Simple past	*ḍarabtuhu*	I hit him.
2. Past definite	*qad ḍarabtuhu*	I did hit him.
3. Negative perfect (+ *mā*)	*mā ḍarabtuhu*	I haven't hit him.
4. Future perfective	*kāna l-yawmu qarīban*	The day will be soon.
5. Contrafactual conditionals	*law ḍarabanī, la-māta*	If he had hit me, he would have died / If he were to hit me he would die.
6. Gnomic (atemporal)	*kāna llāhu 'alīman*	God is omniscient.

Imperfect Indicative

1. Present habitual / present progressive	*yaḍribunī*	He hits / is hitting me.
2. Future[1]	*(sawfa/sa)yaḍribunī*	He will hit me.
3. Past habitual / progressive (+ perfect of *kāna*)	*kāna yaḍribunī*	He used to hit me.
4. + *qad* for "may, might"	*qad yaḍribunī*	He might hit me.

Subjunctive

1. after *'an*	*'axāfu 'an yaḍribanī*	I fear he'll hit me.
2. with *li-* for purpose	*'atā li-yaḍribanī*	He came to hit me.
3. with *lan* for neg. future	*lan yaḍribanī*	He will not hit me.

---

[1] Affirmative explicit with *sawfa* or *sa-*.

4. with *fa-* after prohibition, wishes, requests, &c.	*lā yağḍab fa-yaḍribanī*	Let him not get angry lest he hit me.

Jussive

1. with *lam* for neg. past def.	*lam yaḍribnī*	He did not hit me.
2. with *li-* for hortatory	*li-yaḍribnī*	Let him hit me.
3. with *lā* for neg. imperative	*lā yaḍribnī*	Let him not hit me.
4. possible conditionals	*'in yaḍribnī yamut*	If he hits me, he'll die.
	man yaḍribnī yamut	Whoever hits me will die
	iḍribnī tamut	Hit me and you die.

Appendix J

MANDATORY PHONETIC CHANGES

Following are the mandatory phonetic changes that occur with the "weak" consonants *w* and *y*. The vertical line indicates a syllabic division. The basic rule throughout is as follows: any weak consonant surrounded by short vowels is dropped along with the following vowel, and the preceding vowel is lengthened in compensation if possible (if the syllable is closed, the vowel cannot be lengthened).

-awa|* → *-ā|* (qawala* → *qāla* §18, **irtaḍawa* → *irtaḍā* §60.2)
-awaC| → *-uC|* (**qawalta* → *qulta* §18)
-awi|* → *-ā-* (mawita* → *māta* §18)
-awiC|* → *-iC|* (mawitta* → *mitta* §18)
-aya|* → *-ā|* (sayara* → *sāra* §18, **imtayaza* → *imtāza* §60.1)
-ayī|* → *-ay|* (talqayīna* → *talqayna* §39.1)
-ayu|* → *-ā|* (yalqayu* → *yalqā* §39.1)
-ayū|* → *-aw|* (yalqayūna* → *yalqawna* §39.1)
-iyi|* → *-ī|* (hādiyi* → *hādī* §27.1)
-iyiC|* → *-iC|* (hādiyin* → *hādin* §27.1)
-iyī|* → *-ī|* (hādiyīna* → *hādīna* §27.2, **tarmiyīna* → *tarmīna* §39.2)
-iyu|* → *-ī|* (hādiyu* → *hādī* §27.2, **yarmiyu* → *yarmī* §39.2)
-iyū|* → *-ū|* (hādiyūna* → *hādūna* §27.2, **yarmiyūna* → *yarmūna* §39.2)
-iyuC|* → *-iC|* (hādiyun* → *hādin* §27.2)
-iw-* → *-ī-/-iy-* (biwḍ-* → *bīḍ* §36, **raḍiwa* → *raḍiya* §20.3, **du'iwa* → *du'iya* §53.2)
-uwi|* → *-ī|* (quwila* → *qīla* §53.2)
-uwī|* → *-ī|* (tad'uwīna* → *tad'īna* §39.3)
-uwū|* → *-ū|* (yad'uwūna* → *yad'ūna* §39.3)

**-C/wa- → -Cā-*[1] *(*yuqwalu → yuqālu* §55.3, *'amwata → 'amāta* §76.2)

**-C/wu- → -Cū- (*yaqwulu → yaqūlu* §37)

**-C/wuC/ → -uC/- (*yaqwulna → yaqulna* §37)

**-C/yi- → -Cī- (*yasyiru → yasīru* §37)

**'v'/C- → -'v̄/C- (*'u'minu → 'ūminu* §75.4, **'a'kulu → 'ākulu* §30.6, **'a'mana → 'āmana* §75.4, **'i'ti → 'īti* §49)

---

[1]Except in the elative 'AF'ALU pattern, as *ṭayyib- > 'aṭyabu*, and *qawīm- > 'aqwamu*.

English-Arabic Vocabulary

abide مازال
able, be قدر
abomination منكر
absent, be غاب
accept تقبّل
acknowledge, refuse to انكر
Adam آدم
adopt اتّخذ
adultery, commit زنى
advance أقبل
advise نصح
afflict أصاب
after (conj.) بعد أن
after (prep.) بعد
afterwards (adv.) من بعدُ
against على
age سنّ
alive حى
all كل
almost كاد
alms زكاة

alms, give تصدّق
among من ، بين
angel ملك
announce بشّر
anyone أحد
anything شيء
apostle رسول
appear بدا
appoint as successor خلّف
approach قرب
arise قام
arms سلاح
as كما
as for امّا
ask سال
aspire to ابتغى
astray, go ضلّ
avail نفع
aware, be درى
away, turn ولّى

back, go ارتدّ

back, send/bring ردّ
band طائفة
bar منع
be كان
beast دابة
beautiful جميل ، حسن
become اصبح
before (adv.) من قبل
before (conj.) قبل أن
before (prep.) قبل
beget ولد
behind وراء
behold ابصر
believe in آمن بـ
believer مؤمن
beneath تحت
benefit, be of نفع
better خير
between بين
beware اتّقى
big كبير
bird طير
black اسود
blame لام
bless بارك
blessing بركة
blind اعمى
book كتاب
bow down to سجد
break كسر
bring اتى بـ
bring down نزل بـ
broken, be/get انكسر ، تكسر
brother اخ
build بنى
but ولكن ، الا

call out to نادى
call upon دعا
calm, be اطمانّ
capable of, be قدر على
care of, take نصح
cast رمى
cause of, in the فى سبيل
certainty يقين
charge, put in ولّى
child ولد
choose اختار
city مدينة
clay طين
clear مبين ، بيّن
come اتى
come to pass جرى
command امر
community امّة
companion صاحب
conceal خفى ، اخفى
concluded, be تمّ
conspire كاد
consume اكل
contain وسع

content, be رضى
corruption, work افسد
create خلق
curse لعن

darkness ظلمة
daughter بنت
day يوم
dead ميّت
deaf أصمّ
death موت
deceive غرّ
decide قضى
deed عمل
deity إله
delude غرّ
deny نكر
depart سار ، انطلق
descend نزل
despair of يئس من
devil شيطان
devoted مخلص
devout صالح
die مات
differ خالف ، اختلف
disbelieve in كفر
disease مرض
disengage oneself فارق
disobey عصى
distant بعيد
division فرقة

djinn جنّ
do فعل ، عمل
down, come/go نزل
draw back ادبر
draw near اقترب ، تقرّب
drink شرب
drink, give to سقى
due, give full وفّى
dumb ابكم
dust تراب ، تربة
dwell سكن

each other بعض...بعض
ear اذن
earth ارض
eat اكل
elder شيخ
encourage حرّض
end آخر ، عقبى
endeavor جاهد
enemy عدوّ
enjoy تمتّع
enter دخل
entrust وكل
equal, be سوى ، استوى
eternal خالد
every كل
evidence بيّنة
evil شرّ
evildoer مفسد
example, give as ضرب مثلاً

except إلاّ
exclusion of من دون
exculpate برّأ
eye عين

face وجه
face (v.i.) توجّه
faith ايمان
fall down سجد
far from بعيد عن/من
fast (v.i.) صام
fast, be سرع
father أب
fear خاف
feed أطعم
female انثى
few قليل
fight قاتل
fill (v.t.) ملأ
filled, be امتلأ
find وجد
finger إصبع
finished, be تمّ
fire نار
first أول
flee فرّ
flow جرى
follow تبع ، اتّبع
foolish, be جهل
for لـ
forbid منع ، نهى
forbidden, be حرم
forceful شديد
forget نسى
forgive غفر لـ
forgiveness, ask استغفر
form هيئة
forward, come/go أقبل
free بريء
friend ولىّ
friendly, be أنس
from من
fruit فاكهة

garden حديقة
gate باب
genii جنّىّ
girl بنت
give وهب ، آتى
go ذهب
go back ارتدّ
go down نزل
go out خرج
go out against خرج على
God الله
god, deity إله
God-fearing تقىّ
good حسن
good deed حسنة
good news بشرى
good thing خير
good works صالحات

goodness خير
goods متاع
Gospel الانجيل
great كبير
green أخضر
group طائفة
guard, be on اتّقى
guide دلّ
guided, be اهتدى

half نصف
hand يد
hand over سلّم ، أسلم
happen جرى
harm ضرّ
hasten عجل ، استعجل
haughty, grow تكبّر ، استكبر
he who من
hear سمع
heart قلب
heaven سموات
heel عقب
heir to, be ورث
hell جهنم
help نصر
helper ولىّ
here هنا
high, be علا
hinder منع
hit the mark أصاب
hope, give up يئس
house بيت
how? كيف
however إنّما
humankind بشر
humble, be تواضع
hypocrite منافق

Iblis ابليس
idol صنم
if اذا ، إن ، لو
ignorant, be جهل
ill, fall مرض
in فى
increase (v.i.) زاد ، ازداد
indicate أشار
infidel كافر
infidelity كفر
inform نبّأ
inhabit سكن
inhabitants اهل
inherit ورث
injustice ظلم
innocent برىء
inspire أوحى
invite دعا
itinerant سيّار
judge قاضٍ
judgment, day of يوم الدين
judgment, pass حكم

kill قتل

king ملك
kingdom مملكة
know علم ، عرف ، درى ، خبر
knowledge علم
Koran القرآن

lag behind خلف
land أرض
large كبير
last (adj.) آخر
last forever خلد
laugh ضحك
lead دل ، هدى
leaf ورق
learned men علماء
leave خرج ، ترك
left (hand) شمال
liar, call a كذّب
lie كذب
life حياة
life to come الآخرة
life, this الدنيا
light نور
like (prep.) ك
likeness مثل
little قليل ، صغير
live حيّ ، عاش
look نظر
lord رب
loss, suffer خسر
lost, be/get ضلّ
love أحبّ
lust هوى

male ذكر
man رجل ، بشر ، انسان
many كثير
marry نكح
master مولى
mate زوج
matter أمر
maturity, reach بلغ أشدّه
meaning معنى
Mecca مكّة
memorize حفظ
mention ذكر
merciful رحمان
mercy, have رحم
messenger رسول
might قوة
mighty قويّ
mistake اخطأ
mistaken, be خطئ
month شهر
moon قمر
morning صبح ، صباح
mother أمّ
motion, set in سيّر
mountain جبل

name اسم
name (v.t.) سمّى

narrate قصّ
near to اقترب
near, draw قريب من
necessary, be انبغى
neglect غفل
never ابداً
new جديد
news نبأ ، خبر
night ليل ، ليلة
noble كريم
nobody لاأحد
north شمال
nose أنف
not ما ، لا ، إن ، ليس
nothing لا شيء
number عدد

O يا ، ياأيّها
obedience اطاعة
obey أطاع
observe closely اطّلع
occur وقع
old man شيخ
on على
one (adj.) واحد
one (pron.) أحد
one-eyed أعور
opinion (legal) فتوى
opinion, give an أفتى
oppress ظلم
or يا ، أم
order أمر
orphan يتيم
other آخر
other than غير
over (prep.) على
over, turn قلّب
overturned, be انقلب ، تقلّب

paradise جنّة
pardon عفا
parents والدان
part جزء
part company هجر
partner شريك
pass away (cease) زال
pass away (die) تُوُفِّيَ
pass by مرّ من
pass over مرّ على
patient, be صبر
peace سلام
people اهل
perform (prayer) أقام
perhaps لعلّ ، عسى أن
perish هلك ، خسر
permit أذن
pilgrimage, make a حجّ
pious صالح ، تقيّ
place مقام ، مكان
pleasant, be طاب
pleased, be رضى
plot كاد

poor فقير
possession of, in the عند
possessions مال
possessor of ذو ، صاحب
possible, not ماكان لـ أن
power سلطان ، عزّة
powerful قوىّ
pray for صلّى على
prayer (invocation) دعاء
prayer (ritual) صلاة
prepare هيّأ
prescribe for كتب على
presence of, in the عند
preserve حفظ
prevent منع
prison سجن
prophet نبىّ
prostrate oneself سجد
protect وقى
protection, seek عاذ
punish جزى
purify طهّر
put جعل
put down وضع

question (v.t.) سال
quick, be سرع

rain مطر
rather بل
reach بلغ
ready, get (v.t.) هيّأ
reality حق
reason عقل
recite قرا
reckon حسب
recognize عرف
refuge, take آوى
refuse to acknowledge انكر
relate قصّ
religion دين
repel دفع
repent تاب
requite جزى
resurrection قيامة
retrace one's steps انقلب على عقبيه
return رجع ، عاد
reward جزى
rich غنىّ
right (hand) يمين
rise طلع
rise up قام
river نهر
rock حجر
rule ملك ، سلطان
rule (v.t.) ملك
rush (v.i.) استعجل

sabbath سبت
sacrifice (n.) قربان
sacrifice (v.t.) قرّب
sad, be حزن

safe, be/feel امن
safe, keep حفظ
sake of, for the لأجل
say قال
scare خوّف ، أخاف
see رأى
seize أخذ
send بعث ، أرسل
send forth بعث
separate فرّق
servant عبد
sick مريض
sign آية
sin جناح ، خطيئة
sin (v.i.) خطئ
sincere مخلص
sister اخت
slave عبد
sleep نام
small صغير
smash كسّر
so that حتّى
so-and-so فلان
some بعض
someone أحد
something شىء
son ابن
sorrow حزن
soul نفس
speak to كلّم
spend انفق
spirit روح
spread بسط
spring عين
star نجم ، كوكب
steal سرق
stone حجر
strength قوّة
strike ضرب
strive جاهد
strive for ابتغى
strong قوىّ
subjugate سخّر
submit أسلم
summon دعا
sun شمس
surround أحاط بـ
sustenance رزق

take اخذ
tame انّس
taste ذاق
teach علّم
term اجل
testify شهد
that (adj., pron.) ذلك
that (conj.) أن
that (rel. pron.) الذى
that which ما ، الذى
then فـ ، ثم ، إذاً
there ثمّ ، هناك

thing شيء
this هذا
though, as كأنّ
throw رمى ، القى
thus كذلك
time حين ، مرّة
to الى ، لـ
today اليوم
tonight الليلة
tooth سنّ
Torah التوراة
torment عذاب
touch مسّ
travel سار
tree شجر
tribe قوم
triumph نصر
truth حق
truth, tell the صدق
turn (v.t.) وجّه
turn away from ولّى ، أدبر عن
turn towards (v.i.) اتّجه الى
two اثنان
tyranny ظلم

unbeliever كافر
unfortunate مسكين
ungrateful for, be كفر بـ
universe العالمون ، العالم
unlawful, make حرّم
unmindful of, be غفل عن
use of, make انتفع من

vanquish غلب
verse آية
village قرية
violent شديد
visit the sick عاد

walk مشى
want اراد
wares متاع
watch out for حافظ على
water ماء
water, ask for استسقى
water, give سقى
way سبيل
weep بكى
what? ما
when (conj.) إذا ، لمّا
when? متى
whenever كلّما
where? اين
wherever اينما
which (rel. pron.) الذى
which? ايّ
white ابيض
who (rel. pron.) الّذى
who? من
whole كل ، جميع
why? لم ، لما
wife امرأة ، زوجة

will (v.i.) شاء
wisdom حكمة
wish ودّ ، تمنّى
with بـ ، مع
witness شاهد
woman امرأة
word كلمة
words قول
world عالم
world, the next الآخرة
world, this الدنيا
worse شرّ
worship عبد
write كتب

year سنة ، عام
young صغير

Arabic-English Vocabulary

Words are arranged by root, real or apparent. The number following "A" after nouns refers to the section in Appendix A where the broken-plural type is found. SFP = sound feminine plural; SMP = sound masculine plural; s.o. = someone; s.th. = something

اب *'ab* (A10a) father

ابد *'abadan* (+ neg.) never

ابن *ibn-* (A10a, *banūna)* son

اتى *'atā (I) 'ityān-* come to, bring s.o. (*bi-* s.th.); IV give to

اجر *'ajr-* reward

اجل *'ajal-* (A2a) term, appointed time, instant of death; *li-'ajli-* for the sake of

احد *'aḥad-* (m) (A2a), *'iḥdā* (f) one, someone, anyone; *yawmu l-'aḥadi* Sunday

اخ *'ax-* (A10b/c) brother; *'uxt-* (A10d) sister

اخذ *'axaða (u) 'axð-* take, seize, take hold (*bi-* of); III *'āxaða* take to task (*bi-* for); VIII *ittaxaða* adopt

اخر *'āxir-* (SMP/SFP/A4b) last, final; *al-'āxirat-* the next world, life to come; *'āxaru* (A9) other; II *'axxara* reprieve, put off, delay; V *ta'axxara* come after, be delayed, be late

ادد *'idd-* terrible, horrible

ادم *'ādamu* Adam; *ibnu 'ādama* pl *banū 'ādama* human being

اذ *'ið* when

اذا *'iðā* when, if; *'iðan* then, therefore

اذن *'aðina (a) 'iðn-* permit; IV *'āðana bi-* declare; *'uðun-* (A2a) ear; *'iðan* then, therefore

اذى *'aðiya (a)* suffer harm; IV *'āðā* annoy, harm; *'aðan* annoyance

ارض *'arḍ-* (f) (A10e) earth, land

اسم *ism-* (A10a/e) name; see also √*SMY*

اسى *'asiya (ā)* grieve

اصبع *'iṣba'-* (A11) finger

افرنج *'ifranj-* Franks, Europeans; *'ifranjiyy-* Frank, European

افف *'uffin li-* fie on

اكل *'akala (u) 'akl-* eat, consume

الا *'illā* (+ acc.) except for; but, only, except, just; (+ neg., see §33); *'allā = 'an lā* that …not; *'a-lā 'innā* is it not a fact that

الذى *allaðī* who, he who (§21.1)

الله *allāhu* God

اله *'ilāh-* (A6a) god, deity

الم *'alīm-* painful

الى *'ilā* (+ gen.) *('ilay-)* to

ام *'am* or; see also √*'MM*

اما *'ammā* as for (followed by *fa-*); *'immā* either, or

امر *'amara (u) 'amr-* order, command *(bi-); 'amr-* (A1b) affair, matter; (A1e) order, command; *min/bi-'amri* at the order of

امراة *imra'at-* see √*MR'*

امرؤ *imru'-* see √*MR'*

امم *'umm-* (A10d) mother; *'ummat-* (A3a) community

امن *'amina (a) 'amn-/'amānat-* be safe, secure, trust (*'alā* with); IV *'āmana bi-* believe in

ان *'in* if; not; *'inna* sentence-head particle followed by acc.; *'anna* (+ acc.) that; *'an* (+ subj.) that

انث *'unθā* female

انس *'anisa (a) /'anusa (u) 'uns-* be friendly, on intimate terms (*bi-* with), perceive; II *'annasa* put at ease, tame; III *'ānasa* be friendly with, cordial to; IV *'ānasa* keep company, observe; X *ista'nasa* be sociable, on familiar terms with; *'ins-* humanity; *'insān-* human, person

انف *'anf-* (A1a/b) nose

انما *'innamā* however, rather; specifically

انى *'annā* how?; *'ānā'a* (+ gen.) throughout, during; *'inā'-* pl *'āniyat-/'awānin* vessel

اهل *'ahl-* (SMP/A10e) people, inhabitants, family

او *'aw(i)* or

اول *'awwalu* (m), *'ūlā* (f) (SMP/SFP/*'awā'ilu)* first

اوى *'awā (ī) ma'wan* take refuge, shelter; IV *'āwā* give shelter to, take refuge

اى *'ayy-* (+ construct) which?, whichever?, what kind of?

ايمان *'īmān-* see √*'MN* IV

اين *'ayna* where?; *'aynamā* wherever

آية *'āyat-* (SFP) sign, token, verse of the Koran

ايها *'ayyuhā* (m), *'ayyatuhā* (f) O, vocative particle

ب *bi-* (+ gen.) in, by, with, through; *bi-mā 'anna* inasmuch as, for as much as

بدء *bada'a (a) bad'* - begin, start (*bi-* with)

بدو *badā (ū) budūw-* appear; IV *'abdā* cause to appear

برء *barī'* - (A5b/d) free, innocent (*min* of); II *barra'a* exculpate, make free; IV *'abra'a* heal

برج *burj-* (A3c) constellation

برد *bard-* cold, coolness

برص *'abraṣu* leprous

برق *al-burāqu* Buraq, mythical animal on which the Prophet ascended into heaven

برك III *bāraka 'alā/fī* bless; VI *tabāraka* be blessed; *barakat-* (SFP) blessing

بسط *basaṭa (u) basṭ-* spread, stretch out

بشر II *baššara* announce good news to (*bi-* of); *bušrā* good news; *bašar-* humankind

بصر *baṣara (i) baṣar-* look, see, understand; II *baṣṣara* make see, enlighten; IV *'abṣara* see, behold; V *tabaṣṣara bi-* reflect on; X *istabṣara* be able to see; *baṣar-* (A2a) vision, insight

بضع *biḍā'at-* (A6b) wares, merchandise

بطل IV *'abṭala* talk idly

بعث *ba'aθa (a) ba'θ-* send (*'ilā* for), send forth, resurrect

بعد *ba'da* (+ gen.) after (prep.); *min ba'di* after (prep.); *min ba'du* afterwards (adv.); *ba'da-mā, ba'da 'an* after (conj.); *ba'īd-* far, distant (*min, 'an* from)

بعض *ba'ḍ-* some; *ba'ḍuhum... ba'ḍan/in* each other

بغل *bağl-* (A1b/c) mule

بغى VII *imbağā* be proper, seemly (*li-* for), be necessary (*li-/'alā* for); VIII *ibtağā* strive for, aspire to

بقى *baqiya (ā) baqā'* - remain

بكم *'abkamu* (A8) mute, dumb

بكى *bakā (ī) bukā'* - cry, weep (*'alā* over); IV *'abkā* make weep

بل *bal(i)* nay rather

بلغ *balağa (u) bulūğ-* reach, attain; IV *'ablağa* make reach, announce, inform, deliver; *balağa 'ašuddahu* he reached maturity

بلو *balā (ū) balā'* - put to the test

بنت *bint-* (A10d) girl, daughter

بنى *banā (ī) binā'-/bunyān-* build

بهت *buhita* (pass.) be flabbergasted

بوب *bāb-* (A2a) gate, door

بيت *bayt-* (A1b) house, dwelling

بيض *'abyaḍu* (A8) white

بين *bayna* (+ gen.) between, among; *bayyinat-* (SFP) indisputable evidence; IV *'abāna* make clear, obvious

تبع *tabiʻa (a) tabaʻ-/tabāʻat-* follow; VI *tatābaʻa* follow in succession; VIII *ittabaʻa* follow, pursue, heed

تحت *taḥta* (+ gen.) beneath, under

ترب *turbat-, turāb-* dust, dirt, earth

ترك *taraka (u) tark-* leave, abandon, leave behind

تقى *taqīy-* (A5d) pious, God-fearing, devout

تمم *tamma (i) tamām-* be completed, finished, fulfilled; IV *'atamma* finish, fulfill

توب *tāba (ū) tawbat-* turn away (*ʻan* from), renounce, relent, repent (*'ilā* toward)

تيه *tāha (ī)* wander

ثعب *θaʻbān-* serpent

ثقل *miθqāl-* a small weight

ثم *θamma* there, in that place; *θumma* then, next, afterward

ثمر *θamar-* fruit

ثنى *iθnāni* (m), *iθnatāni* (f) two; *yawmu l-iθnayni* Monday

جبر *jabbār-* pl *jabābirat-* giant

جبل *jabal-* (A2b) mountain

جثم *jaθama (u/i)* lie prone

جثو *jaθā (ū)* bend the knee

جحم *jaḥīm-* hellfire

جدد *jadīd-* (A5c) new

جذذ *juδāδ-* (coll.) small fragments

جرأ *jarī'-* bold, courageous

جرم IV *'ajrama* commit a crime; *mujrim-* (SMP) criminal

جرى *jarā (ī) jarayān-* flow, blow, happen, come to pass; IV *'ajrā* make flow, make happen, execute

جزء *juz'-* (A3b) part, section

جزى *jazā (ī) jazā'-* requite, recompense, reward, punish (*bi-, ʻalā* for); III *jāzā* = G

جسم *jism-* (A3b) body

جعل *jaʻala (a) jaʻl-* put, make

جلد *jalada (i) jald-* flog; *jaldat-* lash

جلل *jalla (i) jalāl-* be great, exalted

جمع *jamaʻa (a) jamʻ-* gather, collect; *jamaʻa l-qur'āna* memorize the Koran; IV *'ajmaʻa* make a consensus, be of one mind; VIII *ijtamaʻa* assemble, be gathered (*ʻalā* for); *jamīʻ-* all, whole, entire; *'ajmaʻīna* altogether

جمل *jamīl-* beautiful, handsome

جنح *junāḥ-* sin, crime (*ʻalā* for) (*'an* to)

جنن *jinn-* (coll.), *jinniyy-* (sing), pl *jānn-* djinn, genie; *jannat-* (SFP) garden, paradise

جهد III *jāhada* endeavor, strive; VIII *ijtahada* work hard, be industrious; *jihād-* "holy war"

جهر *jahara (a) jahr-* raise the voice

جهل *jahila (a) jahl-* be ignorant, not know

جوب X *istajāba* respond

جود *jawād-* generous

جوع *jā'a (ū) jaw'-* be hungry

جوو *jaww-* air, atmosphere

جیء *jā'a (ī) majī'-* come to, bring s.o. (*bi-* s.th.)

حبب II *ḥabbaba* make beloved; IV *'aḥabba* love, like, want (noun: *ḥubb-/maḥabbat-*); X *istaḥabba* consider desirable, preferable (*'alā* over); *ḥabīb-* (A5d) loved one; *maḥbūb-* beloved; *ḥabbat-* seed, grain

حبر *ḥibr-* (A3b) Jewish title of learning

حبس *ḥabasa (i) ḥabs-* confine, imprison, keep back

حبل *ḥablu l-warīdi* jugular vein

حتى *ḥattā* (+ subj.) so that, until (with ref. to fut.); (+ gen.) until, up to

حجج *ḥajja (u) ḥajj-* make the pilgrimage to Mecca; III *ḥājja* dispute with

حجر *ḥajar-* (A2a, *ḥijārat-*) stone, rock

حدث *ḥadīθ-* (A5i) event, report, transmitted narration; II *ḥaddaθa* transmit a narrative account to (*'an* on the authority of)

حدد *ḥadd-* (A1b) border, limit

حدق *ḥadīqat-* (A5e) garden

حرر II *ḥarrara* set free

حرص *ḥarīṣ- 'alā* greedy for

حرض II *ḥarraḍa* encourage

حرق II *ḥarraqa* burn

حرم *ḥaruma (u)* be forbidden; II *ḥarrama* make unlawful, proscribe (*'alā* for); *ḥurum-* (pl) sacred things

حزن *ḥazina (a) ḥuzn-* be sad, grieve; *ḥuzn-* (A3b) grief

حسب *ḥasiba (a) ḥisbān-* reckon, consider; *ḥasaba (u) ḥisāb-* make an account, figure; III *ḥāsaba* call to account

حسن *ḥasan-* beautiful, good; *ḥasanat-* (SFP) good deed; *ḥusn-* beauty, kindness, favor; II *ḥassana* improve, make good; IV *'aḥsana* do good, do well

حشر *ḥašara (u) ḥašr-* gather together (a herd); *ḥāšir-* announcer, herald

حصن *muḥṣanat-* (SFP) chaste woman

حصى IV *'aḥṣā* to count, enumerate

حطط *ḥaṭṭa (u)* decrease, reduce

حظظ *ḥaẓẓ-* (A1b) portion

حفر *ḥafara (i) ḥafr-* dig; *ḥāfir-* hoof

حفظ *ḥafiẓa (a) ḥifẓ-* preserve, protect, memorize; III *ḥāfaẓa ʿalā* watch out for, be mindful of; VIII *iḥtafaẓa bi-* maintain, guard; X *istaḥfaẓa* commit *(ʿalā)* s.th. to the charge of (acc.)

حقق *ḥaqq-* (A1b) truth, reality; right, due; *ḥaqīq-* worthy

حكم *ḥakama (u) ḥukm-* pass judgment (*bi-* of, *ʿalā* on); *ḥukm-* (A3b) judgment, order, decree; *ḥākim-* (A4a) ruler, governor; *ḥikmat-* wisdom; *ḥakīm-* (A5b) wise

حلق *ḥalqat-* ring, hitching ring

حلل IV *'aḥalla* make lawful

حمد *ḥamida (a) ḥamd-* praise; II *ḥammada* extol

حمر *'aḥmaru* (A8) red; *ḥimār-* pl *ḥamīr-* donkey, ass

حنذ *ḥanīð-* roasted

حوج VIII *iḥtāja 'ilā* be in need of

حوط IV *'aḥāṭa bi-* surround; VIII *iḥtāṭa* be careful, on one's guard

حول *ḥawla* (+ gen.) around

حيث *ḥayθu* where, wherever (conj.)

حين *ḥīn-* (A3b) time; *ḥīna* at the time when

حيى *ḥayya yaḥayyu/yaḥyā* live, be alive; IV *'aḥyā* bring to life, revivify; X *istaḥyā* be ashamed; *ḥayy-* (A1a) alive; *ḥayāt-* life

خبر *xabura (u) xubr-/xibrat-* know thoroughly, be fully acquainted *(bi-/-hu)* with; *xabar-* (A2a) news, piece of news

خرج *xaraja (u) xurūj- min* go out of, leave; go out (*ʿalā* against); IV *'axraja* make go out, expel, bring/take out; X *istaxraja* get out, extract; *xarj-* tribute

خردل *xardal-* mustard

خرر *xarra (i) xurūr-* fall down prostrate

خزن *xazana (u) xazn-* to store up, accumulate; *xazīnat-* storehouse, treasury

خسر *xasira (a) xusrān-* suffer loss, go astray, perish

خصف *xaṣifa (a) xaṣf-* to pile on, stick (leaves) onto oneself

خضر *'axḍaru* (A8) green, verdant; IX *ixḍarra* turn green, be verdant

خطأ *xaṭi'a (a) xaṭa'-* be mistaken, make a mistake, sin; IV *'axṭa'a* err, miss, be off target; *xaṭī'at-* (A5g) mistake, error, sin

خطر *xaṭara (i/u) xuṭūr- ʿalā* occur to

خفت III *xāfata* mumble

خفف II *xaffafa* lighten, reduce

خفى *xafiya (ā) xafā'*- hide, be concealed; IV *'axfā* conceal; *xafā (ī) xafā'* hide, conceal (trs.)

خلد *xalada (u) xulūd*- last forever, be immortal; *xuld*- immortality

خلص IV *'axlaṣa* be sincere (*'ilā* to); *muxliṣ*- (SMP) sincere, devoted

خلف *xalafa (u) xalaf*- come after, take the place of; lag (*'an* behind); II *xallafa* appoint as successor; III *xālafa* differ from, be at variance with; IV *'axlafa l-wa'da* go back on a promise; VIII *ixtalafa* differ (*'an* from), dispute (*fī* about)

خلق *xalaqa (u) xalq*- create; *xalq*- creation, created beings, people; *xalīqat*- (A5e) creature; *xalāq*- lot

خلل *xalīl*- (A5d) friend

خمد *xamada (u) xumūd*- to go out, die down (fire)

خمر *xamr*- wine

خوف *xāfa (xif-) (ā) xawf*- fear, be afraid of; IV *'axāfa* scare

خول *xālat*- maternal aunt

خون *xāna (ū) xiyānat*- betray, be false to

خير *xayr*- goodness, (+ *min*) better than; II *xayyara* give a choice to; VIII *ixtāra* choose

دبب *dābbat*- (A4b) beast, four-legged animal

دبر *dub(u)r*- (A3b) the back, rear side; IV *'adbara* turn one's back (*'an, 'alā* on), go backward, flee, run away

دخل *daxala (u) duxūl*- enter (*'alā* into the presence of); IV *'adxala* make enter

درى *darā (ī) dirāyat- bi*- know, be aware of, comprehend; IV *'adrā* make know

دعو *da'ā (ū) da'wat*- call, call to/upon (*'ilā* + verbal noun) to do s.th., pray, invoke; *du'ā'*- (A6a) prayer, invocation

دفع *dafa'a (a) daf'*- push, push away, repel

دلل *dalla (u) dalālat*- lead, guide (*'alā* to), show

دلو II *dallā* to dangle, lead on

دنو *danīy*- low; *ad-dunyā* this world, this life

دور *dār*- pl *dūr-, diyār*- abode

دوم *dāma (ū)* remain

دون *dūna, min dūni* (+ gen.) below, to the exclusion of, up/down to

دين *dīn*- (A3b) religion; *yawmu d-dīni* judgment day; *dayn*- debt

دية *diyat*- bloodmoney

ذخر VIII *iddaxara* store up

ذرر *ðarrat*- (SFP) atom, small particle; *ðurriyyat*- progeny

ذرع *ðirā'*- cubit; forearm, paw

ذكر *ðakara (u) ðikr*- mention, recollect, make mention of; V *taðakkara* remember; *ðakar*- (A2a) male

ذلك *ðālika* that (demonstrative, see §17.1)

ذلل *ðalīl*- (A5j) abject, lowly, mean; *ðull*- baseness

ذهب *ðahaba (a) ðahāb-/maðhab*- go, take away (*bi*- s.th.); IV *'aðhaba* make go away

ذو *ðū*= possessor/possessed of (§31)

ذوق *ðāqa (ū) ðawq*- taste; IV *'aðāqa* make taste

راف *ra'fat*- pity

رأى *ra'ā yarā ra'y-/ru'yat*- see, consider; IV *'arā* make/let see, show; *ru'yā* vision

ربب *rabb*- (A1a) lord, master; *rabbāniyy*- (SMP) rabbin, Jewish title of learning

ربط *rabaṭa (i) rabṭ*- tie

ربما *rubbamā* perhaps

رجع *raja'a (i) rujū'*- come/go back, return; *raja'ū 'ilā 'anfusihim* "they conferred apart"; IV *'arja'a* make return; *marji'*- (A11) refuge, retreat

رجف *rajfat*- tremor

رجل *rajul*- (A2b) man

رجم *rajama (u) rajm*- stone, cast a stone; *rajama bil-ğaybi* guess; *rajīm*- stoned, accursed

رجو IV *'arjā* put off

رحب II *raḥḥaba bi*- welcome

رحل *raḥl*- (A1c) saddlebag

رحم *raḥima (a) raḥmat-/marḥamat*- have mercy on, be merciful; *raḥīm*- merciful; *ar-raḥmānu* The Merciful, epithet of God; *raḥim*- kinship, womb; *waṣala r-raḥima* maintain family ties, take care of those to whom one is tied by family relationship

ردد *radda (u) radd*- send/bring back, ward off, return; reply (*'alā* to); V *taraddada* be reflected, recur, waver, be uncertain, hesitate; VIII *irtadda* go back, revert, apostasize, refrain (*'an* from); X *istaradda* reclaim, get back

ردم *radm*- dam, dike

رزق *razaqa (i) rizq*- provide with sustenance; *rizq*- sustenance

رسل *rasūl*- (A7b) messenger, apostle; *risālat*- (A6b) message; IV *'arsala* send forth

رشد *rušd*- guidance

رضع IV *'arḍa'a* suckle

رضو *raḍiya (ā) riḍwān- ʻan* be content with, pleased with, find acceptable; IV *'arḍā* make content

رعد *raʻd-* thunder, awe

رفع *rafaʻa (a) rafʻ-* raise, erect

رقب *raqabat-* slave

ركب *rakiba (a) rukūb-* mount, ride; *rukbat-* knee

ركع *rakʻat-* kneeling, prostration

رمى *ramā (ī) ramy- bi-* pelt with, cast; accuse

روح IV *'arāḥa* relieve; *rūḥ-* (A3b) spirit

رود III *rāwada* entice; IV *'arāda* want

روم *ar-rūm-* Byzantium, Byzantines, Greeks, Anatolians; *rūmiyy-* Byzantine, Greek, Anatolian

زكو *zakāt-* (A10f) alms

زنج *zanj-* (A1b) Blacks, Ethiopians; *zanjiyy-* Black, Negro

زنى *zanā (ī) zinā'-/zinan* commit adultery, fornicate

زوج *zawj-* (A1a) mate, spouse

زول *zāla (zul-) (ā) zawāl-* pass away; (neg.) continue, abide eternally; IV *'azāla* cause to pass away, take away

زيد *zāda (ī) ziyādat-* be more (*ʻalā* than), increase; IV *'azāda* increase (trs.); VIII *izdāda* increase (int.)

زيل *mā zāla (zil-) (lā yazālu)* (neg. + imperf. ind.) keep on, be still (doing s.th.)

زين II *zayyana* adorn, embellish

س *sa-* (proclitic + imperf. ind.) affirmative future explicit particle

سال *sa'ala (a) su'āl-* ask; VI *tasā'ala* ask one another; *su'āl-* (A6a) question

سبب *sabab-* road, way; *'atbaʻa sababan* take one's way

سبت *sabt-* Sabbath; *yawmu s-sabti* Saturday

سبح *subḥāna* (+ construct) glory be to

سبل *sabīl-* (m & f) (A5c) path, way

ستر *sitr-* covering, shelter

سجد *sajada (u) sujūd-* fall prostrate, bow down (*li-* before); *masjid-* (A11) mosque

سجن *sijn-* prison

سحر *saḥara (a) siḥr-* enchant; *sāḥir-* sorcerer; *siḥr-* magic

سخر II *saxxara* subjugate

سخط *saxiṭa (a)* be angry

سدد *sadd-* mountain, barrier

سدر *sidrat-* lote-tree; *as-sidratu l-muntahā* the heavenly lote-tree

سرب *sarāb-* mirage

سرع *saruʻa (u) surʻat-* be quick, fast; *sarīʻ-* quick

سرف IV *'asrafa* be extravagant, waste, squander

سرق *saraqa (i) sariqat-* steal, rob; VII *insaraqa* get stolen; VIII *istaraqa* filch, pilfer; *istaraqa s-sam'a* eavesdrop

سعر V *tasa''ara* be kindled, lit

سقط *saqaṭa (u) suqūṭ-* fall, drop off

سقى *saqā (ī) saqy-* give to drink, water; IV *'asqā* = G; X *istasqā* ask for water

سكن *sakana (u) suknā/sakan-* inhabit, dwell; IV *'askana* make dwell; *sakīnat-* tranquility

سلح *silāḥ-* (A6a) arms, weapons

سلط *sulṭān-* (A12) power, authority

سلم *salima (a) salāmat-* be safe and sound, intact; II *sallama* keep from harm, hand over intact, + *'alā* greet; III *sālama* make peace with; IV *'aslama* submit, surrender; *salām-* greetings, peace

سمع *sami'a (a) sam'-/samā'-* hear; IV *'asma'a* make hear; VIII *istama'a li-/'ilā* listen to

سمو *samā'-* (m & f) pl *samāwāt-* sky, heaven

سمى *ism-* (A10a/e) name; II *sammā* name, stipulate

سند IV *'asnada* lean

سنن *sinn-* (A3b) tooth, age

سنة *sanat-* (SMP *sinūna*, A10f) year

سود *'aswadu* (A8) black; IX *iswadda* turn black, be blackened

سوف *sawfa* (+ imperf. ind.) future explicit particle

سوق *sāqa (ū) sawq-* to drive

سوء *sā'a (ū) saw'-* be evil, bad; *sū'-* evil, ill (noun); *sayyi'-* evil, bad (adj.); *sayyi'at-* (SFP) evil deed

سوى *sawiya (ā) sawā'-* be equivalent, equal to; II *sawwā* equalize, put on the same level (*bi-* with); VIII *istawā* be even, on a par, stand upright, sit down (*'alā* on), be cooked, mature, ripe, be done right

سير *sāra (ī) sayr-* set out, travel, depart; II *sayyara* make go

شبر *šibr-* (A3b) span, handspan

شبع *šabi'a (a) šab'-* be satisfied, full, satiated

شجر *šajar-* (A2a), *šajarat-* (SFP) tree

شدد *šadīd-* (A5a/d) forceful, violent; *šiddat-* might, violence; VIII *ištadda* be harsh

شرر *šarr-* evil; (+ *min*) worse than; (+ construct) worst

شرق *mašriq-* east, orient, rising point of the sun

شرك *šarīk-* (A5b) partner; III *šāraka* go into partnership with; IV *'ašraka bi-* ascribe a partner to; *širk-* portion; *mušrik-* polytheist, heathen

شرى VIII *ištarā* to buy, purchase s.th. *(bi-* at the price of)

شطر *šaṭr-* half

شفع *šafa'a (a) šafā'at-* intercede (*li-* on someone's behalf); X *istašfa'a 'ilā* seek intercession with

شقق *šaqqa (u) šaqq-* cleave, split; VII *inšaqqa* be split apart, cloven asunder; *šāqq-* harsh

شمس *šams-* (f) (A1b) sun

شمل *šimāl-* north; (f) left hand

شهب *šihāb-* (A6c) shooting star

شهد *šahida (a) šuhūd-/šahādat-* witness, testify (*'alā* against); III *šāhada* witness; IV *'ašhada* cause to witness; X *istašhada* produce as witness; *šahādat-* testimony, testimonial (of faith); *šahīd-* (A5b) witness

شهر *šahr-* (A1b/d) month

شور IV *'ašāra* make a sign, indicate (*'ilā*)

شىء *šā'a (ši'-) (ā) maši'at-* will, want; *šay'-* (A1a) thing, something, anything

شيخ *šayx-* (A1b) elder, old man, leader, chief

شيطن *šayṭān-* (A12) devil, demon

صبح *ṣubḥ-/ṣabāḥ-* dawn, morning; IV *'aṣbaḥa* become (in the morning), get up, wake up

صبر *ṣabara (i) ṣabr-* be patient

صحب *ṣāḥib-* (A4c) companion, master; VIII *iṣṭaḥaba* accompany

صخر *ṣaxr-* (A1b) rock; *ṣaxrat-* rock

صدق *ṣadaqa (u) ṣidq-* speak the truth, be truthful; II *ṣaddaqa* declare as true, affirm; *ṣadaqat-* (SFP) alms; V *taṣaddaqa* give alms, be charitable (*'alā* to)

صرخ IV *'aṣraxa* help

صرط *ṣirāṭ-* path, road

صغر *ṣaġīr-* (A5a/e) small, young; II *ṣaġġara* make small, belittle

صفو VIII *iṣṭafā* choose, select

صلح *ṣāliḥ-* (SMP) good, right, proper, pious, devout; (SFP) good deeds, good works; II *ṣallaḥa* put in order; IV *'aṣlaḥa* promote good, make peace, reform

صلو *ṣalāt-* (A10f) prayer, ritual prayer; II *ṣallā 'alā* pray for

صمم *'aṣammu* (A8) deaf

صنم *ṣanam-* (A2a) idol

صوب IV *'aṣāba* hit the mark; *'uṣība* (pass.) be stricken, afflicted

صوم *ṣāma (ū) ṣiyām-/ṣawm-* fast

ضحك *ḍaḥika (a) ḍaḥk-* laugh

ضرب *ḍaraba (i) ḍarb-* strike, smite, hit; *ḍaraba maθalan* give as an example; VIII *iḍṭaraba* clash, be upset

ضرر *ḍarra (u) ḍarr-* harm, hurt; III *ḍārra* = G; VIII *iḍṭarra* force, compel; *ḍarrat-* wife (relationship of multiple wives one to the other)

ضعف X *istaḍʿafa* despise, belittle

ضلل *ḍalla (i) ḍalāl(at)-* go astray, get lost; IV *'aḍalla* cause to go astray

طعم *ṭaʿām-* (A6a) food, victuals; IV *'aṭʿama* feed; X *istaṭʿama* ask for food

طغت *ṭāğūt-* false gods

طفق *ṭafiqa (a) (ṭafaq-)* (+ imperf. ind.) to begin to, start

طلع *ṭalaʿa (u) ṭulūʿ-* rise (sun); IV *'aṭlaʿa* cause to rise; VIII *iṭṭalaʿa ʿalā* be informed of, observe closely; *maṭlaʿ-* (A11) rising place of the sun or heavenly body

طلق *ṭalāq-* divorce; II *ṭallaqa* divorce; IV *'aṭlaqa* set free; VII *inṭalaqa* depart, proceed, move freely

طمأن QIV *iṭma'anna* be calm, assured, secure, at peace, tranquil

طهر *ṭahura (u) ṭahārat-* be pure, clean; II *ṭahhara* purify; V *taṭahhara* cleanse oneself, perform ablutions

طوع IV *'aṭāʿa* obey; X *istaṭāʿa* have the endurance, capability for, be able to, capable of

طوف *ṭā'ifat-* (A4b) group, band, party

طوق IV *'aṭāqa* bear, endure

طول *ṭawīl-* (A5a) long

طيب *ṭāba (ī) ṭībat-* be good, pleasant; *ṭayyib-* good, pleasant; *ṭīb-* perfume; *ṭūbā li-* blessed be

طير *ṭayr-* (A1b) bird

طين *ṭīn-* clay, mud

ظلم *ẓalama (i) ẓulm-* wrong, oppress, treat unjustly; VIII *iẓẓalama* be unjust; *ẓulm-* injustice, tyranny; *ẓulmat-* (SFP) darkness

ظما *ẓam'ānu* thirsty

ظهر *ẓahr-* back; *ẓuhūr-* loins

عبد *ʿabada (u) ʿibādat-* worship; *ʿabd-* (A1c) servant, slave

عتو *ʿatā (ū) ʿutūw- ʿan* be insolent toward

عجب *ʿajiba (a)* wonder, marvel

عجل *ʿajila (a) ʿajal(at)-* hurry, hasten; II *ʿajjala* hurry (trs.); V *taʿajjala* hurry, be ahead of, precede; X *istaʿjala* be in a hurry, rush; *ʿijl-* (A3b)/*ʿijalat-* calf

عجم *ʻajam-* (A2a) Persians, non-Arabs; *ʻajamiyy-* Persian, non-Arab; *'aʻjamu* (A9a) Persian, non-Arab

عدد *ʻadda (u) ʻadd-* count; II *ʻaddada* number; IV *'aʻadda* prepare; *ʻadad-* (A2a) number; *ʻiddat-* number

عدل *ʻadl-* justice, equity

عدو *ʻadūw-* (A7a) enemy; III *ʻādā* be inimical to, aggress upon

عذب *ʻaδāb-* (A6a) torment; II *ʻaδδaba* torture, torment

عرب *ʻarab-* (A2a) Arabs; *ʻarabiyy-* Arab; *al-ʻarabiyyat-* Arabic (language)

عرج *ʻaraja (u)* rise, ascend; *maʻraj-* (A11) height

عرش *ʻarš-* (A1b) throne

عرف *ʻarafa (i) maʻrifat-* know, recognize; VIII *iʻtarafa* confess; *maʻrūf-* act of favor, kindness

عرى *ʻariya (ā) ʻury-* be naked

عزز *ʻazza (i) ʻizz-* be strong, powerful; *ʻazīz-* (A5d/j) potent, powerful; *ʻizzat-* (SFP) power; VIII *iʻtazza* be powerful

عسى *ʻasā 'an* perhaps

عصى *ʻaṣā (ī) ʻiṣyān-* disobey; *maʻṣiyat-* disobedience

عظم *ʻaẓīm-* (A5a/e) great, huge, magnificent

عفو *ʻafā (ū) ʻafw- ʻan* pardon

عقب *ʻaqib-* (A2a) heel; *inqalaba ʻalā ʻaqibayhi* he turned back in his tracks; *ʻāqibat-* (A4b) end, result; *ʻuqbā* end, final result, reward

عقر *ʻaqara (i) ʻaqr-* wound, hamstring

عقل *ʻaqala (i) ʻaql-* be endowed with reason, be reasonable; II *ʻaqqala* bring to reason, make reasonable; *ʻaql-* (A1b) reason, rationality, intellect

عكف *ʻakafa (u/i) ʻukūf-* be attached, devoted

علم *ʻalima (a) ʻilm-* have knowledge (*bi-* of), know, realize, learn; II *ʻallama* teach; V *taʻallama* learn; X *istaʻlama* seek information; *ʻilm-* (A3b) knowledge, learning; *ʻalīm-* (A5b) learned, knowing; *ʻālam-* (A4b/SMP) world, (pl) universe

علو *ʻalā (ū) ʻalā'-* be high; VI *taʻālā* be exalted, (imperative) come on; X *istaʻlā* rise, tower (*ʻalā* over), master; *ʻalīy-* high; *maʻlan* (A11) high place; *ʻalā (ʻalay-)* + gen. on, over, against, to; *ʻalā 'an* on condition that

عمر *ʻamara (u)* cause to prosper; *al-baytu l-maʻmūru* prototype of the Kaʻba

عمل *'amila (a) 'amal-* do, perform; III *'āmala* do business, trade with; *'amal-* (A2a) labor, deed

عمى *'a'mā* (A8) blind

عنب *'inab-* pl *'a'nāb-* grapes

عند *'inda* (+ gen.) with, in the possession of, presence of

عهد *'ahd-* covenant, pact

عهن *'ihn-* tufts of wool

عود *'āda (ū) 'iyādat-* visit the sick; *'āda (ū) 'awd-/ma'ād-* return

عوذ *'āδa (ū) ma'āδ-* seek protection (*bi-* with); II *'awwaδa bi-* place under the protection of; X *ista'āδa* = G

عوم *'ām-* (A2a) year

عون IV *'a'āna* help

عيش *'āša (ī) 'ayš-* live; *ma'īšat-* living, livelihood

عين *'ayn-* (A1b/d) eye; (A1b) spring

غرب *ğaraba (u) ğurūb-* set (sun); *ğarīb-* (A5b) foreign, foreigner, strange; *mağrib-* west, setting point of the sun

غرر *ğarra (u) ğurūr-* delude, deceive; VIII *iğtarra* be deceived

غشى *ğašiya (ā)* cover

غفر *ğafara (i) mağfirat-/ğufrān-li-* forgive; X *istağfara* seek forgiveness; *ğafūr-* forgiving

غفل *ğafala (u) ğaflat- 'an* neglect, ignore; VI *tağāfala* feign ignorance

غلب *ğalaba (i) ğalabat-* subdue, vanquish; VIII *iğtalaba 'alā* vanquish, gain dominion over

غنى IV *'ağnā 'an* enable someone (d.o.) do without; X *istağnā 'an* dispense with, do without; *ğanīy-* (A5d) rich

غيب *ğāba (ī) ğayb-* be absent, vanish; *ğayb-* (A1b) that which is invisible, supernatural

غير V *tağayyara* change (int.); *ğayru* (+ construct) other than, non-, un-

ف *fa-* and, and then (sequential particle); (+ subj.) lest (hypothetical consequence)

فتح *fataḥa (a) fatḥ-* open; X *istaftaḥa* ask for something to be opened, request admittance

فتو IV *'aftā* give a (legal) opinion, give counsel to; X *istaftā* seek counsel from; *fatwā* (f) (A11) legal opinion; *fatan* pl *fityān-/fityat-* youth, lad

فجر VII *infajara* gush forth, explode

فرد   *fard-* (A1a) individual

فرر   *farra (i) firār-* flee

فرض   *faraḍa (i) farḍ-* ordain, assign

فرق   *faraqa (u) farq-* separate, part, distinguish (*bayna* between); II *farraqa* part, separate; III *fāraqa* disengage oneself from, part with; V *tafarraqa* be separated, split, divided; VIII *iftaraqa* = V; *firqat-* (A3a) division; *mutafarriq-* miscellaneous; *furqān-* epithet of the Koran

فسد   *fasada (u) fasād-* rot, decay, be wicked, vain; IV *'afsada* work corruption, spoil, act wickedly

فسق   *fasaqa (u/i) fisq-* be dissolute

فطر   *faṭara (u) faṭr-* create; V *tafaṭṭara* be torn; *fiṭrat-* innate disposition, natural inclination

فعل   *fa'ala (a) fa'l-/fi'l-* do

فقر   *faqīr-* (A5b) poor

فقه   *faqiha (a) fiqh-* understand, comprehend

فكه   *fākihat-* (A4b) fruit

فلح   IV *'aflaḥa* prosper

فلك   *falak-* (A1a) celestial sphere; *fulk-* ark

فلن   *fulān-* (m), *fulānatu* (f) So-and-So

فم   *fam-* pl *'afwāh-* mouth

فوق   *fawqa* (+ gen.) above

فى   *fī* (+ gen.) in

فيل   *fīl-* (coll.) elephants; *fīlat-* elephant

قبس   *qabas-* borrowed

قبل   *qabila (a) qabūl-* accept; III *qābala* confront, meet; IV *'aqbala* come/go forward, advance (*'alā* toward, on); V *taqabbala* accept, receive; *qabla* (+ gen.) before (prep.); *min qablu* beforehand (adv.); *qabla 'an* before (conj.); *qub(u)l-* (A3b) fore, front part

قتل   *qatala (u) qatl-* kill; III *qātala* fight with; *qatīl-* (A5f) slain

قد   *qad(i)* (+ perf.) perfective particle; (+ imperf.) may, might

قدر   *qadara (i) qadar-* be capable (*'alā* of); II *qaddara* appoint, determine, predestine; *qadīr-* powerful, potent; *qadr-* amount; *miqdār-* extent, amount

قدس   II *qaddasa* bless, make sacred; *baytu l-maqdisi* Jerusalem

قدم   V *taqaddama* to precede, go before; *qadīm-* (A5b) old, ancient

قدو   VIII *iqtadā bi-* emulate, follow

قرء   *qara'a (a) qirā'at-* say aloud, recite, read; *al-qur'ānu* the Koran

قرب *qariba (a) qurb-* draw near, approach; II *qarraba* allow near, let approach; sacrifice; V *taqarraba min* approach, come close to; VIII *iqtaraba 'ilā* draw near to; *qarīb-* near (*min* to), (A5d/e) relative, kinsman; *qurbān-* (A12) sacrifice

قرر *qarra (a/i) qarr-* be cool; *qarrat 'aynuhu* he was happy; *qurratu l-'ayni* delight, joy; *mustaqarr-* habitation, dwelling place

قرن *qarn-* (A1b) horn; *ðū l-qarnayni* epithet of Alexander the Great

قرى *qaryat-* (A3a) village, town

قسط IV *'aqsaṭa fī* be fair to

قسم III *qāsama* to swear to

قصص *qaṣṣa (u) qaṣaṣ-* narrate, tell (*'alā* to); *qiṣṣat-* (A3a) story, tale

قضى *qaḍā (ī) qaḍā'-* decide, foreordain; VII *inqaḍā* be concluded, completed

قطع *qaṭa'a (a) qaṭ'-* cut, be decisive; *qaṭa'a 'amran* make a final decision; II *qaṭṭa'a* cut, hack to shreds; VII *inqaṭa'a* get cut off

قعد *qa'ada (u) qu'ūd-* sit down; *maq'ad-* (A11) seat

قلب *qalaba (i) qalb-* turn over, around (int.); II *qallaba* turn over (trs.); V *taqallaba* be overturned, vanquished; VII *inqalaba* be overturned, changed; *qalb-* (A1b) heart

قلل *qalīl-* (A5a/d/e) little, few, slight; IV *'aqalla* make few; *qullat-* pl *qilāl-* jug

قمر *qamar-* (A2a) moon

قوع *qī'at-* desert

قول *qāla (ū) qawl-* say, uphold, maintain (*bi-*); *qawl-* (A1a) words, speech

قوم *qāma (ū) qiyām-* rise up (*'ilā* for) (*'alā* against), go (*'ilā* to), undertake (*bi-*); II *qawwama* make straight; III *qāwama* oppose, resist; IV *'aqāma* perform; X *istaqāma* stand erect, straight; *qiyāmat-* resurrection; *qayyim-* straight, right; *maqām-* (SFP) place, position; *qawm-* (A1a) people, nation, tribe; *mustaqīm-* straight

قوى *qawīy-* (A5d) powerful, forceful; *quwwat-* (A3a/SFP) might, strength

ك *ka-* (proclitic + gen.) like (prep.); *ka-ðālika* thus, likewise; *ka-'anna(mā)* as though

كبر *kabura (u) kubr-* be big, large; II *kabbara* make big, magnify; IV *'akbara* laud, extol; V *takabbara* be haughty, scornful; X *istakbara* = V; *kabīr-* (A5a/e) big, large, old

كتب *kataba (u) kitābat-* write, prescribe (*'alā* for); III *kātaba* write to; *kitāb-* (A6c) book

كتم *katama (u) katm-/kitmān-* conceal

كثر *kaθīr-* (A5a/e, SFP/SMP) many, much; II *kaθθara* increase, make many; III *kāθara* outnumber

كذب *kaðaba (i) kaðib-* lie (*'alā* to); II *kaððaba* call a liar, repudiate

كرم *karīm-* (A5a/b) noble, generous; II *karrama* ennoble, revere; IV *'akrama* honor

كسر *kasara (i) kasr-* break; II *kassara* smash, shatter; V *takassara* get shattered, broken; VII *inkarasa* be, get broken

كسو *kasā (ū)* clothe

كفر *kafara (u) kufr-/kufrān- bi-* be ungrateful for, disbelieve in; *kāfir-* (A4a/SMP) unbeliever, infidel

كفف *kāffat-* all

كلب *kalb-* (A1c) dog

كلل *kull-* all, every; *kullamā* whenever; *kalālat-* distant heir; *kall-* burden

كلم II *kallama* speak to, address; III *kālama* speak with; V *takallama* speak (*ma'a* with); *kalimat-* (SFP) word

كما *kamā* just as (conj.)

كمه *'akmahu* born blind

كنز *kanz-* (A1b) treasure

كهل *kahl-* man of mature age

كود *kāda (kid-) (ā)* (+ imperf. ind.) be on the verge of, almost (do s.th.)

كوكب *kawkab-* (A11) star, heavenly body

كون *kāna (ū) kawn-* be; *makān-* (A6a/d) place

كيد *kāda (ī) kayd- li-* plot the downfall of, conspire against

كيف *kayfa* how?

ل *la-* (proclitic) really (emphatic particle); *li-* (proclitic + gen.) for, to, because of; (+ subj.) in order that

لاك *mal'ak-, malak-* (A11) angel

لبن *laban-* milk

لعب *la'iba (a) la'b-* play, jest

لعل *la'alla* (+ acc.) perhaps

لعن la'ana (a) la'n- curse; la'nat- (SFP) curse

لقى *laqiya (ā) liqā'-* meet, encounter; III *lāqā* meet with, encounter; IV *'alqā* throw, cast; VIII *iltaqā bi-* meet with

لم *li-ma* why, what for?; *lam* (+ jussive) negative past definite particle

لما *lammā* when (conj.); *li-mā* why?

لو *law(i)* if (contrary to fact); would that, if only (optative particle); *law-lā* were it not for

لوم *lāma (ū) lawm-/lawmat-* blame, reproach; VI *talāwama* blame, scold each other

ليس *laysa (las-)* (defective) is not

ليل *layl-* (A10e) nighttime; *laylat-* (SFP) night

ما *mā* what?; that which, whatever (relative); not; (+ perf.) as long as

ماء *mā'-* (A2b) water

ماذا *māðā* what?

متع *matā'-* (A6a) goods, chattel, wares; II *matta'a* equip, make enjoy (*bi-*); V *tamatta'a bi-* enjoy; X *istamta'a bi-* enjoy, relish

متى *matā* when?

مثل *miθl-* (A3b) likeness, similarity; *miθla* (+ gen.) like (prep.); *maθal-* (A2a) likeness, parable, simile; *timθāl-* pl *tamāθīlu* image, likeness; II *maθθala bi-* make like; III *māθala* resemble; VI *tamāθala* resemble each other

مجس *majūs-* magi; II *majjasa* make Mazdaean

مخلص *muxliṣ-* see √XLṢ

مدن *madīnat-* (A5c/e) city, town

مرء *imru'-, al-mar'-* man; *imra'at-, al-mar'at-* woman

مرر *marra (u) murūr- 'alā* pass by, over; *marrat-* (SFP) time, instance

مرض *mariḍa (a) maraḍ-* fall ill, be sick; *maraḍ-* (A2a) sickness, disease; *marīḍ-* (A5f) sick, ill, diseased

مسس *massa (masis-) (a/u) mass-/masīs-* touch

مسك IV *'amsaka* to hold fast, hold up

مسكن *miskīn-* (A12) poor, unfortunate

مشى *mašā (ī) mašy-* walk, go on foot

مطر *maṭar-* (A2a) rain; IV *'amṭara* rain down

مع *ma'a* (+ gen.) with

مكن II *makkana* make firm, establish; IV *'amkana* be possible for; V *tamakkana min* be able to; *makān-* (A6a/d) place (√KWN)

ملء *mala'a (a) mal'-* fill; VIII *imtala'a* be filled, full; *mala'-* council of notables, chiefs

ملاك *mal'ak-* see √L'K

ملك *malaka (i) mulk-* possess, rule, reign (*'alā* over); II *mallaka* put in possession of, make king; *malik-* (A2d) king; *malikat-* (SFP) queen; *mamlakat-* (A11) kingdom; *malak-* see √*L'K*

ملل *millat-* (A3a) community, sect

مما *mimmā = min mā*

ممن *mimman = min man*

من *min* (+ gen.) from, out of, among (partitive); *man* who?, he who, they who, whoever

منع *mana'a (a) man'-* hinder access (*min* to), prevent (*min* from); III *māna'a* put up resistance to

منو V *tamannā* wish for, desire, make a wish

مهد *mahd-* (A1b) cradle

مهل *muhl-* molten metal

موت *māta (mit-) (ū) mawt-* die; IV *'amāta* cause to die; *mawt-* (A1a) death; *mayyit-* (A5f/1a/ SMP) dead

مول *māl-* (A2a) property, possessions

مؤمن *mu'min-* see √*'MN* IV

ميثاق *mīθāq-* see √*WθQ*

ميد *māda (ī)* sway

نار *nār-* (f) (A10c) fire

ناس *nās-* people, humans

نبء *naba'-* (A2a) news; II *nabba'a bi-* inform of

نبى *nabīy-* (SMP, A2a) prophet; *nabawiyy-* of or pertaining to the prophet

نجم *najm-* (A2b/d) star

نخل *naxīl-* dates

ندو III *nādā* call, cry out to, proclaim

نذر IV *'anðara* warn; *naðīr-* (A5b) warner

نزل *nazala (i) nuzūl-* go/come down, bring/ take down *(bi-);* II *nazzala* send down; IV *'anzala* send / bring / take down; *manzil-* (A11) station, stopping place

نسى *nasiya (ā) nisyān-* forget; IV *'ansā* make forget; *nisā'-* (pl) women

نصح *naṣaḥa (a) nuṣḥ-* take good care of, advise

نصر *naṣara (u) naṣr-* help, assist (*'alā* against); VIII *intaṣara* be victorious, triumph (*'alā* over), take revenge (*min* on); X *istanṣara* ask for assistance; *naṣrāniyy-* pl *naṣārā* Christian; II *naṣṣara* Christianize

نصف *niṣf-* half

نطق *naṭaqa (i) nuṭq-* speak

نظر *naẓara (u) naẓar-* look, regard; III *nāẓara* argue, debate; IV *'anẓara* respite; VIII *intaẓara* wait, expect; *manẓar-* (A11) watchtower

نعت *na'ata (a)* describe

نعم IV *'an'ama 'alā* show favor to; *ni'mat-* favor; *na'am* yes

نفخ *nafaxa (u) nafx-* blow, puff

نفس *nafs-* (f) (A1b) soul; (A1d) self

نفع *nafa'a (a) naf'-* be of benefit to, avail; III *nāfa'a* benefit; VIII *intafa'a* avail oneself (*bi-/min* of)

نفق III *nāfaqa* be hypocritical, dissimulate; IV *'anfaqa* expend

نكح *nakaḥa (i) nikāḥ-* marry

نكر *nakira (a)* not recognize, not know, deny, disown; IV *'ankara* refuse to acknowledge, disavow, disclaim; *munkar-* (SFP) objectionable act, abomination; *nukr-* awful

نكس *nakasa (u) naks-* turn over, turn upside down; *nukisa 'alā ra'sihi* he was confounded

نهر *nahr-* (A1a/d) river; *nahār-* daytime

نهى *nahā (ā) nahy-* forbid someone (*'an* s.th.); VIII *intahā 'ilā* reach, end up at

نور *nūr-* (A3b) light; II *nawwara,* IV *'anāra* make light, illuminate

نوق *nāqat-* pl *nūq-, niyāq-, nāqāt-* she-camel

نوم *nāma (nim-) (ā) nawm-* sleep; *manām-* dream

هبط *habaṭa (i) hubūṭ-* go down

هجر *hajara (i) hajr-/hijrān-* part company with, be separated from; III *hājara* migrate; VI *tahājara* desert one another

هدد *hadda (i) hadd-* be decrepit, in ruins

هدهد *hudhud-* hoopoe-bird

هدى *hadā (ī) hidāyat-* lead, guide aright; VIII *ihtadā* be led, guided, shown the right way; *hudan* right guidance; *hadīyat-* (A5g) gift

هذا *hāðā* this (demonstrative, §17.1)

هرول *harwala* (Q1) *harwalat-* run, walk fast

هل *hal(i)* interrogative particle

هلك *halaka (i) halāk-* perish, die; IV *'ahlaka* destroy, ruin; X *istahlaka* exhaust oneself

همم *hamma (u) bi-* intend

هنا *hunā* here; *hunāka* there

هود *hāda (ū) hawd-* be, become Jewish, practise Judaism; II *hawwada* make Jewish

هوى *hawan* (A2a) lust, passion

هيء II *hayya'a* prepare, make ready; V *tahayya'a* be prepared, in readiness; *hay'at-* (SFP) form, shape

وثق *mīθāq-* covenant

وجب *wajaba (i) wujūb-* be necessary, imcumbent (*li-, 'alā* for)

وجد *wajada (i) wujūd-* find, *wujida* (pass.) exist; IV *'awjada* bring into existence

وجه *wajh-* (A1b) face; II *wajjaha* make face, turn (*li-, 'ilā* toward); VIII *ittajaha* turn towards, set out (*'ilā* for); *wajīh-* eminent, illustrous

وحد *wāḥid-* one (adj.)

وحي *waḥy-* inspiration; IV *'awḥā* inspire (*'ilā* someone) (*bi-* with)

ودد *wadda (wadid-) (a) wudd-/mawaddat-* wish

ودع *wada'a (a)* let, allow (+ imperf. ind.)

(وذر) *yaðaru* (no perf., imperf. only + imperf. ind.) let

وراء *warā'a* (+ gen.) beyond, behind

ورث *wariθa (i) wirāθat-* inherit from, be the heir of; IV *'awraθa* make heir

ورد *warada (i) wurūd-* reach (water); *wird-* thirsty herd

ورق *waraq-* (A2a), *waraqat-* (SFP) leaf

ورى III *wārā* to conceal, keep secret

وسع *wasi'a (a) sa'at-* contain, hold, have the capacity for; II *wassa'a* expand; *wasī'-* vast

وسوس *waswasa* (Q1) *waswās-* to whisper

وصد *waṣīd-* threshold

وصى *waṣīyat-* (A5g) bequest, legacy, directive, commandment; II *waṣṣā*, IV *'awṣā* recommend, charge (*bi-* with), bequeath

وضع *waḍa'a (a) waḍ'-* put down, lay aside; VI *tawāḍa'a* be humble

وعد *wa'ada (i) wa'd-* promise; *wa'd-* (A1b) promise

وفد *wafd-* (A1b) herd

وفى II *waffā* give full due, give full share of; V *tawaffā* take, get one's full share of, receive fully, *tuwuffiya* (pass.) die

وقع *waqa'a (a) wuqū'-* fall, befall, occur

وقى *waqā (ī) wiqāyat-* ward off; VIII *ittaqā* beware, be on one's guard, fear (God)

وكل *wakala (i) wakl-/wukūl-* entrust (*'ilā* to); II *wakkala* authorize, put in charge (*bi-* of); V *tawakkala 'alā* rely, depend on; VIII *ittakala* = V; *wakīl-* (A5b) warden, guardian

ولد *walada (i) wilādat-* beget, give birth, *wulida* (pass.) be born; *walad-* (A2a) child, son; *wuld-* progeny; *wālid-* (SMP) father, progenitor; *wālidāni* parents

ولكن *walākinna* (+ acc.), *walākin* (+ vb.) but

ولى *walīy*-(A5d) friend, helper, supporter; II *wallā* turn aside (*'an, min* from), put in charge of; V *tawallā* turn away; *mawlan* (A11) master, patron; *walāyat*- friendship

وهب *wahaba (a) wahb*- give

يا *yā* O, vocative particle

ياجوج *yājūju wa-mājūju* Gog and Magog

ياس *ya'isa (a) ya's*- despair, give up hope (*min* of); IV *'ay'asa* deprive of hope; X *istay'asa* be despondent

يتم *yatīm*- (A5g/h) orphan

يد *yad*- (f) (A1d/10e) hand

يسر *yusr*- ease, leisure

يقن *yaqīn*- certainty

يمم *yamm*- sea, river

يمن *yamīn*- (f) (A5h) right hand, oath

يهد *yahūd*-, *yahūdiyy*- Jew, Jewish; see also √*HWD*

يوم *yawm*- (A1a) day; *al-yawma* today; *yawma* on the day when; *yawma'iðin* on that day

يونان *yūnān*- Greeks, Ionians; *yūnāniyy*- Greek

Index of F'L Patterns

Arranged in Arabic alphabetical order. For broken-plural patterns see Appendix A.

استفعال ISTIF'ĀL- 77
استفعل ISTAF'ALA 77
أفاعل 'AFĀ'ILU 36.1
افتعال IFTI'ĀL- 59
افتعل IFTA'ALA 59
أفعال 'AF'ĀL- 10
إفعال 'IF'ĀL- 75
افعالّ IF'ĀLLA 81.3
أفعل 'AF'ALA 75; 'AF'ALU 36
افعلّ IF'ALLA 81
أفعلاء 'AF'ILĀ'U 10, 40.1(3)
افعلال IF'ILĀL- 81
افعنلل IF'ANLALA 82
افعنلى IF'ANLĀ 82
افعوعل IF'AW'ALA 82
افعوّل IF'AWẆALA 82
أفلاّء 'AFILLĀ'U 40.1(4)
انفعال INFI'ĀL- 58
انفعل INFA'ALA 58

تفاعل TAFĀ'ALA 79; TAFĀ'UL- 79
تفعّل TAFA''ALA, TAFA''UL- 67
تفعلة TAF'ILAT- 64
تفعيل TAF'ĪL- 64, 65

فاعٍ FĀ'IN 27.2, 40.2
فاعل FĀ'ALA 78; FĀ'IL- 23, 27.1, 40.2
فالّ FĀLL- 27.3
فعال FA''ĀL- 70; FI'ĀL- 10, 40.1(2), 78; FU'ĀLU 94; FU''ĀL- 40.2
فعالة FA'ĀLAT- 28(5)
فعاة FU'ĀT- 40.2
فعل FA'ALA 13, 28(1–2), 30.1(1); FA'ILA 13, 28(1–2), 30.1(2); FA'ULA 13, 28(1–2),

30.1(3); FA'L- 28(1); FA'IL- 10; FU'L- 80.1, 93; FU'AL- 36.1; FU'ILA 53; FU'UL- 10, 93; FA''ALA 64
فعلاء FA'LĀ'U 80.1; FU'ALĀ'U 40.1(2)
فعلل FA'LALA 87
فعلة FA'ALAT- 40.2; FA'LAT- 85; FI'LAT- 85
فعلى FU'LĀ 36.1
فعول FU'ŪL- 10, 28(2)
فعو *FA'AWA 20.1; *FA'IWA 20.3
فعى *FA'AYA 20.2; FU'IYA 53.5
فعيل FA'ĪL- 40.1(1); FU'AYL- 62
فلفل FALFALA 87
فيل FĪLA 53.2

متفاعل MUTAFĀ'IL-, MUTAFĀ'AL- 79
متفعّل MUTAFA''IL-, MUTAFA''AL- 67
مستفعل MUSTAF'IL-, MUSTAF'AL- 77
مفاعل MUFĀ'IL-, MUFĀ'AL- 78
مفاعلة MAFĀ'ALAT- 78
مفتعل MUFTA'IL-, MUFTA'AL- 59
مفعال MIF'ĀL- 84
مفعل MAF'AL- 83; MAF'IL- 83; MIF'AL- 84; MUFA''IL-, MUFA''AL- 64; MUF'IL-, MUF'AL- 75
مفعلّ MUF'ALL- 81
مفعلة MAF'ALAT- 83; MAF'ILAT- 83
مفعول MAF'ŪL- 24
مفول MAFŪL- 27.4
مفيل MAFĪL- 27.4
مفيول MAFYŪL- 27.4
منفعل MUNFA'IL- 58

يفعل YAF'ALU 30; YAF'ILU 30; YAF'ULU 30; YUF'ALU 55, 75; YUF'ILU 75

General Index

All numbers refer to paragraphs.

Other Titles of Interest from Ibex Publishes

Introduction to Persian, 3rd Edition (CDs) / W. Thackston
Nine audio CDs for this book
ISBN 978-1-58814-055-5

An Introduction to Persian, 4th Edition / W. Thackston
Revised edition of this book.
ISBN 978-1-58814-055-5
ISBN 978-1-58814-054-8 (Key to Exercises)

The Gulistan (Rose Garden) of Sa'di / W.M. Thackston
Bilingual English and Persian Edition with Vocabulary
ISBN 978-1-58814-058-6

A Millennium of Classical Persian Poetry / W.M. Thackston
A guide to the reading and understanding of Persian poetry from the tenth to the twentieth century
ISBN 978-0-936347-50-9

Persian-English English-Persian Learner's Dictionary
Transliterated dictionary for students of Persian
ISBN 978-1-58814-034-0

1001 Persian English Proverbs
In English and Persian compiled by Simin Habibian
ISBN 978-1-58814-021-0

Introduction to Koranic & Classical Arabic
By W.M. Thackston
ISBN 978-0-936347-40-0

Introduction To Syriac
By W.M. Thackston
ISBN 978-0-936347-98-1

PERSIAN (FARSI) ALPHABET POSTER
Color 18 x 24 poster
ISBN 978-1-58814-094-4

HOW TO SPEAK, READ & WRITE PERSIAN (FARSI)
Book & 4 Audio CDs
ISBN: 978-0-936347-05-9

AN ENGLISH-PERSIAN DICTIONARY / DARIUSH GILANI
22,000 entries
ISBN 978-0-936347-95-0

RUBAIYAT OF OMAR KHAYYAM FOR STUDENTS OF PERSIAN
Bilingual Khayyam with transliteration
ISBN 978-1-58814-083-8

PERSIAN FIRST GRADE READER
ISBN 978-0-936347-34-9
ISBN 978-0-936347-36-3 (TEACHER'S MANUAL)

A LITERARY HISTORY OF PERSIA / EDWARD G. BROWNE
The classic history of Persian literature
ISBN 978-0-936347-66-0

A DICTIONARY OF COMMON PERSIAN AND ENGLISH VERBS
ISBN 978-1-58814-030-2

LEARNING PERSIAN: BOOK ONE
Includes an audio CD
ISBN 978-1-58814-052-4

LEARNING PERSIAN: BOOKS TWO & THREE
Includes two audio CDs
ISBN 978-1-58814-069-2

ACCELERATED PERSIAN
ISBN 978-1-58814-140-8

THE POEMS OF HAFEZ BY REZA ORDOUBADIAN
ISBN 978-1-58814-019-7

THE POEMS OF ABU SAID BY REZA ORDOUBADIAN
ISBN 978-1-58814-039-5

SELECTED POEMS FROM THE DIVAN-E SHAMS-E TABRIZI
ISBN 978-0-936347-61-5

THE DIVAN-I HAFIZ / H. WILBERFORCE CLARKE
Complete literal translation of Hafez's divan with copious notes.
ISBN 978-0-936347-80-6

THE HAFEZ POEMS OF GERTRUDE BELL
ISBN 978-0-936347-39-4

PERSIAN COOKING: A TABLE OF EXOTIC DELIGHTS
ISBN 978-1-58814-087-6

THE CANNON [TUP]
Translation of Gholam-Hossein Saedi novel
ISBN 978-1-58814-068-5

MALAKUT AND OTHER STORIES BY BAHRAM SADEQI
Translated by Kaveh Basmenji
ISBN 978-1-58814-084-5

AFSANEH, A NOVEL FROM IRAN
Ravanipour novel translated by Rebecca Joubin
ISBN 978-1-58814-095-1